1

CORNWALL
Village Book

THE VILLAGES OF BRITAIN SERIES

Other counties in the series include:

A list of the volumes currently available can be obtained
from the publisher

The
CORNWALL
Village Book

*Compiled by the Cornwall
Federation of Women's Institutes from notes
and illustrations sent by Institutes in the County*

Published jointly by Countryside Books, Newbury
and the C.F.W.I., Truro

🍁 FOREWORD

From Torpoint to the Lizard, and Morwenstow to Lands End, W.I. members are very proud of their Cornish heritage, and the love and affection of their villages and countryside is shown only too clearly in the contributions in this book.

We have thoroughly enjoyed researching, and delving into the past and often came up with surprising discoveries! History, legends, folklore and traditions, Cornwall has in abundance while no area of the South-West is as rich in the relics of the Celtic era.

We have been delighted to have the opportunity to put into print the special knowledge members have of their county, and there has been plenty to record. A county of contrasts from the severe and dramatic north coast with its rugged cliffs and rocky terrain to the mild and gentle south of wooded valleys and winding rivers with the sea encompassing three sides of our beautiful coastline.

But perhaps most importantly we have been able to record the special tales and exploits of local characters, synonymous only with Cornishmen. Our visitors are welcomed by a different scene at every mile, a compulsive delight for their yearly pilgrimage but as this book relates, these are experiences which we are privileged to enjoy for the whole year, in our county.

Sheila Goldsworthy
County Chairman

FOREWORD TO THE SECOND EDITION

Cornwall retains its unique place in the lives of its residents and the many tourists who visit the Duchy.

We are pleased to have had the opportunity to update the drawings and information in this new edition of the Village Book. We hope you find it interesting and will be encouraged to visit, or revisit, the villages of Cornwall.

Annabel John
County Chairman

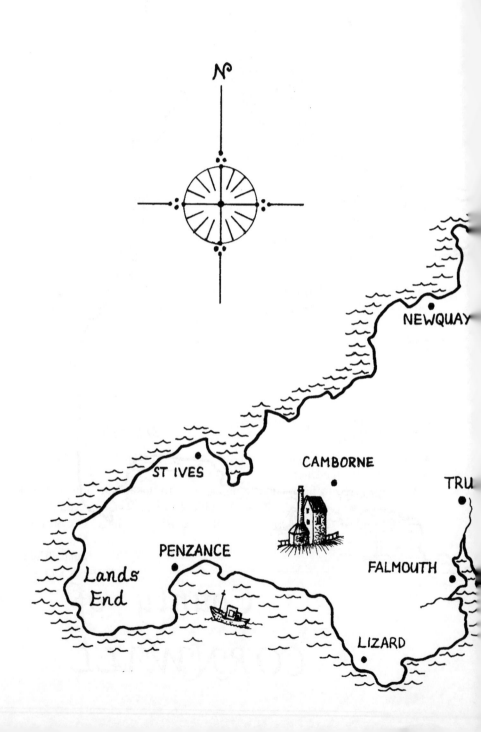

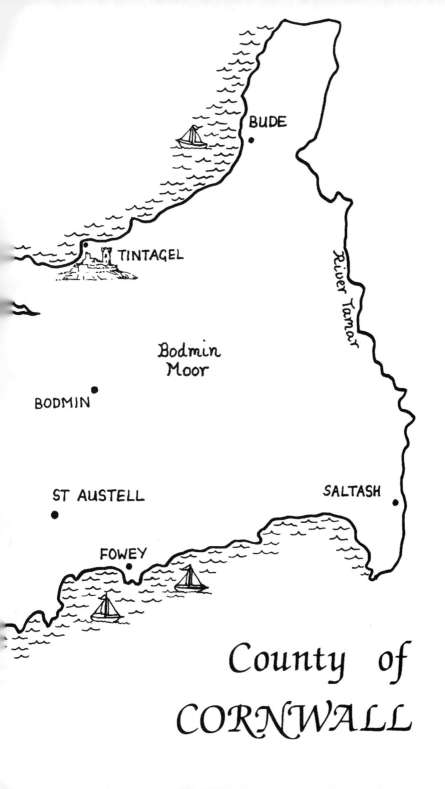

BUDE

TINTAGEL

River Tamar

Bodmin
Moor

BODMIN

ST AUSTELL

FOWEY

SALTASH

County of
CORNWALL

🍁 ACKNOWLEDGEMENTS

The Cornwall Federation of Women's Institutes wishes to thank all Institutes whose members have taken part in this book by providing material and illustrations of their villages.

Special thanks are due to the co-ordinator of the original project, Rosemary Slee, and to Shirley Morrish for the new edition.

The Cheesewring

❧ ALTARNUN

Once upon a time, as all good stories begin, St Nonna or Nonita, the reputed mother of St David, happened upon this pleasant place and it is her name which draws modern day travellers, be they holidaymakers thundering their way down the A30 or 'Cousin Jack's' relatives from overseas seeking out his birthplace in the 'old country', to visit Altarnun or Altarnon. The spelling of the village name can cause confusion. Some say different religious factions sponsored the alternatives – who knows? The essence of Altarnun remains and it has been three times winner of the Tidy Village trophy in the Britain in Bloom competition, as well as being judged the Best Kept Village in Cornwall for 1999.

Its fine church, the 'Cathedral of the Moors', supports the largest parish in Cornwall, and among its many treasures the ancient glass in the east window sports a portrait thought to be a likeness of St Nonna herself. The waters from the holy well were believed to help in curing madness and epilepsy, although the methods used in realising these cures were rather suspect.

Methodism can claim fame here too. Did not John Wesley himself preach at nearby Trewint? Indeed a fine bust of him, carved by a famous son of Altarnun, Neville Northey Burnard, the sculptor, holds a prominent place in the village today and is much photographed by summer visitors.

Set in wolfram and tin mining country, Altarnun has always enjoyed a busy community. In those times the miners and their families had an almost self-sufficient economy with notably cobblers, slaughterhouse and butchers, a tailor and the mill at Penpont providing not only locally grown ground corn, but at water-wheel cleaning time a tasty dish of eels. Happily there are still village shops and a post office, but in common with most rural communities, these days the lure of the supermarkets and department stores in local towns draws the housewife.

Markets have been a feature of life hereabouts for many a long year, and until recently customers travelled from all over the country to attend pony and cattle sales and the Lamb Fairs.

The 'new bridge' over the river aptly named Penpont Water was built in the 1950s. Many remember crossing over by the old packhorse bridge to enjoy themselves at the Empire Day celebrations with the colourful maypole dancing on the village green, and after the Second World War setting the foundations of Altarnun's carnival week, which for over 50 years remained very much the high spot of the village year.

Imagine if you will, an excited clamour of children marching away from their old school rooms in 1935 to settle themselves into a grand new building.

Maybe they celebrated when they won a shield for singing at the Music Festival held later that year in nearby Launceston. Those same old school rooms became the Church Hall and are used for meetings and fundraising activities, including the famous Altarnun teas which attract visitors from far and wide each Thursday in the summer months. The village hall opposite the Methodist church hosts a wide range of activities, from a playgroup, Brownie pack, badminton and youth clubs for the youngsters, to line dancing and short mat bowling for the older folk. There is also an active Women's Institute in the village and never a shortage of things to do.

🍁 ALVERTON

Alverton derives its name from Alwardus or Alward's town, dating back to Edward the Confessor and documented in the Domesday Book 1086. One of the earliest references states 'The lord of Alverton manor was executed for rebellion in 1327.'

Today's traveller passes two thatched houses, one known as Tredarvah Farm, the other Hawkes Farm, both well below the present road level. The latter, owned by the Daniel family in 1600, was once the home of a Madam Woodhouse, whose grandson the great Admiral Pellow (Viscount Exmouth) was reputed to have lived there.

George Daniel built a house in Love Lane and today one can see the old lintel dated 1675, preserved when the house was rebuilt in 1843. Nearby the Pirate inn, once a farmhouse, has two inscribed stones in the side of the building dated 1674 and 1701.

Between Alverton House and the Orchard (now the YMCA) stood a woollen cloth mill, closing in 1830. Also in the area was a serge factory that closed about 1810. In later years at Alverton, near the Pirate inn, a tannin or fellmonger's factory existed. Also, on the outskirts, a rope business was in operation.

Between Buriton House and Wellfield, a popular venue for fairs, was a well where a local character sold water, charging one quarter pence or halfpence a pitcher. During a dry season water was taken by cart from the Alverton brook, also sold by the pitcher, having to cross a ford before the bridge was built in the 19th century,

A boundary stone, opposite Alverton House, erected in 1686, is still used for the ancient ceremony of beating the bounds, originating when Penzance became a borough in 1614.

The main thoroughfare through the village, once a pathway lined with trees, today is the main A30 to Land's End. Farm fields are now a large housing estate.

The inhabitants are fishermen, builders, or involved in local government, general services and tourism.

🍁 ANTONY

The boundaries of Antony stretch from Wilcove in the south to the stream at Sunwell valley in the north, to St John in the east and down through Blerrick Farm in the west to the right-hand side of Wacker. A cottage at Blerrick is said to have stood on the boundary of Antony and Sheviock and because of this a problem arose on the death of the occupant as to which parish he should be buried in, his feet being in one parish and his head in the other. The village covers 947 hectares, and the population at the last census was 453.

There are many small farms around the village and some still survive as family farms while others have been taken over by the Antony estate as the elderly tenants have retired. Most of these houses are very old and many have an historic past. Antony House is now owned by the National Trust and is open to the public from Easter onwards, a beautiful house standing in gardens with woodland around the perimeter. There is a beautiful woodland walk and fetes take place occasionally through the year in aid of charity. The Carew-Pole family live in the house as their ancestors have done for generations before them and Mr Richard Carew-Pole is the County Councillor for Rame. In 1644 Sir Alexander Carew was beheaded on Tower Hill for treason.

Antony Church Town, as it was first known, had Torpoint and Maryfield as its parishes, and Antony was part of the diocese of Exeter in 1269 when the church of St James was rededicated. It was enlarged in 1420, but there was a church probably made of wood long before this. Mothering Sunday at Antony, the mother church, is still celebrated with the two daughter churches from Torpoint and Maryfield.

The first school at Antony was completed in 1766 and was built with money from a bequest in the will of Sir Coventry Carew to teach twelve poor children to read and write. The remains of this school are now a store for the council. A new school was opened in 1928 and a new wing was added in 1958. It has been improved over the years and is now educating 105 full time pupils. The school motto is 'Manners Maketh Man'.

The village has two forts, one at Tregantle and the other at Scrasdon, known as 'Palmerston's Folly' and built in 1867. Both forts are still used today by the Armed Forces for training and exercises. Social life in the village is provided by the institute built around 1923 and leased to the village by the Carew-Pole family. The committee run discos at New Year and there is also a darts team known affectionately as the 'Tea and Bun Club' by others in the darts league. The other social centre is the village pub, once known as the 'Plasterer's Arms' but now the Ring o' Bells.

The pound in the village was once used to hold fortnightly cattle markets and held any straying livestock. A fine had to be paid before the livestock was released. The pound is now used by the council to store materials for road repairs.

🍁 BLISLAND

Sheltering under the western edge of granite-bound Bodmin Moor, less than three miles from the busy east-west A30 artery, the village of Blisland retains, almost untouched, its age-old character.

Known in ancient times as Bluston and Bliston-juxta-Montem, the village is referred to in the Domesday Book as Glustone. It is the only village in Cornwall to have a village green with trees, around which cluster granite houses and cottages, some of them of considerable antiquity.

The beautiful parish church is dedicated to St Protus and St Hyacinth, brothers of servile origin who were martyred in AD260. Although these two saints are well known in Italy, this is the only church in England with such a dedication. The remains of St Hyacinth were discovered as recently as 1848 in the catacombs although the body of Protus, which had originally been buried here, had long since been removed. Referred to as 'dazzling and amazing' by Sir John Betjeman, his favourite church has retained much of its pre-Reformation colour and grandeur. The chief glory of the church must surely be the rood screen. Executed in the baroque style it is the work of F.C. Eden and was installed in 1894 by Vernon Collins, the squire-parson at that time, to replace an earlier 15th century screen. The Collins family have been in continuous residence in the parish since the middle of the 18th century.

St Pratt's feast is celebrated on the first Sunday after 22nd September. In years gone by, a large gathering headed by a silver band would process from the church down to St Pratt's Cross where flowers were laid. The following day the Blisland sheep fair was held in a field next to the church. Farmers drove their sheep down from outlying farms on the moor and this would be a great opportunity to renew old friendships and criticise the quality of a neighbour's sheep! The next day a marquee was erected on the green where tea was served and a sports day held. All in all, this was one of the most memorable weeks in the Blisland year. The children of the village still take flowers to St Pratt's Cross on his Holy Day but this is all that is left of the three days of festivity.

A short walk from the centre of the village lie the ruins of a chapel where John Wesley preached on one of his many visits to the county.

Due east is Jubilee Rock, a curiosity well known in this corner of Cornwall. In 1809 this large granite boulder was used by Lieutenant John Rogers of Pendrift to celebrate the 50th anniversary of George III. The Royal Coat of Arms together with the figure of Britannia and various other inscriptions were carved on its face and painted in appropriate colours. In 1999 the brass plaque which disappeared about 100 years ago was handed in to Truro Museum. It is now on display in Bodmin Museum.

In ancient times panning for tin was carried out in the many streams which criss-cross the moor. This, combined with tenant farming, gave a living to some of the inhabitants whilst many men trudged across the moor to nearby slate and granite quarries. The whole community was dependent on the vagaries of the climate and geology of the moor for its wellbeing. In the late 19th century deposits of china clay were discovered at Carwen and Durfold and a water wheel, said to be the largest in the land, was constructed at Durfold to drive the necessary machinery. The clay deposits were worked out soon after the end of the First World War and the wheel fell into disrepair. It was finally removed in the 1970s and is awaiting reconstruction for exhibition in Wales.

Blisland is fortunate in having a thriving village school and the Blisland Inn. Sadly the post office/village shop closed in 1999 but we have a part-time service run by volunteers. The vicarage has been sold and the Rector looks after four churches. The chapel holds a service once a fortnight.

Many non-Cornish people have been attracted by the attributes of this village and have settled within its boundaries. The community of Blisland seems to have the happy knack of assimilating these changes without losing its character or robust Celtic individuality.

🍁 BOSCASTLE

Boscastle, on the north coast, is a picturesque old fishing village and port where cargoes of coal, salt, beer, bricks and limestone arrived and slates, minerals, china clay and corn were taken away.

The narrow entrance to the harbour is bounded on one side by Willapark and on the other by the Profile Rock which resembles Queen Victoria. Nearby is the blowhole which explodes in a shower of spray when the tide is right, and is sometimes called the 'Devil's Bellows'. The inner jetty was rebuilt by Richard Grenville in 1584. The merchandise was loaded onto horse-drawn carts to be transported inland. They had to struggle up the steep old road through the village and must have been grateful for a drink of the cool water from the river Jordan at Gunpool, which was the main watering place for the upper part of the village.

Many of the cottages are over 400 years old, and are still occupied. Fore Street holds memories from the past, two halves of a granite cider press now being used as stepping stones to the cottages. By the seat in the war memorial garden is a 15th century granite corn measure – the spout is broken, but the measure is still recognisable. Behind the war memorial is the cattle mound – site of Bottreaux Castle dating back to 1080, and from which Boscastle takes its name.

Boscastle was a manor estate and the lord of the manor employed local tradesmen for the upkeep of the property. This meant that the village was mainly self-sufficient and most of the people found employment locally. This came to an end in 1946 when the estate of 1,450 acres, comprising the village and including all the properties, inns, farms, smallholdings, cottages, building sites, harbour, cliffs and woodlands etc, was sold for £90,000. It was soon divided and sold off in individual lots. Remaining evidence of the feudal system is to be seen on the cliffs behind the church at Forrabury. Here you will find the 'stitches', a rare relic of Celtic tenure of land. The narrow strips, which are owned by the National Trust, are rented out to local farmers, and are grazed in winter and cultivated for the remainder of the year.

At the top of the old road is the Napoleon Inn, while at the lower end is 'Boney's' rival, the Wellington, a posting hotel till the early 1920s. Here the coach passengers could obtain a meal or a night's lodging. This was re-enacted in 1990, when the sound of a post horn heralded the arrival of the coach from Bude.

Times change and many traditional village activities have been lost. Gone are the floral dances and the annual torchlight procession through the village in November, when the Carnival Queen led a parade of wonderful tableaux on waggons, accompanied by flaming torches and brass bands, to finish with a fireworks display. Perhaps there are echoes of this past in the highly successful annual old time music halls of recent years and the duck-race days in May when the children, at least, continue the floral dance tradition.

Boscastle is divided into two parishes by the river Jordan which meets the river Valency in the harbour. St Symphorian's church is high on the cliffs in Forrabury parish. It is sometimes known as the church with the silent tower, as a ship carrying bells for the church capsized and sank in a storm.

Hidden away in a hollow in the beautiful Valency valley, surrounded by ancient trees, carpeted with bluebells and daffodils in the spring, is the church of St Merthiana in the parish of Minster. It is built on the site of a priory and a holy well is to be found in the churchyard. There is a pair of scissors carved halfway up the western face of the tower. Nobody knows their origin or purpose. From the church there is a path through Peter's Wood owned by the National Trust, which winds down to the river Valency. Here Thomas Hardy walked with his Emma, from St Juliot to Boscastle, and found inspiration for his novel *A Pair of Blue Eyes.*

Little has changed over the years, but the harbour still retains its old world charm, and the walks through the valley and on the cliffs can still be enjoyed. In 1994 a Visitors' Centre was opened. Situated in the public car park, it is managed by the North Cornwall Heritage and Countryside Service.

🍁 BOTUS FLEMING

Botus Fleming is one of the smallest parishes in Cornwall. Long and narrow, it is bounded all round by water – by the Lynher to the west and the salt water of a Tamar creek to the east. It is cut across the middle by the Saltash to Callington road, which more or less divides the parish between Botus Fleming village with Moditonham, and Hatt.

In 1524 a tax was levied, and 24 men are listed in Botus Fleming, including Edward Crosman – could he be the man from Cross, the beautiful old farmhouse at the main crossroads in Hatt? Did Henry Pawly own Pawley's Park? John Slade appears in another subsidy list of 1544 and Sladeland is still the name of a house and several fields.

Maybe other fields get their names from earlier inhabitants too: Richard Skin, tenant farmer of Swiftaford, was Overseer of the Poor in 1827 (Skin's Field); there are a number of Hodges recorded between 1608 and 1698 who left their name to the house and the orchard still called Hodges.

In Queen Elizabeth I's time musters were held of all able men to assess the strength of a defence force, and to list the armour and weapons available. In the muster of 1569 there are 12,000 names in Cornwall, Botus Fleming having only nine men listed as able! John Barrett had a bow and a sheaf of arrows – could he be the man who gave his name to Barrett's meadow?

When the Armada came within sight of our coast they reported (July 1588) they had been seen by the Cornishmen 'where upon they made fires and smokes'. Beacons had been in existence 250 years before that, so they were a familiar sight on the hilltops over a very long period. Beacon Park in Hatt is the highest point of the parish. The old farmhouse now known as Bicton was called Beacon only 150 years ago.

William Martyn, once Mayor of Plymouth, bought land in Botus Fleming in

1706, and his son, a Doctor of Physic of Plymouth, inherited it. There is no evidence that Dr Martyn ever lived here but in his will he specifically asked to be buried without pomp 'in the most elevated part of and as near the middle of the field as may be. I desire that there may be erected over my grave a plain marble monument.' Several years before his death he prepared the long inscription to be carved on the tomb. And there it still stands, in a prime position looking out over the Tamar. This field has been known as Burial Field ever since.

Several field names are obviously repeated on different farms, such as Back Door, Gratton (stubble), Home, Bramble, Furze and Well (plenty of springs in this area) and Mowhay (pronounced Mooy) where ricks were/are stacked before thrashing. However the commonest name is simply Orchard. From over 350 fields in the parish 60 were orchards in the 1830s. There are very few productive orchards now, but in living memory there were apples, cherries and pears grown, often with soft fruit under. Many orchards were close to the farmhouses, for their own use, but the majority of cherry orchards were down the sheltered valley towards the Tamar.

Cherries from here were famous – sweet and dark. The older people remember the days spent up long ladders picking the cherries, and packing them for market but they also remember with joy the wondrous sight of the village in blossom time.

🍁 BOYTON

Boyton or Boietone may be either from the Cornish word 'byu' or from the French word 'bois', a wood, which agrees well with the situation of Boyton, at one time in the midst of woods. The Abbot of Tavistock had purchased Boyton before the Norman Conquest and the Domesday survey in 1086 claims that Earl Moreton had taken Boietone unjustly from him. In 1540, it was acquired for the Duchy of Cornwall by an exchange effected by Henry VIII. The Duchy disposed of the land in 1947.

The parish church, situated in the centre of the village, dates back to the 13th century. There are signs that a chapel existed there before 1288. William Symons of Bradridge gave £100 towards building the tower, which was completed in 1696. Boyton Methodist church celebrated its centenary in 1989.

Boyton Revel and Fair was 'high day' of the year. In addition to sale of cattle etc, there was wrestling for prizes in the meadow opposite the church, sports and games for children and a dance in the Duchy Arms barn, bringing the day to a close with a pot of ale or cider and handshakes all round.

Sadly, the Pound House no longer exists. Here, the farmers made their surplus apples into cider. At a 'sample time' six of the regular 'tasters' knelt around the cider-well and using a long handled saucepan, dipped it into the cider and passed it around for opinions. Cider was the main thirst quencher during harvest time.

The Duchy Arms, opposite the church, is no longer an inn. A staunch Methodist converted it into a temperance hotel, much to the dismay of local inhabitants, especially the church bell ringers who nipped across to quench their thirst at the Duchy Arms after ringing the bells.

The blacksmith's shop has been in use in the village for years. No longer are horses shod there but farmers come with their machinery for repair and in spring and summer it is a hive of activity.

Farming has always been the main source of employment. At one time Boyton could boast of having two carpenters, an undertaker, two grocer's shops, two shoemakers, a family-run tailor's shop and a butcher. After the First World War, a post office, two petrol pumps and a cycle repair shop were added. The shed still stands in the village which was used years ago by the Launceston postman who brought the mail by horse and trap to the village before the days of the post office. He sorted the mail in the shed. It was then collected by two men who travelled around the parish on foot or cycle to deliver it. The horse spent the day in Temperance Orchard until 4.30 pm when it took the Launceston postman with the outgoing mail back to Launceston.

An old custom observed was shooting at the apple trees on old Twelfth Night to drive away evil spirits and hope for a good crop of apples next season. The Harvest Supper, often celebrated on Christmas Eve, was given to all who had helped in any way with harvest. The 'Ash Faggot' was bound with several binds and a bind allocated to each of the boys, and he who got his bind burnt through first had the prize offered by the master.

The old pump and trough still stands outside the blacksmith's shop, a reminder of when it supplied every cottage in the village with their daily water requirements.

Just over Boyton bridge, under which the river Tamar runs, is Boyton mill where farmers took their corn for grinding. Now a private residence, the mill wheel exists which as once operated by the force of water from a nearby weir. Nearby is the now dry course of the Bude Canal and there was a wharf at Boyton bridge.

Agnes Prest, the Boyton Martyr, lived at Northcott hamlet, also in Boyton parish. Because of her religious beliefs she was burned at Southernhaye, Exeter in November 1557.

Old landmarks are fast disappearing but nostalgic memories remain. Houses and bungalows are springing up in and around the village. The church hall is the centre point for local activities.

Breage & District

Breage (pronounced by villagers to rhyme with 'vague') was named after a saint called Breaca who escaped persecution by the Irish and landed in Cornwall during AD700.

The 12th century church in the village is called St Breaca's and has 15th century frescos on its walls uncovered in 1955. The Queen's Arms, the only pub in the village, dates from the 14th century and has a vast collection of decorative plates hung on every beam throughout the bars and restaurant.

Tin mining was the main source of employment for villagers until the last mine was closed in the mid 1930s. Older villagers recall with great pleasure the days when Breage was busy and bustling, with miners coming to collect their wages and staying to spend them in the many and varied shops the village then possessed. There were also three inns, very well used on pay days!

Ponies and traps called 'jousters' supplied the village regularly with fresh food, including one which came regularly from Porthleven bringing fish straight from the fishing boats. When the driver called 'fresh herring and fresh mackerel', it really was fresh!

The first china clay discovered in Cornwall was found by a mineralogist named Cookworthy on Tregonning Hill, which is about one and a half miles from Breage. The deep pits made when the clay was taken are very evident to this day.

Breage has a thriving Church of England school with pupils drawn from all over the district. The village has a silver band originally formed in the 1920s and still very popular today with the young and not so young.

Breage village hall was in very poor condition when the village bought it in 1960. Now, it is in use throughout the week and popular at weekends.

Breage today is a very quiet village with a small development of modern bungalows. Many of the older mine houses and cottages have been bought and modernised by sailors and airmen from the nearby naval air station called Culdrose. The village has a post office, village stores and a small hairdresser's. There are still a few working farms in the area and there is a little fishing but no other work now that mining is finished.

Breage Fair is always held on the third Monday in June. Once it was a real fair with roundabouts and sideshows. Sometimes there was a circus and cattle, sheep and horses were brought for sale in the main street. Breage Feast Day is 26th December.

The village has its own litany which runs as follows: 'From Praa Sands and Breage Hands, dear Lord deliver us'. Its origin seems to be lost in the mists of time!

☘ BUDOCK WATER

Budock Water takes its name from St Budoc, a Breton monk who founded a religious community at the head of the pleasant south-facing Budock valley in about AD470. Today, the church of St Budock sits square on the hill above the village. Nothing is left of the earliest buildings, the present fabric dates mainly from the 15th century with later restorations. Tradition says the right hand of the saint was embalmed and used as a means of receiving a blessing. There is a figure of the hand in the porch and the churchwardens' staves are carved to show the hand. There is a brass memorial on the floor of the chancel to John Killigrew, who was appointed by Henry VIII as Governor of Pendennis Castle. The Killigrew family were responsible for much of the early development of Falmouth. This family-orientated church has an enthusiastic bell-ringing team, Mothers Union, Wives Circle and a Guild of Azenor.

The village nestles in the valley of the Budock river which tumbles down through the woods and fields to flow into the sea at Maenporth, not two miles away. Surrounded as it is by steep pastures and wooded downs, it is hard to believe that the busy port of Falmouth is just over the hill. There are several farms around the village producing meat, milk, grain, vegetables, eggs and flowers. Some of the names of the farms and fields are the same today as those in the records of the 14th century. A network of footpaths crosses the area and are walked regularly by groups led by members of the parish council.

The oldest houses are mainly in the centre of the village, the newer developments of houses and bungalows extend along the valley and also up the lower slopes. Of the large houses in the parish, Penjerrick retains its garden full of interesting plants and is open to the public on certain days. This is one of the many properties owned by the Fox family, who took a benevolent interest in the village.

Where the Budock river flows under the road a redundant chapel has been turned into a meadery, and farther along the busy village hall hosts many activities. Still farther along stands the post office, which is also a newsagents and general store. Here is also found the village inn, the Trelowarren Arms, a typical country pub with an oak tree on the forecourt and bright tubs of flowers. Besides the library and fish and chip vans, there is a mobile wet fishmonger, a mobile butcher, a greengrocer and a hairdresser servicing the village.

Many of the local work-force have employment in Falmouth, mainly in the hotels, shops and offices, local government or the dockyard. Some still work in agriculture and horticulture but not nearly as many as in the past. Some work in building and allied trades, quite a few own their own small businesses. Some of the farms and houses in the area offer accommodation for tourists.

The village has a high proportion of senior citizens and many of the bungalows have been bought by retired people. There is a flourishing Over Sixties Association which holds monthly meetings and organises outings. There is one nursing home for the elderly, Roscarrack.

True to Cornish tradition, the village is associated with two choirs, the Budock Singers and the Treverva Male Voice Choir which has achieved countrywide fame.

Older villagers have seen many changes in their lifetime. The village has almost doubled in size, new roads have been made, a public water supply and electricity were installed, and a new sewerage scheme was completed in 1972. In April 1991 came street lighting in the main road. In spite of changes, the friendly spirit of the village persists among the inhabitants and newcomers are accorded a hearty welcome into the community. Every year the village holds a Fun Day in June in the playing field, and a garden show in July in the village hall. Feast Sunday is the Sunday nearest 19th November, and is followed by a Feast Night Concert the next evening.

❧ Bugle

Bugle is a place name which has puzzled many people. Some say it derived from brass bands. On some deeds it was called Carnswerry and others called it Carnerosemary or Carnsmerry, hence the name given to the council houses built just after the Second World War.

From accounts and cuttings taken from various newspapers and books the popular theory is that Bugle got its name because of the Regulator coach which stopped at the inn – which was described as 'attractive to neatness and comfort' and had a good stabling and a lock-up coach house. This information came from *Life in Cornwall in the Mid 19th Century* extracted from the West Briton newspaper. As the coach left the inn, the guard would blow a bugle for the ostler at Bilberry Farm to bring the horses to the main road where they were exchanged.

It was also reported that when the roof of the Bugle inn was being put on they heard of a public execution that day at Bodmin. The roofers downed tools and went to see it. Also reported in the *Western Morning News* – 'The inhabitants of the hamlet of Bugle bore so evil a reputation it was necessary to have a county policeman in residence there; but a revival was taking place at the Bible Christian chapel – good attendances recorded and it was hoped it would do permanent good'.

Early in the 1900s two or three men gathered at the local bootmaker's shop to play rings and draughts etc. It was decided to build a men's institute in which to carry out these activities. In 1908 the foundation stone was laid. After a few years of hard work money was still needed for the building and in 1912 the West of England Bandsmen's Festival was formed and some of the profits from this venture were used for the purpose. The Festival is still held every year the third Saturday in June and is Bugle's big event of the year, and unique in the fact that it is the only Festival to hold a Royal Trophy. The working men's institute is still the meeting place for young and old.

The Bugle Music Festival was started in 1951 and has gradually increased during the years. It is held each year in May. Sport also plays a big part in the life of the village. There is a football club formed in 1901, bowling club (for men and women) set up in 1948, and a cricket club.

The other important buildings in the village are the Methodist church dating back to 1858, the school and the Legion Hall (now called the village hall). Many shops have closed (there used to be 16) but some have expanded and grown. The main occupation of the inhabitants is working in the clay industry. This has altered considerably over the years and many redundancies have taken place.

Many customs have been dropped mainly because of the influx of new people to Cornwall. The older generation recall the famous Snail Creep with fife and drum band which used to start at Molinnis and parade through the village; the Sunday school outings with big saffron buns and stalls erected in the road for Good Friday and feast days.

The railway from Par to Newquay runs through Bugle. Years ago the station would be packed for an outing to Newquay but now it is almost derelict, owing to the change of transport – many people having cars. The Cornwall Mineral Railway was built to carry china clay trains from Goonbarrow to Gunheath. Mr Dan Warne built many of the clay work chimney stacks around the area and also built the Great Western Hotel at Newquay and Carnsmerry Crescent in St Austell.

❧ CALLINGTON

Callington is a small town with a village atmosphere, in present times rapidly expanding. From various points in the town can be seen Bodmin Moor, Kit Hill and the wooded valleys of the rivers Lynher and Tamar.

'Ten miles from anywhere' – this rather derogatory phrase used to describe

Callington in fact highlights the town's position on the crossroads of the north/south and east/west routes in this part of East Cornwall. This position also helped in its rise as an important market town for the surrounding parishes. The market flourished until 1965 and is commemorated by the name of the residential home built on the site – Chyvarhas means Market House.

Callington's origin lies in the Celtic past of Cornwall. Its earliest name was Celliwic; over the centuries there have been many variations including Killiton and Calweton, this last being interpreted by the Cornish language expert Oliver Padel as 'the town by the bare hill', ie nearby Kit Hill. Gates at its four entrances enclosed the town and in the days of the turnpikes provided an income for the gatekeeper.

One of Callington's most prized possessions is the parish church of St Mary built in the early 15th century, restored by the Victorians in 1859 and 1886.

Callington never had a resident lord of the manor, only various absentee owners. From 1558 to 1832 it was a 'pocket' or 'rotten' borough, returning two members to Parliament (according to the political choice of the owner). The writer Horace Walpole was one of these; his sister-in-law Lady Orford was then 'Lord' of the manor and his father Sir Robert Walpole, England's first Prime Minister.

The town now spreads far beyond the 'bound stones' which marked the limit of the borough. These may still be found in Liskeard Road, Saltash Road, Tavistock Road, Haye Road and at Newport. The title of Portreeve, originally appointed as chief steward to the lord of the manor, has survived into present day Callington in the person of the chairman of the local council.

The modern secondary school, Callington Community School, is sited on part of the old Callington Common, as is also the industrial estate at Moss Side. The new southern bypass, built with financial help from the European Community, follows the line of a very old bridleway which served the same purpose hundreds of years ago.

The annual Honey Fair, held on the first Wednesday in October, is a revival of the old fair which was originally a three day event held in March. It involves the whole town with a street market, displays and competitions, and special stalls in all the local halls. The emphasis of the exhibition is on the production and sale of honey, with hives and their products on view.

On Midsummer's Eve the Old Cornwall Society organise the annual bonfire ceremony on Kit Hill, lit by the Portreeve in the presence of The Lady of the Flowers, after prayers in Cornish; this bonfire is the last of a chain of fires throughout Cornwall. It was also lit on the occasion of the Queen's Silver Jubilee in 1977.

Copper mines once flourished, then struggled at several points in the parish of Callington. A particularly interesting mine near Newbridge south of the town produced rhodanite.

The ruins of the mines of Kit Hill add to the mystery of the place – given to the people of Callington by Prince Charles, Duke of Cornwall, to celebrate the birth of Prince William. From the summit can be seen the whole of Callington and beyond.

Alongside members of families which have lived in the area for generations are newcomers attracted by its proximity to the large city and industries of Plymouth – across the river. Once the Tamar bridge was built in 1961, and recently the road tunnel opened, the expansion of the town was an inevitability.

The industrial complex on the east side of the town holds many developing light industries, and the largest employer, Ginster's pasty factory, makes its presence known by the unmistakable aroma of baking pasties at any time.

In and around Callington are many craft-workers maintaining their skills in what used to be known as cottage industries – leather work, spinning and weaving, wood carving etc.

However diverse the occupations and origins of the inhabitants of Callington, the community spirit is almost palpable; as is seen at the many events held by different organisations throughout the year.

🍁 CALSTOCK

One of the most pleasant and attractive walks in the Tamar valley is alongside the river, namely Lower Kelly. In the 1800s and early 1900s Lower Kelly was then only a track, with the Calstock incline plane railway coming across the lower end of it, from the hill above, and ending up running down on wooden trestles to the quay. This is now an attractive house and garden, the garden stretching 450 ft alongside the river.

In the ground itself the occupants have found two deep holes with the wooden remains of trestle legs which held up the final rails of the incline railway as well as – at different levels – numerous lumps of coal, clay pipes, old bottles, ashtrays and pieces of china. They have also, to their delight, been able to expose parts of the original cobbled quay.

The river certainly would not have been the peaceful place it is now, where there can be seen otter, mink, heron, cormorants, coots, dab chicks, mallards and nesting reed warblers, but full of sailing boats, barges and paddle steamers, manoeuvring for berths alongside the noisy, bustling and dirty quays from Danescombe up to Calstock.

They would have shipped out copper, lead ore and granite, as well as the stone for Dover South breakwater – no doubt first trundling down on the incline railways on the first part of their journey. More attractive loadings would have been of strawberries, cherries, daffodils, narcissus and anemones that grew in abundance on every available piece of ground along here.

Loaded off ships on to the old quay, would have been lime and the street sweepings and offal from the slaughterhouses in Plymouth, where it had been stacked on to Tamar wharf to Maker and then shipped up here to be spread on the strawberry beds. Coal was also unloaded here.

A few yards out from this spot is a large sandbank, known in the 1800s as Kelly Rock sand shoal. Here the paddle steamers *Empress* and *Aerial* once raced each other down the river with their passengers cheering, only for *Aerial* to catch her paddlebox on the shoal and smash it. Another time, the *Aerial* actually sank at the same spot and was patched up at low tide and floated again as the tide rose. The owners of Incline House, as the old quay is now called, have seen quite a few boats touch here and then had to wait for a rising tide to float them off. In the 1950s, there was a small sailing boat, the *Aphrodite*, who came up every year at low tide to this sand shoal just to scrape the barnacles off her bottom. On the sand shoal itself – explored by adventurous youths – have been found ginger beer bottles.

It is known that in the one main street of Calstock, there were eleven pubs and many shops, including a baker's, a millinery shop, post office, restaurant, butcher's and many others. Adjoining the Tamar inn, there is now a delightful patio area where boat visitors and others enjoy food and drink, particularly in the summer months. Do they know that this area used to be where the mortuary was situated? Another well-known feature of Calstock, especially to the trippers, is the Archway Chip Shop. This, as late as the 1940s, used to be a pub called the Devonport inn and below the new flooring are the original slates of the bar area.

At the bottom of the hill, entering the village itself, are some lovely old and very large houses. The main one of these used to be the Commercial Hotel and has many rooms, and further down the row the house known as The Cuddy was a doctor's surgery.

There were at least three large thriving chapels available to the miners of olden days. One has been converted into four very attractive flats with beautiful river views, the second also having been converted into flats – which whilst being converted caused quite a stir as old graves were disturbed under the flooring. These were removed and laid to rest in other sacred places, by checking old records that identified them – alas the bones found in the garden of the Old Manse next door cannot be identified! The third chapel has now been converted, with the aid of Lottery money, into a Poets Centre.

There are many other places of interest in Calstock if you have the time to wander – especially the beautiful old church of St Andrew situated at the top of the village and whose churchyard is a history book in itself. Beautifully kept, it contains pages and pages of life in the old days – numerous deaths of children and indeed whole families who died of cholera and other chilling diseases and names of men who left Calstock to mine in other parts of the world and upon their death at quite early ages, were returned to lie with the families they left behind. One particular headstone is well worth reading – the tale of a sailor who drank too much and fell off his boat the worse for wear and met a watery grave!

CANWORTHYWATER

The village of Canworthywater, pronounced Kenerywater is in the parish of Warbstow. In the past it was a busy place. It had a mission church, two chapels – Methodist and Bible Christian only a few hundred yards from each other, a post office, a pub, butcher, thresher proprietor's, and a blacksmith where farmers took their horses to be shod and implements repaired. At Tuckingmill was a corn mill worked by a water wheel, farmers bringing corn to be ground. The undertaker and his helper would make the coffins for people in the parish.

You can imagine how Canworthywater got its name, where three rivers meet. The village was often flooded after heavy rain, when the roads were impassable for many hours. The river authorities finally thought that if the rivers were straightened this would stop the flooding and it did.

Christmas was always a happy occasion when a family of eleven, who all played an instrument, would load up the farm waggon with an organ and go around singing the old Cornish carols. Another great time was the Sunday School Anniversary, when before tea on the weekday the children led by the superintendents marched along the village singing and carrying banners.

There was great excitement when the first motor car went through the village. It could be heard coming half a mile away, and it contained the vicar of Jacobstow, driven by his chauffeur to Tresmeer station (now gone).

One of the chapels, the mission church, blacksmiths, undertaker and pub have all gone, but there is a shop and petrol station and an agricultural engineer's. The village has so far not had much development, but now there are plans to start building.

🍁 CARGREEN

The name Cargreen is generally believed to be derived from Carrecron – Cornish for 'seal rock'. However, it must be a very long time since seals were common hereabouts. The village, in the parish of Landulph, looks east across the Tamar river and is protected from the south-westerly gales by a shoulder of hill.

The prefix 'Lan' in Landulph denotes the monastic settlement of a Celtic saint. St Dilpe (or Dilph) is believed to have travelled by water from Ireland, establishing himself by a well near to Kingsmill Lake, and his church was built close by. The medieval covering to St Dilph's well is long gone, as are traces of the port which flourished for about 50 years in the 15th century and from which pilgrims to St James at Compostella sailed to Spain. The Black Death is reputed to have decimated the population and the remainder fled over the hill to Cargreen. Thus, this Cornish church is nearly a mile distant from its village. Kingsmill Lake is largely silted up and the marshes are a favourite haunt of over-wintering birds – and 'twitchers'. The church has been rebuilt many times over the years, the last such major restoration being at the beginning of the 20th century. The carved bench ends and the brass commemorating Theodore Palaeologus, said to be the last direct descendant of the Byzantine emperors, are of particular interest.

The main occupation locally was farming, with fishing (and smuggling) as subsidiaries. The village was surrounded by orchards and rubbish brought from Plymouth by boat (sweepings of the streets, markets and dockyard) was spread over the fields as manure. People sometimes found coins, and still find clay pipes and other artefacts, as the ground is worked. The generally warmer micro-climate of the Tamar valley encouraged cultivation of strawberries and flowers. As there was next to no access beyond the steep stony lanes, produce was moved by river or by taking the row-boat ferry to the Devon side and then walking the two miles uphill to the station at Bere Ferrers to catch the train for Plymouth, returning with one's purchases the same way!

Up to 1990 the most eyecatching views of the parish came in the spring when travellers round Saltash caught sight of the brilliant fields of daffodils grown around Neal Point and Kingsmill Lake. Sadly the fields are now returned to general cultivation but the special varieties, named after places in the valley, will long remain.

Electricity for light and power came in the early 1950s and the narrow entry roads were metalled making vehicular access possible and the ferry uneconomic. The Tamar road bridge encouraged development throughout south-east Cornwall and the village enlarged slightly, attracting pleasure-boat owners who are now the principal river users. However, without private transport, the parish and village two miles from the main road remains a pleasant riverside rural island and the Devon bank (25 miles away by road) a foreign land.

🍁 CARHARRACK

Carharrack (meaning fortification of Harthok or Great Rock) is three miles from Redruth and nine miles from Truro and Falmouth. In the early 1700s it consisted of a few cottages, nestling on the south-eastern side of Carn Marth (Mark's Carn). Little Carharrack was probably the original Carharrack as it lies on the pilgrims' route from St Day to St Michael's Mount. A farmhouse at Little Carharrack was used for accommodation and entertainment of these travellers, but tradition has it that the farmhouse was also the site of a chapel used after St Day's church fell into disrepair.

The last 150 years or so has seen the village rapidly expanding, several rows of houses being built about 1830. The pound is situated at crossroads close to the boundaries of Manors St Day and Carharrack. To the west of the pound, Lower Carharrack Stamps were active until about 70 years ago.

An ancient cross at Ting Tang was mentioned in deeds of 1731 as the White Cross (White Stile), known also as Penhaligan's Cross. A granite post with a small cross now marks the original site, the cross having been removed to Scorrier. The white cross marks the entrance to Trevince and Churchtown, funeral processions passing here on the way to Gwennap church. It was probably the point of rest for the coffin bearers. Stories abound of a ghost appearing at this stile.

Carharrack owes its existence to the mines. Copper was the principal mineral extracted, but tin was the first to be raised. Streaming was the usual method before underground mining took place. In 1748 John Williams instigated the building of the Great County Adit which drained the whole area and enabled deeper shafts to be sunk with the aid of the steam engine, which led to the copper boom of 1750-1850. James Watt was supervisor at Ting Tang in 1777 and William Murdock was also a frequent visitor to the area. The mines began to prosper and the opening of Wheal Damsel in 1795 led to its being the richest mine in the parish. The years up to 1840 saw the area become the wealthiest square mile in the mining world, but by 1860 copper mining was failing and by 1870 Carharrack's place as the centre of mining ceased.

Railways sprang up in conjunction with the mines, the Redruth/Chacewater railway opening in 1825, the first in Cornwall. It ran through Carharrack; a small cutting with a foot-bridge at the top of the village has been restored by the parish council. The Devoran Railway was constructed for United and Consolidated Mines and was used for transporting the ore to the port at Devoran and so to South Wales.

The mission church was erected in 1884 and dedicated to St Piran, the patron saint of tinners. It now contains the original organ from St Day's church. The Methodist church is on the site where John Wesley is reputed to have preached to villagers on 3rd September 1743. He did not preach at the famous Gwennap Pit (three quarters of a mile away) until 5th September 1752. He continued to preach at the Pit until 1789 when he was 89 years old. This was his last visit as he died two years later. A museum depicting Methodism in Cornwall is sited in this church. The third chapel in the village was built by Billy Bray, who was born at Twelveheads in 1794. A later church built to his memory was demolished in 1986 to make way for new development.

With villages having to make their own entertainment, various activities took place. The St Day and Carharrack Silver Band attained a very high standard at national level and is now booked for many functions. The Carharrack Show was run on similar lines to other Cornish shows, but sadly through lack of interest was discontinued. A carnival was staged every year, proving popular for a while before it, too, was discontinued, but happily it has been revived in recent years. A tea treat was held every year in the playing field; various stalls were set up, and a character known as 'Jam Pot Moyle' would sell goldfish, the customers providing their own jam pot. The Serpentine Walk around the village ended the day and included a walk through the Maze.

Today's modern village with improved transport, both public and private, means access to the larger towns, which has resulted in a lot of local shops closing. However, village life hasn't changed much, as various clubs and organisations are thriving.

🍁 CARLEEN

The name Carleen is probably derived from Caer – a Celtic word for fortified homestead. Carleen is a very small village nestling under Tregonning Hill – which was inhabited certainly by the Bronze Age peoples, if not by their predecessors in the New Stone Age. It was probably the Bronze Age people who began building the large fortification on the summit of the hill known as Castle Pencaire.

In about AD 500 a band of Irish holy men and women landed at Hayle with St Breaca and made their way to Tregonning Hill. Just on the fringe of Carleen she established her church between what are now two farmsteads, Chynoweth and Tolmennor. She later moved to the lowlands and built another church in an area which has perpetuated her name, the village of Breage.

Carleen is in the parish of Breage and since the 18th century has grown into a village because of the tin mines. It was the home of the biggest tin mine in Cornwall during the 19th century – Wheal Vor, which employed around 1,200 men, women and children in about 1850. Many of the new inhabitants were Methodists and a huge chapel and Sunday school were built in 1833. A smaller chapel opposite this site, built in 1762 soon after John Wesley visited the area, had become inadequate. The old chapel soon became a village shop and remained so until 1979. Many of the old cottages were built from cob – a mixture of clay and straw – and had their roofs thatched with reed.

Carleen's industrial past also involved china clay quarrying. It was on Tregonning Hill where William Cookworthy, in 1746, discovered the ingredients to perfect hard paste porcelain. When purer china clay was discovered near St Austell, the local china clay industry declined. A brickmaking company was then formed, and the late 19th century kiln still stands.

Much hardship was experienced when the Wheal Vor mine closed in the 1870s. Many men went overseas to try and get a living – some never to return to their families. Many of the mine shafts have now been capped.

One well known local character was Henry Magor, an accomplished horseman who worked for Mr Will Tyack. Mr Tyack kept a large number of horses which were used to pull huge consignments of timbers, coal and mine equipment to the mines. Harry could command upwards of 20 horses in harness which pulled a large wagon through the very narrow lanes to their destination. He would often get drunk, climb on the wagon and fall asleep – the horses bringing him back home to Carleen!

Sadly, the chapel has closed. The Apostolic church has served the village for many years. It is now known as Carleen Community Church and really lives up to its new name.

An old lady called Eleanor Wills made little brushes from 'griglans' – an old Cornish dialect word for heathers. She bound the griglans together to make a small hand brush which was used to clean the clome ovens and open hearths. She walked from Carleen across Tregonning Hill to Penzance to sell her wares.

During the great blizzard of 1891, another old lady who lived on the outskirts of the village had come to the shop to get some groceries. On her way back to her little cottage in Wheal Vor Road, or Black Road – so called because of the black tin found in the mine – she stopped to shelter. The blizzard came in so thick that she died of exposure under a gorse bush. Her name was 'Lizzie Figgy' and it has been immortalised in this area in that anyone suffering from the cold is referred to as 'being like Lizzie Figgy'.

The village shop sold everything from hobs for boots to dried fish from Newfoundland. On entering the shop one was bombarded by an aroma of vinegar, oranges, dried fruit, candles, vegetables in sacks – all these smells created one delicious fragrance. What a wonderful meeting-place to catch up with all the village gossip! A second shop opened some years afterwards, and there was a certain amount of rivalry over customers. A little row of cottages known as Gilbert's Row was built by a relative of former proprietors of this shop, which has now closed, but there is a daily bus service. There are plans for a new village hall.

Long may the village remain sheltered under the shadow of its proud industrial past, and its residents continue to preserve what is left for future generations.

🍁 Carnkie

Carnkie started life as a cluster of cottages, mostly inhabited by workers from the quarries at Mabe and Longdowns, about four miles and one and a half miles away.

There was a surprisingly large shop, selling a wide variety of goods, and two carpenters who were also the local coffinmakers. 'When you heard the nails being hammered into the coffin, you knew that someone in the area had died. Those nails had a different sound to the others.'

There was also a forge standing conveniently close to the public water pump, in the centre of the village. The pump was the place where neighbours exchanged news and gossip as they waited to fill their buckets with the clear spring water, while the children played and teased around them, gleefully hiding the buckets and containers – presumably to the exasperation of their elders!

Two unique features of the village were the monkey puzzle trees which could be clearly seen from the hill tops around the village. No one knows how or why these unusual trees came to be planted in Carnkie.

The shop closed in 1986 and is now a house, the carpenters and the blacksmith are gone, and the pump fell silent when mains water was brought to the village in 1967. The monkey puzzle trees have also disappeared. Bungalows gradually sprang up along the road that runs through the village – some of the cottages were demolished to make way for them – and the village slowly grew a new face.

The chapel was built in 1900, its rather sombre exterior belying the warm intimacy of the inside of the building, where a small number of members and the Sunday school meet every Sunday. Our playgroup meets at Halwin school. The WI meet in the village hall and hold their annual craft and produce show there in September.

The whole village turns out for the annual barbecue, when the very old and the very young come together to share in an old-fashioned evening of friendliness and fun. Listening to the Wendron band playing here on a warm summer's evening, in the company of family and neighbours, is a truly special experience.

During the 19th century Carnkie was one of the villages known for its midnight revelries, but now the rather more sedate events are confined to the popular cricket club, which enjoys a reputation for being one of the best clubs in the district, with a variety of amenities to appeal to members of all ages.

The friendly garage owner has taken over from the blacksmith, and a visit to the village hairdresser takes you into a charming olde-worlde cottage, no chrome and glass reception here, just a warm and friendly welcome. A strong sense of family unity still prevails, and in times of trouble neighbours don't hesitate to knock on your door with offers of help, while being equally eager to share the joyful occasions.

🍁 Coads Green

Coads Green is in North Hill parish in North Cornwall, and has a panoramic view of the Cornish hills.

Before 1826 when the first Methodist chapel was erected on a site supplied by a generous benefactor for a fee of 30 shillings, there were few houses, although some of the outlying farms are of great age. But long memories can recall life as it was here about 80 or 90 years ago, some with great amusement.

Then there were butchers, fishmongers, a blacksmith, saddler, mason, carpenter, seamstress, midwife and wart charmer. Jobs were mainly agricultural, plus several men who worked at the ochre pit just outside the village. Ochre was used in making camouflage. The fishmonger, known as 'Blind Weekes', travelled by pony and trap 22 miles to Looe for fish, the trap driven by a lad who was his guide. The saddler repaired leather goods, but had a golden rule that at 3 pm daily he would stop work for a pipe of tobacco, and until it was finished his customers just had to wait. The blacksmith's forge was a centre point of the village. Here he would make, among other things, 'scoots' from donkey shoes for the men's hobnail boots.

A chapel caretaker, grave digger and horseman, a real strong man, was known to have started to dig a grave at 4 am, do a day's work, and complete the grave all in a day. On one occasion, having toothache, he persuaded a friend to pull the offending tooth out with pliers! To prevent him working after he sustained broken ribs, his wife was obliged to hide his clothes.

Another remembered character was 'Dr' Hick who lived in an old cottage (still standing) in the centre of the village. He made embrocation, mainly for animals, which he took around the district in a donkey and cart. On his return he would release the donkey and let it have a jolly good roll in the middle of the road. Locals swore by his 'cure', the formula of which he kept a guarded secret.

Local carpenters made coffins, and a continuous 'tap, tap' from the workshop denoted a death. Coffins were carried low by teams of six men at a time, and a timekeeper would accompany the cortege to signal time for a changeover. This was before the advent of cars.

Most housewives made bread and cakes with wheatflour ground at nearby Ruses Mill. Cookers were old black ranges requiring much black lead polishing. Today there is a choice of electricity, Calor gas or solid fuel cooking.

Water supply came from the village pump above a 60 ft deep well at an annual rental of three shillings, until 1953, thereafter four shillings. This entitled paid up members to attend any 'Deep Well' meetings. When water was low, it was rationed to two buckets a day, after which the pump was locked! It fell into disrepair, but was restored by the WI in 1985. The telephone exchange was installed in 1929.

Mains water, electricity and council houses came to the village in 1954. The population in 1977 was 145, in 1990 it was 175. Although quite small, it is a very busy community supporting many organisations. The chapel was later used as a Sunday school, then a day school in 1867, with twelve children on the register. The primary school today has over 80 children. The school bell was rehung and rung after 40 years to mark the Millennium, and is now in daily use. There is a Methodist church and resident minister, shop and post office, garage, social centre hall, telephone kiosk, and a bus shelter serving the Launceston-Plymouth route. There has never been a village pub.

An annual pantomime of local talent, started in the 1960s and well known for miles around, contributes to many charities.

🍁 CONNOR DOWNS

Connor Downs lies on the eastern edge of the district of Penwith, four miles west of Camborne and two miles east of Hayle. It is a village of linear shape which has developed around the route of the former A30 trunk road which ran through the centre. It is in the parish of Gwithian.

The downs were originally named Connorton or Connorton Downs and these names are mentioned in the Domesday Book. Apparently Connorton referred to a wide area which included Gwithian and Hayle and it is said that it could originate from the Irish word Conair meaning 'a haven', which would have referred to the natural harbour of the Hayle estuary. It was very much a farming community with one or two large farms and many smallholdings. This meant that most of its inhabitants were involved in agriculture, though some were miners who travelled by donkey and shay to East Pool Mine and Dolcoath Mine at Camborne to work. Local people were also employed at the nearby explosive works at Upton Towans during the First World War.

The mission church served as the first school in Connor Downs with children walking to school from the neighbouring villages of Gwithian and Angarrack and also from the outlying areas. For some children this meant a walk of between eight and ten miles a day. In 1908 the present school was built and at that time it catered for children between the ages of five and 15.

The village was almost self sufficient with a variety of shops and services. These included a butcher's, a barber's, a blacksmith, a newsagent, a fish and chip shop, a garage, a post office and a carpenter's and undertaker's. Water was supplied by a series of wells, about six in number, which were at various points around the village. Most of these have now been filled in.

There is a rhyme connected with the village:

'Connor Downs happy land,
Spalling stones and selling sand.'

This obviously referred to the three stone plats in the area where cartloads of large stones were delivered. A workman using a large mallet broke up the stones which were then used for roadbuilding. Sand was sold at a halfpenny a bucket and was used by housewives for cleaning the cement floors of their homes. The sand was sprinkled over the floors and then brushed up.

These days there is still a pub, a post office, a newsagent's, a signwriter's, a petrol station and two garages selling cars – a far cry from the 1920s when there was only one car in the village and this was owned by Mr Jory the local undertaker. Most people used a horse and trap or had to walk to Gwinear Road station to catch a train.

Over the years many changes have taken place; several housing estates and individual houses have been built which consequently has used up much of the farmland. The village has also been bypassed which has greatly reduced the volume of traffic passing through and of course the new road has taken away farmland as well. The original road through Connor Downs was a turnpike road which was constructed in 1829 and it had a toll gate. Most of the present day inhabitants work in neighbouring towns and the majority of the children of secondary school age attend the comprehensive schools in Camborne or Hayle. Generally now the emphasis is on horticulture rather than agriculture with many fields of broccoli, bulbs and cabbages and there is also a pick-your-own fruit farm in the area.

🍁 CONSTANTINE

Lying between Falmouth and the Lizard and about two miles from the Helford river, Constantine is a granite village built on a hill. It boasts a butcher, an electrical shop, a new art gallery/estate agent and two general stores, one of which incorporates the finest wine merchant in the area. The parish church of St Constantine, built on the site of a Celtic monastery in the 15th century, and the Italianate Methodist chapel are both constructed of granite, as are the old terraced houses, built when the local quarries were the main employers. This is no longer so and those of the 1,500 or so inhabitants who are not retired have the same variety of occupations as any rural community. Other recent changes include the loss of the police house and the village 'bobby'; the exchanging of the old vicarage for a modern house half a mile from the church, and the building of a fine new surgery for the local practice instead of the Old Doctor's House. The chapel was recently bought for use by the community, and is now called 'The Tolmen Centre'.

The village has a thriving silver band which plays at local charity events and leads the carnival in August and the carol singing at Christmas. For over 100 years the Garden Society has staged its annual show in July and a younger organisation, the Arts Society, holds a summer exhibition. There are also numerous clubs and societies catering for all ages and interests. The social club, two public houses and a small restaurant provide refreshment for both locals and visitors but generally Constantine is not a holiday resort but a working community.

Streams and underground waterways run down through the wooded valley to Polwheveral creek where they join the Helford river at Calamansack.

The past has not always been so peaceful, for in the 1960s an elderly farmer was robbed and murdered at Nanjarrah Farm by two young men, one a local who later paid the extreme penalty. In earlier days the ghost of an ancestor of the late Sir Peter Scott, who lived at Trewardreva, was reputed to gallop through the village followed by his pack of hounds. Superstition also tells of travellers to Constantine being 'pixie mazed' or led astray by mischievous little folk. The only way to break the spell was to turn a garment inside out. More recently on Constantine's Feast day in March, stalls were set up on either side of Fore Street selling all kinds of delights including delicious Cornish Fairings. Unfortunately this custom, together with tea treats, is no longer with us but the village still lives as a busy and friendly community, virtually self contained.

🍁 COVERACK

Coverack is a small fishing village situated on the south-east corner of the Lizard peninsula in an Area of Outstanding Natural Beauty. It has a nucleus of indigenous families but also a large percentage of retired people, most of whom have spent many holidays in Coverack in their youth. A number of houses (including the old Headland Hotel) are used for holiday occupation only.

Reached via Helston or Gweek over the Goonhilly Downs (the BT earth station), steep hills unsuitable for caravans or long vehicles lead to the village. The 'new' road, and better access, is the B3294 (fork right after Zoar garage).

Once the haunt of smugglers, now the village is a centre for windsurfing, crabbing, diving and pleasure fishing. It has two beaches and sand and rock pools at low tide; Mill beach in the village (the mill has disappeared!) and Mears to the west of Chynalls Point (an Iron Age fort) reached by the coastal path from Sunny Corner beside the chapel. It is safe bathing, but care is needed in amateur navigation as it is a dangerous coast – the Manacles have claimed many a victim, even to the present day.

All year round facilities include a sub post office, general stores (off licence and groceries), the Paris public house named after a famous local wreck, the Bay Hotel and a Youth Hostel. In season there is Archie's Loft (specialist ice cream made locally), the Seine Loft (pottery, casual clothing, souvenirs), the Mill Shop (souvenirs and ice cream), the Harbour Lights cafe, an art gallery, and a craft and art exhibition. Places of worship are St Peter's church and the Methodist chapel.

Coverack is an area for 'switching off' rather than for organised entertainment, but there are the usual village activities – including weekly bingo, a carnival, a regatta and Lifeboat Day (the lifeboat had an impressive record of service but was disbanded in 1972), and the Coverack Singers have a summer show.

🍁 CRAFTHOLE

In the early 1900s Crafthole was a small village situated on a hill between the sea and a valley. There were about three farms and approximately 40 houses and cottages, two of which were thatched. Most families kept fowls and some reared a pig.

It boasted a small post office, a butcher's shop and a dairy belonging to one of the farms where village folk fetched their milk in jugs. Right opposite there was a bakery where one could buy home made bread and delicious dough cakes, mainly baked in a clome oven, also groceries. Children loved to pop in for a pennyworth of sweets, done up in a greaseproof screw of paper. Later on, a grocery store opened up by the New Inn, now renamed the Finnygook Inn, then a small sweet shop appeared on a lawn in front of another cottage.

The Wesleyan chapel, situated in the centre of the village, was built in 1867. At one time the lower room was used as a day school and now meetings are held there. Recently table tennis teams have been formed, catering both for juniors and seniors, and all have gained success playing in League games. There is also a thriving Sunday school and Sunday Club for the youth.

Crafthole has two historic monuments, one the cross at the top of the hill, where markets and a fair were once held; an important place for travellers to rest awhile and where monks paused to worship during their pilgrimage down through Cornwall. The cross used to stand in the middle of the road, but with the coming of the motor car it had to be moved to the side of the hedge for safety. The other monument is the village pump, where villagers had to draw their water for drinking, now no longer in use because in the 1930s piped water was brought through the village.

In 1920 the Sheviock parish recreation room was opened and it soon became the centre of activities. Meetings, concerts, whist drives and dances were held. The dances were mainly 'sixpenny hops' when music was supplied by piano and drums. The one big event of the year was the sports and carnival, when every house was dressed overall with bunting and flags and anyone who could play an instrument joined in to lead the fancy dress parade around the village. The whole proceedings ended with a grand dance, when a special dance band was engaged to supply the music. Events continued until 1962 when the owner of the recreation room passed away and so the parish lost a great asset, and events as far as possible were then held in the Methodist schoolroom. In the meantime, a fund had been set up for a new hall and eventually in 1976 the Sheviock parish memorial hall came into being, built mainly by voluntary labour. The Carnival and Flower Show have been successfully revived with added attractions.

More estates have been built now, so the number of people living in the village has greatly increased. The working population commute to Plymouth mainly, and the children are taken by bus to schools in Antony and Torpoint. The farms have been amalgamated and the barns converted into houses. There is a post office, along with a well stocked shop, milk is brought to the door and a fishmonger calls once a week.

Crafthole is still a lovely village in which to live, with the sea not too far away, moors in the distance, fantastic views and the lights of Plymouth shining bright and clear at night.

❦ CURY

Cury is a geographically divided village on the Lizard peninsula, just south of the Royal Naval Air Station at Culdrose. Divided, because the public house and post office are at Cury Cross Lanes and the churches, schools and most houses are at Cury Churchtown, Whitecross and Nantithet a mile or so away. This was not always the situation, originally the pub was next to the church where the cottage now called The Old Inn House stands, plus a long gone cluster of cottages. Surrounding this area was a deer park called Parc Cury. In the little hamlet of Nantithet is a picturesque cottage called Cobblers, which was originally a shoemaker's shop and before that a 'kiddley-wink'.

The area is mainly a farming community – dairy, sheep, beef, potatoes, broccoli and the new crop of asparagus. Because of the closeness to Culdrose and the Goonhilly earth satellite station some of the inhabitants of the village are newcomers.

From airships to spring water and wind turbines could be the story of the Bonython estate at Cross Lanes. If the necessary planning permission is received, up to 15 wind turbines could occupy the site that was once known as the Mullion Royal Naval Air Station. This station was commissioned in June 1916 for the operation of airships against the German U Boats. Records show that one airship patrol lasted a record 19½ hours and then came down in the sea at Mullion Cove. Each man's rations for this trip were salt bacon sandwiches, six Horlicks tablets, a quarter lb Cadbury's chocolate and a quarter pint of tea. There must have been some very thirsty men on board when you consider the sandwiches and the small amount of fluid. Most of the buildings have disappeared, but there are anchorage points for the 'Blimps' still to be found.

There are three school buildings still standing near the church; the oldest dates back to 1812 and is now a farm store. The second, dating from 1849, has been converted into a delightful cottage and the third, a modern building, was opened in 1967.

A former vicar of Cury, Paul Foot BA, wrote a book on the history of Cury. The stories go back many centuries, but one of interest is about the great tree on the village boundary road just north of the Wheel inn near Gwealeth. Apparently this ash tree spread its branches to a diameter of 70 ft and had a trunk of 27 ft in girth. Under this tree meetings took place and also the great fight between miners from Wendron and Breage over the spoils of a wreck. It seems a long way to come to get wreckage, but it appears that a hefty bal maiden, 'Prudy the Wicket' killed a man called Gluyas with her iron-shod patten. The branches of this large tree fell in 1857 and the trunk was removed in 1862. The roots had been sustained by a spring of water which is still there, although slightly altered during recent road improvements.

Another story is about John Jewell of Trevergy, a very superstitious man who feared goblins and ghosts. The Boaden brothers who lived across the valley decided to play a practical joke on him when he passed their farm on his way home from Helston market. They obtained a disused wheel from the old mill at Millewarne, took it up the hill and filled it with furze, dry bracken and branches. When evening came and John Jewell plodded home, the brothers set alight their giant Catherine Wheel and set it off down the hill. It went faster and faster, jumping and bumping over every obstacle. John Jewell turned and saw what he thought was the Devil himself coming after him. He and his horse went straight through his farm gate without even opening it and never stopped until he reached his door, fainting and half dead with fright. Next day the whole neighbourhood turned up to view the evidence and tracks.

🍁 CUSGARNE & FROGPOOL

Cusgarne Wartha in Cornish, Cosgaran or Crane Wood, and Frogpool, in the parish of Gwennap, lie in a sheltered valley on the edge of the famous tin and copper mining area of United Downs. Here in the past were many industries; flour mills, wool, paint, linen and candle factories to name a few. The candles, very important, were used in the early mines. There were also several general stores dotted around the villages.

Cusgarne Wartha House, built in 1629, was rented to James Watt, the famous engineer, and his family in 1780-1800. Tradition has it John Wesley visited and stayed in this house when preaching at Gwennap Pit.

The village school was a board school built in 1877 and is still flourishing today.

Many of the inhabitants emigrated all over the world during the slump in tin and copper mining. One boy, John Verran, who went from Cusgarne, became Premier of South Australia.

The parish church of St Wenap is in Gwennap village one to two miles away. It was built on the site of a monastery which is believed to have stood there about 1,400 years ago. The churchyard is closed for burials but the present cemetery is situated in Frogpool.

The Methodist chapel in Frogpool was built in 1843. Adjacent to it is the Sunday schoolroom erected in 1908. This was built on old foundations of an 1828 chapel building and is a busy centre of village activity. The old Cornish tradition of an annual tea treat has died out. There was a parade behind the Wesleyan banner through the villages followed by entertainment in a nearby field.

The village shop-cum-post office and off licence sell all the essential goods without people having to drive out of the village. A local farmer has made a success of organic farming methods. You can buy fresh vegetables at a farm gate in the middle of Frogpool. The Cornish Arms merits mention – good food, beer and entertainment always available.

This is and always has been an area of small farms. There are also several small businesses in the villages; carpenters, builders, car mechanics plumbers and hairdressers to name a few. Many people commute to neighbouring towns and many more are retired.

Several interesting people have lived here. Mr John Coster, the inventor of the useful machine in mines, the Whim, was observed by some of his friends to be engaged in making something new; when questioned he replied, 'I have a whim in my head'; hence the origin of the name.

This lovely sheltered valley, where many rare plants grow, is a delightful place to live, with something for everyone to enjoy. With numerous footpaths and country lanes for recreation, Cusgarne and Frogpool remain quiet and secluded villages.

❧ DELABOLE

Mention the name Delabole to anyone and they will usually say 'Oh yes, that long straggly village shrouded in mist. I didn't stop'. Being only a mile or so from the magnificent North Cornish coastline, and over 600 ft above sea level, it does receive more than its fair share of sea mists. Hidden here in the lunar landscape is a history and way of life almost unchanged in centuries. There's not a lot of tourism, this is a working village, and that large gaping open wound is the life force of Delabole. Stop and visit this famous quarry and its museum, but watch the edge – it is over 500 ft deep and a mile in circumference. Its history dates BC and it is mentioned in the Domesday Book. Slate from here was used to roof Winchester Castle in 1314, and many examples of slate old and modern can be seen today facing and roofing important buildings all over the world.

Talk to the people and you will find generations of families who have relied on the quarry for their employment, the methods of their work changing very little over the years. Men still sit in their 'bench' and hand split slate with a bettle and chisel. Call in the local pub, named for these workman's tools, and you will find young men enjoying their ale, darts and dominoes as did their forefathers. The talk will be of Countesses, Wide Ladies, Randoms and Peggies. Who are these infamous ladies? Sorry to disappoint you, they are all sizes of slates. A lovely example of Delabole slate can be found enhousing the bar of the Bettle and Chisel. The table tops and the bar counter are all made from sheets of polished slate. Quarry tools and artefacts hang around the walls of the bar, which is now owned and run by locally born people, as are many of the shops in the village. Wherever you turn in Delabole you will find evidence of its long established industrial history, even the altar in the parish church is made of slate.

It is interesting that Delabole village didn't exist before 1893. Prior to that date it was three separate hamlets, Pengelly, Medrose and Churchtown, supporting between them five chapels. The coming of the railway changed it all, and the hamlets amalgamated taking the name of the quarry as their collective name. Little evidence of this busy railway line can now be found, though traces are still around. The hamlets in turn grew and became an entity, though the roads leading up to the quarry still bear the names of Pengelly and Medrose.

The quarry and Delabole village are inseparable, each relying on the other for its existence. It is still a close community, though it has seen its disasters, as when the Poppet Head at the edge of the quarry collapsed in 1869, taking with it 10,000 tons of slate, killing 15 men and injuring six others. You can still talk to men in the village whose grandparents told of the 'Great Disaster' which to them equalled the great Levant mine disaster.

Delabole is not a pretty village, but linger and chat and gain a slice of Cornish history, you will be very glad you did so.

🍁 DOBWALLS

Dobwalls is situated three miles west of Liskeard with a population of over 1,500, but in the old days it was less than 200. It is generally believed that the name derives from the word 'Cobwalls', maybe because the majority of the cottages were built of cob at that time.

Originally it was just one straight road with five narrow lanes branching off, leading mostly to farms, one crossroad being at the top and the other near the lower end. One lane however led down to five cottages; the bottom one standing alone was affectionately called 'The Salt Box'.

There were two carpenter's shops, two chapels and a mission church; there is now one Methodist and St Peter's church. There was also a blacksmith and two shops – the Co-operative stores and a private family business. There are still only two shops, although Rowe's garage shop can supply almost all one's needs. The old Co-op is now a hairdresser's and one of the carpenter's shops a flourishing florist.

Dobwalls once boasted an harmonica band and a village concert party, both being greatly in demand, travelling near and far giving concerts for charity etc.

Water was supplied by two chutes, one at the top and the other in the middle of the village, the lower end being supplied by a well. A large fig tree grew about halfway down the village and produced a good crop of figs every year.

Of course village life wouldn't be complete without a few odd characters. One old lady always did her washing and housework by night. She would light up her boiler when most folk would be going to bed, but she was an excellent cook and was noted for her fruit cakes. One old chap was nearly always to be found leaning over his garden gate – weather permitting – and would shout 'Marnin' to everyone passing. The majority would say 'Morning' in reply, but should there be a stranger who ignored him, he would say 'Come from up country I s'pose'. Then there was 'Neddy'. He had a little wooden hut by the lower crossroads where he repaired bicycles, clocks and also sold sweets! The strong smell of solution, carbide and rubber greeted you as you entered, but there was never a grumble from Neddy if he had to stop in the middle of mending a puncture to serve – often with filthy hands – a hap'orth of rats tails, or a ribbon of liquorice. Who ever heard of hygiene!

Dobwalls now looks very different. Eight housing estates have been built and in 1954 a splendid Victory hall was erected in memory of the men lost in two wars. The village is quite a thriving place. There is a butcher and the post office, and your laundry can also be brought and collected from there. For many years there was no pub but in 1963, in spite of stiff opposition, a private house became the Highway inn, recently renamed the Highwayman.

Dobwalls is situated on the main London to Land's End trunk road and naturally the traffic is very heavy, though there are traffic lights and a pedestrian crossing, as well as two 'bollard' crossings. Villagers live in hope that the long promised bypass will one day be a reality.

🍁 DULOE

Duloe lies above and between the East and West Looe rivers. One could be forgiven for driving through, on your way perhaps to Looe, and only seeing a quiet street with a garage, post office cum shop, Jubilee Centre, pub and church, with houses of various styles. What you might not see is the humming activity of village life behind those doors.

Duloe started long, long ago in the Bronze Age and has its very own stone circle of six eight foot high quartz stones which glint in the sunlight and stand eerily waiting by moonlight. A burial urn and Bronze Age bracelet have been found in the area. Several of its old manors were mentioned in the Domesday Book, all of which survive today although rebuilt as farmhouses.

For generations it has been a farming community and still today a large number of the villagers are connected in some way with farming, with tourism creeping in here and there. In the last half of the 1800s the nearby hamlet of Herodsfoot was a thriving and prosperous mining community. Although little remains of its mining past it hasn't disappeared, unlike Carglonnon of which typhoid fever and mine closure took its toll.

St Cuby's church stands squarely against the ravages of weather and time, built in the 1300s probably on the site of an Iron Age fort. Inside its walls the memorials, effigies and tombs tell of those people who shaped the village in the past. Always a centre of activity of one sort or another, when the tower was restored in the 1850s because it leaned dangerously, 'whispers' say it was because of the weight of contraband once stored beneath! The six bells have rung out over the land since the 1750s and were only silent during the Second World War.

St Cuby's Well, as with many holy wells, has its legend. Originally it had a circular bowl or font of granite with a griffin and dolphins carved around it. The legend says dire misfortune would attend anyone who moved it, this being 'proved' when a farmer with a team of oxen came to move it and one of the oxen fell down dead! When it was moved to Trenant Park, Squire Peel had to pledge to provide pensions for the families of any who fell dead during the operation. The bowl now rests quietly in St Cuby's church.

The Plough inn with its chequered past is another place where you can glimpse village life. At one time it was combined with a butcher's shop – very convenient for its patrons to enjoy fried steak washed down with ale. Then the licence was not renewed and it became a temperance hotel, then a private house and has now come full circle and again its patrons can enjoy a meal and a drink.

The WI hall at the green was for a number of years the focal point for village activities, from Flower Shows right across the board to a drama group. Now village life is thriving in the purpose-built Jubilee Centre.

Duloe is a survivor, it keeps its heart and traditions but bends and sways with the winds of time, keeping the old but including the new.

🍁 EGLOSHAYLE

The parish of Egloshayle derives its name from the church, meaning church on the estuary. There is no record when the church was founded, but it is presumed that the benefactor was Robert Earl of Morton or his son William. The church is said to have been dedicated to St Petroc, which could have been possible as he travelled between Padstow and Bodmin.

Egloshayle is a parish by the river Camel and is bounded in part by the river Alan. The river Kestell flows nearby and empties into the Alan. The parish contains the villages of Washaway, Ford, Sladesbridge, Gonvena, Bodieve and Egloshayle.

Egloshayle church is a building of Early English and Perpendicular styles. The western tower is 82 ft high containing a clock and eight bells, five of which were recast in 1756. In the churchyard are the graves of Nevell Norway and his wife. Nevell Norway was returning (riding horseback) from the market at Bodmin, and at Washaway he was murdered by the Lightfoot brothers who lived at Burlawn. The brothers were hanged at a public hanging at Bodmin in 1840. Legend has it that sometimes a ghostly white rabbit can be seen in the churchyard.

Vicar Lovybond was given permission by the Bishop of Exeter to build a bridge, with the mason John de Harlyn, across the river Camel. Foundations were first laid on sandy ground and were washed away with every tide. Lovybond despaired of ever building the bridge until he laid 'Pakkes of Woole' for the foundations on which the bridge was built. This took place in 1450 onwards. Before the bridge was built there were chapels on both sides of the river where people would give thanks for a safe journey across.

Behind the church is Court Place which was sold in 1807 to a William Norway. Nearby is the old inn, the Earl of St Vincent, so named after a naval officer who was at the battle of Trafalgar with Lord Nelson.

Egloshayle bell ringers were the best in the county in the 1800s, winning contests wherever they went. Their names were Humphry Cradock, John Ellery, John Pollard, Thomas Cleave and, captain of the tower, William Richard. A song about them ('The Ringers of Egloshayle') was recorded in January 1932 by the organist of St Breocke church and sung by William Richard, aged 81 years old at the time and with 54 years bellringing experience. Descendants of the above are still living in the district.

Many new housing estates have been built in the district. At the top, Trenant Vale is the town's industrial estate with the North Cornwall council offices nearby. Wadebridge sports centre and the town's football field are in Bodieve Road. On the playing field are bowling greens, tennis courts, a cricket ground, a play school and a children's play area. The rugby ground is across from the church. There is a men's and ladies' choir and a theatre company in the town. At the end of August a four day craft fair is held in the church when a folk festival is held in the town.

EGLOSKERRY

There is no doubt that 'Eglos' comes from the old Celtic word for church, but about the rest of the village name there are differing opinions. One authority derives it from the Cornish 'caer', a stony place; others hold that it comes direct from one of the myriad of Cornish saints, Keri – 'about whose life', as a recent vicar said, 'little is known'. The church shares its dedication to St Keri (or St Cyriacus) with St Petroc, although the Ordnance Survey maps attribute it to St Corantius. Much of the history of Cornwall is shrouded in its characteristic mist.

The origins of the church are Norman but from this period only a doorway remains, the main construction dating from the 15th century. There are still some people in the locality who remember the disastrous fire of 1922. A path leads through the village 'square' to the holy well, the water from which was used for baptisms at the church font. There is also a small Methodist chapel.

Close by the church is the village shop and post office, notice board and public telephone, also a pleasant area of flowering shrubs and grass with a seat originally donated by the WI. Many of the local houses are built of Cornish stone, quarried within the parish. The school nearby has been housed in temporary buildings since about the time of the First World War! It has an average roll of 50, many of the children coming by bus from surrounding areas. The 19th century school building is now the village hall where parish council and WI meetings are held, as well as other regular activities. The old mill, now a private house, is sited near the river Kensey in the valley, along which ran the North Cornwall branch of the railway from Launceston to Padstow, opened in 1892 and closed in 1966. The former station is now a private dwelling with a garden stretching along the line and still including the old name board.

Like many parishes in Cornwall Egloskerry has a compact village centre, but many of the 254 adult inhabitants live in the outlying hamlets and farms up to two miles away. The population has remained fairly stable for the last 150 years or so, the occupants of new bungalows replacing depleted farming families. Some employment is found on local farms, in the rural workshops and in home industry, but most is in the industrial estates, shops and offices of Launceston five miles away.

Within the parish is Penheale Manor, one of the Cornish manors held from the King at the time of the Domesday Book, in which the village was named Eggoscrue. Little remains of the medieval buildings. The estate was not always well maintained, having many absentee owners. One who lived on the spot in the 19th century was the 'Squarson' (who combined the office of squire with that of parson) Rev Simcoe, after whom the inn (now, alas no more) was named, the Simcoe Arms. Captain Colville, who had bought the estate soon after the First World War, entrusted restoration to Sir Edwin Lutyens, whose new wing is in keeping with the beautiful Jacobean house. The extensive gardens well known for magnificent camellias, rhododendrons and azaleas are open to the public in spring and early summer. The present owner Mrs Diana Colville, now resident in the Dower House, the Barton, has recently held the office of High Sheriff of Cornwall. The estate now farms the greatest amount of arable land in the area, with fields enlarged for ease of working. Most of the smaller scattered farms keep to the old hedgerow-patterned smaller fields for grazing; a flock of sheep or a herd of cattle is not an uncommon sight on the village roads.

🍁 FEOCK

Feock, once known as St Feock until the post authority wanted the shortened form, lies on the western shores of the river Fal, up which the saint whose name still remains is said to have sailed as a missionary about 1,500 years ago. Nothing definite is known about him, or maybe her, but the day is kept on 2nd February as Feock Feast and he is remembered in Truro Cathedral on Thursdays. A well in the area known as La Feock is said to be where he lived in his bee-hive hut and called the few inhabitants to prayer. Footpaths lead from

Loe Beach, Feock

the beach to this spot. Now the bell from the 13th century bell tower, which is separated from the parish church dedicated to St Feock, calls the parishioners to the parish Eucharist at 10.15 am on Sundays.

Feock is approached by a minor road off the Truro/Falmouth road (A39) or from the King Harry ferry or by boat up the river Fal. Heavy traffic builds up, especially during the summer months. At the weekends, the steep hill leading to the beach gets congested with cars and trailers, bringing windsurfers, trailing dinghies and craft of all kinds, including the rowing gigs which race from the beach. The number of craft increases soon after 1st April when the oyster dredging season ends and remains high until 1st October when the season opens. It is an ideal spot for windsurfing and sailing in the Carrick Roads.

Prettily snuggling into the side of the hill above Cowlands Creek on the river Fal stands Tregew, or 'the farm on the good land'. The site is thought to be the oldest in the parish, and was first mentioned in the taxation of the vicarage of Feock on the 23rd August 1315.

Charles Henderson, writing in the 1920s says 'It still has the appearance of a gentleman's seat, with its park-like surroundings, interspersed here and there with rows of stately elms'. Sadly, the elms are no longer there, but the same impression remains. The Edmonds family who owned Tregew in the 17th century was probably responsible for the transformation from farmhouse to gentleman's residence, and although since that time the property has known both lean and prosperous years, it still stands today as one of the most interesting and impressive buildings in Feock.

There is good reason to believe that the present house stands on the site of an ancient monastery which at different times housed both monks and nuns. The present owners of the farm and their parents have all seen ghosts on numerous occasions during the past 60 years. It is their belief that the benign spirits which are abroad are both those of the monks and nuns of medieval times and those of former owners who have been happy to live at Tregew.

🍁 FOUR LANES

There are Bronze Age remains on Gregwartha Farm dating from 600 BC. The area was originally known as Hawton Downs and Four Lanes is the self-explanatory name given because of the crossroads, though pensioners, with a smile, say it is because of the so-called 'lanes'; Deep Lane, Rooks Lane, Duck Lane and Mammy's Lane.

The village stands 750 ft above sea level with excellent views overlooking Camborne, Redruth, the North Cornish coastline and nearby Carn Brea, which

Victoria Inn, Four Lanes

has an Iron Age fort dating from 200 BC. The more modern television mast is now a landmark in the village. Agriculture, mining and quarrying were the main occupations, West Wheal Bassett being the nearest mine. Mining was carried on under Stannary Laws between the years 1100 and 1800.

St Day used to be the market town in those very early days. People travelled there via Deep Lane – carts carrying meat usually had a boy sitting in the back, armed with a cleaver, with instructions to use it if anyone tried to help themselves. The market house in Redruth opened for local farmers to sell their produce in 1824.

In 1880 the local smithy was in the yard behind the Victoria inn. Later it was transferred across the road and was a thriving business for many years. Records show a post office was in existence by 1880 situated opposite the Central Garage. The latter was opened in May 1935 by Mr Prisk. In 1945 it was taken over by Mr A.J. Tresidder who then incorporated the smithy into his business. During the 1920s and 1930s there were several shops, often started by the womenfolk, sometimes in their kitchens. Men had to seek their fortunes in distant lands because so many mines closed.

Four Lanes always had a good carpenter's shop with wheelwrights, and at least a couple of large families were very active in the building trade. There were also two butchers, three greengrocers, a bootmaker, barber and two monumental masons.

It is thought an inn existed at the Four Lanes crossroads before the time of Oliver Cromwell, known as the Four Lanes inn. About the year 1644 some Roundhead soldiers came this way en route to attack St Michael's Mount. They stopped at the inn to rest, where the locals got them drunk and put them to death, afterwards disposing of the bodies in a bog.

Cockles Court was held every Illogan Feast day. Beer, in a bath, was kept at the back of the Victoria inn and the locals could dip and drink as they wished. People passing through the village had to make a contribution to keep the bath replenished.

Four Lanes Methodist church was built in 1856. Not only did it provide for spiritual needs, but as in most 19th century villages, it was the centre of social life.

Sometime in 1944 a small group of village men sang in aid of the 'Welcome Home Fund' for servicemen, under the leadership of the late Mr S.W. Brown. This led to the formation of the now very successful Four Lanes Male Choir with 65 choristers under the musical directorship of Mr R. Brown, a nephew of Mr S.W. Brown. The choir has achieved success at festivals in Blackpool, Cheltenham and the prestigious Elgar Festival held in Worcester Cathedral in 1988. On three visits to Llangollen International Eisteddfod creditable placings were obtained. Much enjoyed are the annual summer harbour slipway concerts at St Ives, and the traditional Cornish carols in the village square on Christmas morning.

St Andrew's church at Pencoys was erected in 1880, built of stone and granite in the Decorated style, consisting of chancel, nave, porch and a western bellcote containing one bell. As is so often the case there is a pub next door, well known as 'The Sportsmans' or 'Duck pub'.

🍁 FOXHOLE

Foxhole is one of a complex of clay villages, and although once self-sufficient in shops, it now has two general stores, one with a post office. There is a gas supply shop, a chip shop and several small businesses. The social life of the village centres round the football club, with its various sports facilities, and the Working Men's Club. There is also a cricket club. The Methodist chapel and the primary school are in the centre of the village.

The village is overshadowed by Watch Hill, with its four ancient tumuli, on the east side, and on the west side by St Stephen's Beacon. This was called King Pippin's Mount in ancient times, when Pippin is said to have been buried in a barrow within a fortified enclosure at the summit of the beacon. The whole structure was destroyed by miners seeking stone to build an enginehouse – remnants of which can still be seen today.

The first recorded settlements at Foxhole date back to the Middle Ages, when the moors all around the village were worked for tin lodes cropping out at the surface. In Tudor times the tin works around Foxhole included Carpalla, Chygwyn, Goverscailt, Stennagwyn and the Fox Hole mine, from which the village takes its name.

In 1748 William Cookworthy visited the district and noticed a white scar on the beacon which turned out to be an opencast tin mine. His investigations revealed the ground contained fine quality china stone and clay which he used to patent the manufacture of hard paste porcelain and so was responsible for the start of the whole china clay industry in this district.

In 1775 the great potter Josiah Wedgwood visited Foxhole and took leases on china clay-bearing land. Cookworthy's clay pit leases were bought in 1782 by the New Hall Company of Shelton, Staffordshire, makers of the famous New Hall china. When Josiah Wedgwood died in 1795, his three pits were taken over by his son Josiah Wedgwood II. The Carloggas pit, one of these three, was then bought by yet another famous potter, Josiah Spode, whose father had invented bone china.

The Methodist chapel was built in 1894. A newspaper and a newly minted penny were placed beneath the chapel foundation stone when it was built. The school opened in 1911, and at present has well over 100 pupils aged from four to eleven.

The post office is built with fine granite stone and is one of the oldest properties in the village. Both the chapel and post office have 'bench marks' (shown as a vertical arrow) establishing the height of land above sea level.

The Union Hall was little more than a wooden shed in 1920, but was replaced by a building housing the Transport and General Workers Union in 1933. Later it was used as a village hall for concerts, dances and whist drives. It is now a doctors' surgery.

Foxhole Silver Band was originally formed at the end of the 19th century. It was revived during the First World War as a territorial band to encourage men to join up. It entered various contests and during the 1930s won the Prince of Wales trophy three years in succession. In the Second World War, the band was kept going by men too old or too young to fight. It was finally disbanded in 1963.

The weather is probably the most talked-about subject in Foxhole. Winter comes late and goes early. The wind is the most adverse weather condition, but fog can often be seen swirling round the old granite cottages and new commuter-belt bungalows.

🍁 Fraddam

This tiny village, just three miles from Hayle, now only contains 14 houses but in an earlier era boasted over 30. For many years the heart of the village was dominated by the pub, the Half-Way House, so called from the journeys made by monks travelling from St Michael's Mount. Since then the myth has grown to include a half-way mark between Penzance and Redruth, Lands End and Falmouth. This road is now called Pilgrims Way.

At the beginning of the century this was a bustling little community, the inhabitants of the cottages mainly servicing the local mines and quarry, and working on the rich agricultural land surrounding the village. The blacksmith David Pascoe was renowned nationally as being the only person able to sharpen the special drills to bore the holes for blasting the famous Blue Elvan stone, reputed to be the hardest in the United Kingdom, at the adjoining Carpenter Quarry. The quarrymen would split the stones with spaling hammers then transport the stones in carts to various points along the road. The smithy was extremely busy, shoeing horses and mending implements, welding the iron with

Halfway House, Fraddam

the heat of the furnace.

A carpenter created further employment; a huge saw-pit was dug to enable large trees to be cut, by placing a tree over the pit with one man pulling the saw up and another man in the pit pulling the saw down. What strength.

Music played an extremely important role in the village. Two choirs and two bands practised regularly in the band hut and Deveral chapel, and the 'om-pa-pa' took on a particular fervent note for the tea treats. One of the villagers composed music which was often included in their repertoire and the chapel resounded with lusty Cornish voices.

In sharp contrast the pub was always popular, and one particular family loved a Saturday night fight – that was their entertainment! An unusual feature was the landlord's chained monkey that ran up and down the drainpipe, a puzzling sight for the inebriated. One jolly character was reputed to have said his feet couldn't pass by the pub door, only through it!

The roads and ditches in Fraddam were kept immaculate by one much loved roadman named Bert Riddington from Carleen, who was known to everyone by his mammoth red handlebar moustache and whiskers. His original patch was from Sithney School to Fraddam, but nearing his retirement he was given an extra mile to St Erth Praze. He had a pasty every day, and wore out a hook every year.

So what of the future of Fraddam? Hopeful and optimistic. The former pub and more recently Butterfly World has been converted to a very pleasant private home. Fraddam Garage is a busy petrol station and MOT centre, and there is also a vehicle repair garage. The trout farm is still very popular and the surrounding farms are successfully producing market garden crops, cereals, flowers, milk and beef. Some have diversified into providing livery stables for the increasing number of horse owners.

The legendary witch of Fraddam who was reputed to be the most powerful witch in the West Country, concocting poisonous brews and creating great mischief, must indeed feel thwarted today with this enterprising and industrious little village.

🍁 FRADDON

Fraddon is situated on what is believed to be the oldest road in Britain, the Stanna Way dating from 2000 BC, first used from Penzance to Dover, now the main A30.

Blue Anchor was most probably a separate hamlet in the early 20th century. The former Blue Anchor police station (now St Margaret's Hotel) served a large area – the whole St Enoder parish and beyond, including Mitchell. The Blue Anchor Hotel was the local beer house or inn, with records back to 1795. Today it is completely modernised, with additions.

Fraddon has its one chapel, the former Bible Christian (Bryanite). The Bible Christian movement was quite strong in St Enoder; in 1890 the founder, William O'Bryan, preached at 'Luke's Shop' on the Goonbell's Road. There was a former small chapel in 1857 at Fraddon, but the present chapel dates from 1877. As a point of interest note the chapel yard. These were a must in nearly every chapel of that period, reserved for chapel-goers to park trap or jingle, and tether their ponies. Rings for tethering and even drinking troughs can be seen today at some chapels.

The first house at the junction of Parka Road, near the chapel, was once occupied by the great evangelist Gipsy Holland, a member of the well-known travelling gipsy Holland family. Their elegant show caravans lined the top of the Summercourt Park at the annual fair. From here he became converted to Christianity, preaching throughout Cornwall at many crowded Revival meetings; his weekly converts matching in a small way those of Billy Graham. Often he took the service the night before the Monday fair, before a thousand people, with hymns played by the great fair organs.

My-Lords Road leads off from St Margaret's Hotel, named after the lords of the manor. There were small manor houses at Trewheela and Burthy, but Chytane was the larger, described by Joseph Polsue as a handsome and pleasantly situated property, the modern residence of Captain Retallack, and before Retallack, Francis Nicholas Bassett.

It was the Rev Doctor W. Borlase who first discovered the exposure of china clay near the Blue Anchor inn, and in 1819 a Mr Pearce Rogers, solicitor, took a 21 year lease for these new found deposits and the clay industry was begun.

Blue Anchor had its blacksmith's shop, owned by the late Arthur Yelland, and later by his son Curwen Yelland, opposite the Blue Anchor Hotel. This was brisk business in those days, keeping the horses and ponies shod, laying coulters for the plough, keeping the harrow tines well pointed and much more for both the farming community and residents, including making ovens for the old black/brass stoves.

At Barton Lane junction there was the grocer's shop operated by Maggie Yelland, wife of the blacksmith. Opposite Fraddon Garage was the Potato Hot Chip Shop (no fish in those days – just chips) owned by the late Jack Bullock; a pennyworth in a cone-shaped bag and two or three pennyworth in the oblong paper bag.

The Fraddon Garage as it is known today was founded by the late Harris Hawkey, and the big business people of the late 19th century and early 20th century were R.B. Hore & Sons. Their large furniture and hardware store adjoined the Oakdene Terrace, all built by them, with the present large shop and post office, opposite the Parka Road junction. This was a thriving grocery and drapery store, with the cattle food stores adjoining, operating horse-drawn delivery waggons before the age of motor transport.

Most of Higher Fraddon is 20th century, with just a few 19th century buildings, as are most of the dwellings up to the end of Fraddon – the Immanuel chapel is in Indian Queens. This boundary was marked up until the 1940s with the ancient 'Long Stone', believed to be a burial place. Quite a dispute raged for years involving Whitehall, London and preservation societies, but it was moved by road improvements and can now be seen in St Francis' churchyard.

🍁 GERMOE

The village gets its name from St Germoe, who came over from Ireland in the 5th century to bring Christianity. He landed on the north coast, made his way upstream, round Tregonning Hill to a well and a settlement in a valley and decided to stay.

From then on mines were dug and prosperity brought the building of houses with thatched roofs for the workers. There were two pubs in the village, the Cornish Mount and the Dolphin – both long gone, a mining counthouse, a shop, a bakery and a cobbler's shop. There were several tin mines in the area including Great Work and Wheal Reath which gave plenty of work. China clay was dug from Wheal Gray pit and taken by horse-drawn carts to Porthleven to be shipped away. The disused pit is now a fishing lake.

The village well became disused at the beginning of the 20th century because it was not clean and a pump or chute was installed further upstream for drinking water. Every household had to fetch their own and they relied on the rain for other water. In times of drought the fire brigade was called to fill up tanks. Water was fetched by horse-drawn carts until 1939. There is now mains water, but the well has been restored as a feature.

There is no record of a church as such before the 12th century but the present church is very well maintained. A special feature is St Germoe's Chair, situated in the churchyard. There is speculation that St Germoe's bones were buried there. It has long had connections with Palm Sunday, when the clergyman, followed by the cross-bearer and congregation carrying palms, read the lesson and sang a hymn at the Chair. The custom is still carried out.

Germoe Feast is always held on the first weekend in May. It was held on the green outside the church until 1896. There were stalls, teas and the hurling of a 'silver' ball between the two pubs. The Feast has been revived and is now held in the church hall, originally built as a Sunday school. Between the wars there was an annual sports day in one of the Trethewey Farm fields with a band and procession, but this was discontinued when war came.

The highest point in the parish is Tregonning Hill, where the war memorial stands. The hill was a landmark for sailors. At one time wreckers used to put a light there to lure sailors ashore and after they were wrecked everyone went down to Praa Sands for the loot. There was also a signalling station there during the Napoleonic Wars. There is a preaching pit on the hill which is still in use at Whitsun.

The post office dates back to the 18th century, originally just a sorting-shed for the mail brought on horseback. One postmistress was Mrs Bright. When a telegram arrived all the village knew the contents before the recipient because she had to wait for someone to come into the shop who was going in the right direction to deliver it.

Now there is no post office or shop in the village, the nearest is at Praa Sands. There is a bus stop at Germoe crossroads for buses to Helston or Penzance. There were two farms in the village with cattle, flowers and broccoli, but they have been sold and the farm buildings changed into houses. Several bungalows have also been built.

The first small telephone exchange was in the post office, but just before the Second World War one of the first automatic exchanges in Cornwall was built at Germoe crossroads. This has now been rehoused opposite and the original building has been turned into a thriving community centre.

The village school was started on 15th January 1877 with 32 children. A fee of up to ninepence per week had to be paid. Originally the building was very cold and bare, but improvements have been made over the years.

🍁 GERRANS & PORTSCATHO

Anyone travelling the Roseland peninsula and nearing the end of their journey, experiences a thrill at the sheer beauty of the location of Gerrans and Portscatho. Situated on a ridge of land which slopes down to the little harbour, it has all the charm of Cornish scenery. This isn't a sleepy old-world village, it is one of friendly people happy to share the sailing, fishing or birdwatching with all who come.

The village grew up as two settlements 4,000 years ago, when Bronze Age people transported tin and copper across to Gaul; they left their burial urns near Gerrans. The land was not the bright patchwork of fields we see today but covered with scrub-oak and strewn with rocks. One thing, however, we have in common is an abundance of water. Streams run down to the river and springs still emerge from rocky places; they can even bubble up through tarmac roads.

Over a thousand years later a Celtic tribe arrived. With superior iron weapons and tools they took over, cleared the land into small fields and raised stone hedges to enclose animals. Their chieftain built a defensive ditch and earthworks, part of which remains. During the time they were here places were given descriptive names; Porth-Scatha means a harbour of boats.

It was not until monks and hermits arrived from Ireland to spread the gospel that Christianity prevailed. They built their oratories near the old healing wells and incorporated pagan rites into Christian festivals. This happened all over Cornwall. Old stories of the saints arriving on millwheels are quite logical. A heavy quern-stone was placed in the bottom of the boat as ballast, and where more convenient for the passenger to sit, out of the rowers' way!

Gerran, or Geraint, grandson of King Marc of Cornwall, gave his name to the little wooden church at the top of the hill. His Celtic cross still stands near the porch. In times when life was a struggle for all, the dedication of these early Christians was remarkable. Soon a larger stone church was built, then, in Norman times, rebuilt. The font is in use today. In 1450 the octagonal spire which guides travellers to the village was erected as a daymark for the fishermen. Church records of the 16th century show causes of death: fever, drowning, consumption, 'died after drinking brandy', but the commonest was 'the bloody flux' or dysentery, showing the insanitary living conditions in those days.

Nevertheless the people of this remote village were resourceful. Seaweed and shells enriched the soils in Gerrans; Portscatho fishermen toiled in all weathers. There was a tidemill on the river and a windmill at Penwithen. There was clay for dishes and withies for lobster-pots. There were two or three inns, several alehouses, but the wages were very low.

Great changes followed the mission of the Wesleys. New hope surged. Several chapels were built, Friendly Societies flourished, drunkenness decreased. Victorian reformers altered attitudes of landlords who set to and rebuilt dilapidated cob cottages and in 1860 the church school was opened. It served the whole parish and had 130 pupils, twice the number of the present day.

There had always been distinct differences between Gerrans and Portscatho – the seafarers, robust and independent, looked down on the agricultural labourers of 'up Gerrans', but the latter were no less caring and hardworking. Soon housing spread along from the Churchtown and along the cliff edge and up to Highertown. Roads improved a little although coal still came up from Percuil on the ancient tin route. All trades were here: carpenter, cobbler, dressmaker, baker and blacksmith.

And what of today? The holidaymakers have really put the village on the map. Since the climate is kind and it is not always windy, many retired people have come to join us. Some young people have to find work away, but that has always been a Cornishman's lot; most families have a relative in Canada or Australia.

Godolphin Cross

If you pause in the dip between the hills of Tregonning and Godolphin and face east, your eye will be carried across a rolling expanse of farmland to the jagged, higgledy-piggledy outline of buildings which form the outskirts of Camborne. If the day is a clear one you'll notice Carn Brea but you'll probably not have noticed the little village of Godolphin nestling in the valley immediately before you. Only a few roofs are visible, the majority are either hidden in the valley or are obscured by the trees which border the lanes and surround the vicarage and cemetery.

Had you stood here at the beginning of the century you would have been in the midst of the clatter and clamour of the daily routine of the Wheal Breage and Wheal Wreeth tin mines whilst from the valley would have been heard the constant thud of the tin stamps. The small cluster of houses of that era were the homes of tradesmen, farmers, farm labourers, workers and miners most of whom were tenants of the Duke of Leeds.

It can only be supposed that the village name is derived from being situated on and near the crossroads en route to the estate of Godolphin, formerly the home of the famous Godolphin family. The manor house which today attracts a great number of tourists dates back to the 15th century and has many important historic links. However in 1740 Mary, the youngest daughter of Sir Francis Godolphin, married Thomas Osborne, fourth Duke of Leeds and the family moved from Cornwall. Since there was no male heir, properties passed to the descendants of the Duke and remained in their possession until well into this century although the manor estate was to have a number of different owners.

The manor and the village are linked, as in former times, by an impressive avenue of trees under which in the late spring a wonderful carpet of bluebells borders the roads and adorns the adjacent banks.

It used to be a busy, almost self sufficient village. It had a Bible Christian church which in 1932 merged with the Methodists and by 1935 they had extended the building, opening a new chapel and using the former one as its Sunday school. The Anglican church is no longer in use but is a short distance from the chapel, and both are equidistant from the Godolphin Arms! During the 1920s Landlord Pope kept the pub and is remembered as being a kindly man who 'never touched a drop hisself' and willingly displayed the Band of Hope posters on his forecourt.

There were two shops, a post office, a seed merchant, a wheelwright, a carpenter, a blacksmith and beyond the manor, a flour mill. Farmers and smallholders produced their own milk, cream, butter and eggs and supplied the local cheese factory, which was situated behind the pub. Pigs were fattened and killed and joints were shared with neighbours. During the war some prime cuts found their way into the most unlikely hiding places, and not because the fridge was not yet available!

Water was fetched daily, in either earthenware pitchers or galvanised pails, from Horsepool or Afterwashes. Folk who came from Carleen (a neighbouring village) or Wheal Vor generally came with a horse or donkey-drawn water butt (or barrel) to fill; a metal chute was kept at the Horsepool for their use. Washing water could be fetched from different points along the stream though sometimes it was necessary to wait until it flowed clear after Granny Body's ducks had had their splash!

Situated right on the corner of the village square, the blacksmith must have known more of the movements of village folk than even the postmistress. His work attracted young and old to stand and stare and pass the time of day. The young were often privileged to be allowed to pass into the smokey, dark confines to turn the handle which operated the bellows. They would only abandon the place if and when the steamroller arrived.

Like most villages, change has come to Godolphin. Additional houses have been built, the one shop remains and incorporates the post office but does not need to supply paraffin for lamps as we have mains electricity and water. Nevertheless, the water from Horsepool is still enjoyed by many as the only 'fit to drink'. Each Christmas there is an impressive display of lights, which is enjoyed by visitors from far and wide.

🍁 GOLDSITHNEY

Goldsithney is well-documented as being on the route taken by pilgrims on their way to St Michael's Mount. St James' House is popularly thought to be the site of a hospice where pilgrims could partake of rest and refreshment.

History has it that the Trevelyan family were largely responsible for the foundation of the community. One of the local hostelries carries the family coat of arms, and on Charter Fair Day a glove, which legend tells was stolen from Sithney, a nearby village, is hung over the pub sign.

Goldsithney Charter Fair, held on the first Saturday in August, has recently been revived, having fallen into abeyance during the war. This is supposed to commemorate the granting of the 'Royal Charter', but whether this refers to Sithney or Goldsithney is a matter of conjecture. The money raised by all participants, village organisations and freelance stall holders (who pay rent), goes to the upkeep of St Piran's hall, which was built to augment St James' Hall (the Tin Tabernacle). Most organisations meet in the new hall.

Goldsithney has changed over the years. There is no industry as such though relics of the mines are still evident, particularly when house foundations disappear! The main source of employment is farming, but with the influx of new people living on new estates there is a very happy mix of lifestyles.

Goldsithney was small, quiet and full of community spirit, which hasn't changed – even though it is now more of a town without town facilities. There was a band, and village processions were popular, adults carrying banners and the children flowers and flags. These were followed by tea treat buns, etc, and games on the field, which is the site of the Meadow View estate. No mains water was available until 1951, and supplies were carried from a well at East End – the quality was far better than now! Locally produced entertainment was popular, especially dances and pantomimes. The Methodist church was built in 1985.

Shops have changed hands or disappeared, ie the fish and chip shop – now there is a weekly van. The old village school has been converted into private dwellings, known as The Folly. Luckily there is one shop, a post office and a Gallery, and several mobile shops call each week.

🍁 GORRAN HAVEN

Gorran Haven is an old fishing village which has grown rapidly in spite of the unfortunate decline of its fishing industry. The main employment is now in the building, tourist and china clay industries – also rather uncertain!

The present village runs down to the beach and sea with cliffs each side and the original cottages huddled in between. The beach and picturesque walks make it very popular as a holiday resort with the four summer months seeing it crowded with visitors. A long hill leads to the village of Gorran Churchtown where the parish church is situated.

Other places of worship include a Methodist church, built in 1830 and having celebrated its 160th anniversary with a Flower Festival in 1990; a chapel of ease, St Just, situated on the cliff edge above the beach and notable for its rather chequered history which included being a fish cellar at one time, though more recently for having a five-sided tower and a lovely stained glass window with a picture of the village in it; and an Independent church called Mount Zion.

Most of life's day to day essentials are to hand with a general store and bakery (whose owner really is called Cakebread!), butcher's shop, newsagent, post office, hairdresser, and – in case of need – a doctor's surgery. As might be expected in a popular tourist village, there are several places for refreshment including two hotels, the Llawnroc and the Smugglers, two cafes and two tea rooms. The Smugglers is situated in Rattle Street, a very old part of the village and so called because of the cobblestones which, unfortunately, were removed when the main water pipes were installed. There is also a village institute built as a memorial to the men who were killed during the Second World War.

Another present day essential is the car and in the middle of the village is a field which nowadays is a large car park but which was a cornfield years ago.

In the past coal was brought to the village by boats which 'beached' on the high tide and when the sea receded horse and carts came onto the beach to carry away the coal – any pieces of coal dropped on the sand being picked up by children. It was a day of great excitement to see a large boat, the *Diligent*, on the beach.

There were once two 'mangle houses' in the village where local women went to mangle their clothes. The mangles were rollers beneath huge boxes shaped like coffins with weights in and which were moved to and fro by turning a handle, the boxes would then turn the rollers with the clothes wrapped around them.

The quality of Gorran Haven-built fishing boats was well known – even as far away as the East Coast – and though the yards are now gone (two went to Flushing) several of the boats built by them are still to be found locally. When there were a lot of boats, especially crabbers, working from the Haven there was a Fishermen's Cooperative Society. After crabs and fish were brought in and packed the Society's own lorry would take them to St Austell to catch the 2.15 pm London train.

The two original limekilns have been partly filled in and one now houses a store and the doctor's surgery, the flat roof of the store being used as a vantage point where people may sit and watch the activities on the sea and around the harbour.

For the 75th birthday of the WI the bells of Gorran church were rung and then a tea was held outside the church rooms, in the sunshine. Although there

Rock beach, Gorran Haven

have been many changes within the village over the years, this event perhaps typifies life in Gorran Haven – simple pleasures in lovely surroundings to be enjoyed by all.

🍁 GRAMPOUND

In the dim and distant past the little white river, part of the upper reaches of the river Fal which runs under the bridge at the bottom of Fore Street in Grampound, was a deep and busy waterway with a Roman encampment nearby. About 1,600 years ago the Romans built a great bridge here; in Norman times the bridge was called Grand Pont, by which name the village was known and from which its present name has evolved.

The community flourished and by 1332 Grampound was given its charter

by Earl John of Eltham which gave the townspeople the right to 'hang convicted thieves' and to exemption from taxes and tolls on the repair and building of other bridges. Most importantly they were granted the right to hold 52 markets a year without payment of dues. The seven-sided market cross still remains in Grampound outside what was once the market hall. The clock tower, now a landmark on the A390, was a symbol of the status of the borough in later years.

The tanning of leather in Grampound goes back to medieval, perhaps even Roman, times and the large cattle markets supplied the hides. At one time there were five tanneries in the area, which was a centre for leather. From 1711 the Croggan tannery flourished in Grampound and still produced high quality leather by one traditional oak-bark method until it closed in early 2000.

The church of St Nun was built in 1370, close to the market hall, as chapel of ease for the convenience of worshippers. It was rebuilt in 1869 into the delightful church it is today.

A small dark chamber behind the market hall was the gaol. Perhaps it was used quite often, as later in its history Grampound became a notorious 'rotten' borough, with much buying and selling of votes. It was once described as 'one mass of notorious corruption' but, as it was also described elsewhere as 'a place of great privileges and very poor inhabitants', maybe the temptations were hard to resist.

The village possessed a mill, mentioned in the Domesday Book, located at the end of what is still called Mill Lane. In 1501 there were spinning mills, in 1653 fulling mills and later, in 1801, these became woollen manufacturers. From 1816 the industry changed to glove manufacturing.

With all this industry, the inhabitants, visitors and the community from the 21 outlying farms became very thirsty and in the village, clustered around the main street, were six public houses. Nor was that all! The private enterprise of villagers who went in for brewing in their homes necessitated the presence of an Excise Office. Of the six public houses only the Dolphin inn remains, a welcome sight halfway up Fore Street. The village, which was once a town centred around the bridge and the market and is now divided by the main A390, annually cocks a snook by stopping the heavy flow of traffic with its carnival procession.

Modern Grampound is a mixture of old Cornish families and newcomers. Of the population of about 600 a quarter is over 60. Nevertheless, the playgroup and the local school are well attended and a Rainbow Group is thriving. The local football team, playing on the ground where American soldiers were camped during the Second World War is becoming very successful, as is the bowling club with its reputation for excellence. During 1998 a further two rinks were added to the green making a six rink square, and a new pavilion built.

There is a visiting library and the local medical group practice has a surgery, built on the site of the ancient poorhouse. There is a general store/post office, a butcher, fishmonger, bakery, a garage and of course, the ubiquitous antiques shops. There are two restaurants, one of which is perhaps the most celebrated Chinese restaurant in Cornwall, and on the day of its opening the teachers brought all the local children to see the Chinese Dragon dancing and weaving to a Chinese band; the other being an Indian restaurant which is also a takeaway. Old and new live happily side by side in Grampound and long may they continue to do so.

❀ GRAMPOUND ROAD

Had it not been for the railway there would have been no such place as Grampound Road. The railway ran more or less down the middle of Cornwall and existing villages like Grampound had to be served by stations some distance away. It was not deemed suitable to call them by the names of the places for which they were built as the distance was too great, so they were called 'The Road to … village', or in this case 'Grampound Road'. There had been a hamlet in the area since Saxon times called High Lanes which happened to coincide with the station.

The station is gone now thanks to the infamous Doctor Beeching but the village continues to grow and at times prosper. Two new building estates have swelled the number of children at the school, which at one time had so few pupils that it was feared it might close. There is an active pre-school play group in the beautiful village hall. This hall was given to the village before the war by Robert Harvey of Trenowth who was the biggest landowner in the area. It is an unusually attractive building designed by Wheatley, who also built the neo-Georgian Trenowth House.

At about the time the hall was being built, Charles Williams of Caerhayes gave the playing field to the village. It is now the home of Grampound Road Cricket Club, which for many years has had one of the most famous and successful village teams in the South West. Right opposite the playing field is the Victorian building of the Church of England primary school. This convenient juxtaposition enables the children to have excellent sporting facilities for a village school.

Grampound Road is in Ladock parish but until recently was split between Probus and Ladock. There is, therefore, no church but a chapel of ease is attached to the school. There is also a Methodist chapel built in 1866 and the two congregations unite to hold ecumenical services.

In Cornwall the traditional building material is stone and brick building was rare until recently, so it is surprising that at one time there was a brick works in Grampound Road. Occasionally the hand-made bricks still turn up marked 'G. Rd' in the frog.

Cornwall is renowned for its saints. Most of them lived in the early years of Christianity but one, St Cuthbert Mayne, was martyred during the Reformation and canonised recently. He was captured at Golden Manor which is near Grampound Road and taken to Launceston where he was hanged, drawn and quartered for his faith.

Walter Rail of Trenython near Grampound Road was a famous showman of horses before the Second World War. His stable was converted into the Co-op shop and again changed into an establishment selling swimming pools, but is now our village shop and post office. One of his horses, *Progress*, held the National Highest Jumping Award at Olympia for a number of years and was probably more famous than any other inhabitant before or since.

The population of Grampound Road is about 800. In the past most of the men would have been engaged in farming, china clay work or the railway with the few employed in what local industry there was such as the saw mill, warehousing and agricultural merchanting. Nowadays in addition to these traditional occupations many of the villagers commute to Truro or St Austell and a number of service families have been welcomed into the community.

Several small businesses have set up in recent years, some in the new industrial estate. There used to be two pubs in the village but now there is only one. Grampound Road is the centre of a very large postal area so there is a busy post office adjoining the excellent stores. Years ago a blacksmith had his shop half way up the hill. There is no sign of it now but its place has been taken by a garage dedicated to servicing trucks. A once thriving woodyard and builders' merchant's has become a small housing estate. Grampound Road may not be the geographical centre of Cornwall but it can be regarded as the crossroads of the county, only four miles from the A30 and one mile from the A390, the two main east/west roads.

🍁 GULVAL

Gulval, situated in the valley where the Trevaylor and Rosemorran streams meet, has always been a beautiful village, once known as 'the little village among the trees'. The origin of the name Gulval is unknown, but is believed to be from St Gudwal, who, though born in Wales, brought Christianity to the area from Brittany in the 6th century. St Gulval-in-Lanisley is recorded in the Domesday Book.

The village developed around the church (where in 1890 the old thatched cottages were pulled down and the residents housed in new barns until the granite houses were built) and at Trevarrack, near the streams, and the chapel. The only thatched houses remaining are Trenow and Rosemorran.

Agriculture has always been the main industry. Years ago men worked in the Ding-Dong mine in the north-west of the parish (but that closed in 1880), the smelting works at Chyandour, the ice-works and the two mills, powered by the streams before the days of electricity. Nowadays with modern transport, many work in nearby towns. On the lower land near the main road and the sea are Europe's first Heliport, an industrial estate, two supermarkets, a residential caravan site and a night club. Just over a mile from Penzance, Gulval is nevertheless a country village, served by a regular bus service.

The lovely church, built in the 12th century and later enlarged, has eight bells in its 15th century tower (unique in that half-way up, the steps change direction from anti-clockwise to clockwise!). The best remembered vicar, the Rev William Wingfield, came because of ill health as a young man and remained for 73 years.

John Wesley preached at Gulval and had great influence. The first chapel was built in 1822 (now Wesley Villa, a private house). The present Methodist church, built in 1884, has the Sunday school room underneath, which is often used for secular meetings and entertainments. The primary school, which still uses the original buildings, has been enlarged on several occasions and modernised in recent years.

'Ye Olde Inn', built in 1895, became the Coldstreamer in memory of Captain Michael Bolitho, killed in the Second World War. The almshouses, standing around their green, have been modernised, and are now comfortable homes for elderly local people. There is a modern, well stocked shop-cum-post office. Older residents can remember when there were four or five small shops, some in back kitchens, but catering for all needs – from groceries to 'chimneys' for oil lamps, and even fish and chips!

Many of the granite houses in both parts of the village were built around the turn of the century, largely by Mr R.E. Bolitho of Ponsandane (now a home for the elderly) who was also responsible for the almshouses and Lanisley Hall – currently being refurbished. Very few new houses were built then until the 1960s, when Pendrea was developed, followed later by Trevarrack, Helnoweth, Ridgevean and more recently 40 Housing Association dwellings.

Gulval Feast is on the nearest Sunday to the 12th November. On Feast Monday the Western Hunt meets at Churchtown, and the chapel has its anniversary bazaar and concert. The church holds a Feast supper and coffee morning.

There is a flourishing cricket club, with its own ground and pavilion, and a village football team.

Gulval Well, once one of Cornwall's most famous but now lost, was located southwards of the church. It was supposed to have the unusual quality of answering the wellbeing of absent friends or relatives by the appearance of its water.

Trevaylor (now also a home for the elderly), Rosemorran and Kenegie (a holiday complex) were amongst the older manor houses. Kenegie was said to be haunted by the ghost of 'Wild Harris', one of its less reputable past residents, and also by the spirit of an elderly scolding housekeeper, whose knitting needles could be heard clicking! Rosemorran, once a religious house, was haunted by a monk – an old story said that at midnight the two stone pillars at the bottom of the park changed places!

Gulval Carn was a favourite haunt of Humphry Davy as a young man. Here he read, studied and painted. A large rock shaped like a reading desk is still known as Davy's rock. Over the years the village may change but this magnificent view over Mounts Bay will always remain.

🍁 GUNNISLAKE

Prior to the opening of the Tamar road bridge, linking Plymouth with Saltash, in 1962, the lowest road crossing of the river Tamar was over the picturesque 15th century New Bridge. Over the centuries the bridge has posed on numerous occasions for paintings and photographs and its portrait, painted by Turner, hangs in the Tate Gallery. During the Civil War it was barricaded by the Royalists in Cornwall against a possible invasion by Roundheads. Today a different style of 'invader' comes streaming over it during the summer months, with caravans and boat-trailers replacing the gun-carriages of their ancient forefathers.

Climbing the hill from the bridge on the Cornish bank the old village of Williamstown, named for the local Squire Williams, enjoyed a life of rural tranquillity, the river providing easy access to and from the area. As the 18th century drew to a close, however, the first mine opened and the size and character of the little settlement changed almost overnight. Indeed, even the name of the village was changed in 1828 to Gunnislake, 'gunnis' being the term for a mine adit. One by one the mines opened: Drakewalls Mine, Gunnislake Old Mine, East Gunnislake Mine, Hingston Down Consols. Wealth beyond the wildest dreams of the average man was produced (Drakewalls, the oldest and richest of the mines yielded over £350,000 during its lifetime) whilst the wretched miners and their families struggled to survive on poverty-level wages and in miserable and overcrowded housing.

Throughout the 19th century the village bustled: it supported no less than 45 shops and its churches, chapels and public houses thrived. In 1876 the roll of the village school was 150 pupils. Though conditions for the miners were harsh, the community which grew up around them was supportive and organised.

With the dawn of the 20th century came the railway, which still provides an important link between Gunnislake, from which circular walks are most popular, and Plymouth. It took away the freight traffic from the river, but as this declined a new use of river transport grew up – the day trip. This activity gradually expanded until, between the wars, there were no less than 14 paddle steamers regularly coming from Plymouth up to Weir Head. The man who ran this service was Mr Worth and his daughter still lives in the village today.

Soon after the turn of the century, however, the mines started to close and the miners were forced to move away. They left in their droves, heading all over the world in search of work and prosperity. The village post office still notes a high turnover of letters bound for the mining areas of far continents as their descendants take advantage of modern communications to keep in touch. Even the mining equipment itself was removed during the First World War, for the manufacture of armaments.

With the departure of the miners much of the heart went out of the village and many of its customs died out, among them the carnival and the once thriving male voice choir. New Year still arrives on 1st January, but it is no longer rung in as it once was by Mousy Southcott, who each year would dress up and walk all around the village with his bell. Through the rest of the year there was a proper Town crier, by the name of Charlie Vinnard. Contemporary with these characters was Willie Wales, a devout Roman Catholic who lived in a tiny cottage in Bealswood Road. Willie, dressed in his usual garb of Army surplus clothing, tramped many miles in his self-appointed task of visiting all the prisons in the area. He walked everywhere, even to Plymouth, and local folk were amazed when he died to find that he left a small fortune in money, stocks and shares.

The houses down beside the river are, of course, vulnerable to flooding, but in 1954 the centre of the village was flooded too. This was caused by a large pond on a farm at Higher Dimson, which burst over its banks. The water came cascading down through the village, swept through the school and all the shops in Fore Street, and took with it the beer barrels from the Buccaneer, thus turning the flood into a major disaster.

The flood through Fore Street today is of traffic: the main road running through its centre causes its share of problems to the village. Following incidents during the 1950s when runaway lorries crashed into the post office, an escape lane was created at Sandhill. Sadly this has not prevented subsequent tragedies on the main road in the village centre.

Today the working population of the village mainly travels to employment in towns and cities which include Tavistock, Launceston, Callington, Plymouth and Exeter. The village supports a nucleus of shops and all everyday commodities are available here. The modern health centre is built on the site of an old mine shaft and the village supports two playgroups in addition to the thriving primary school.

Many new houses have been built. Tiny cottages have been knocked together to provide more spacious accommodation than that enjoyed by the miners, and old outhouses and barns have been converted into luxury homes. After the departure of the miners the village seemed for a time to be dying, but now a new and quieter prosperity has settled back over the community which stretches up the hill from the ancient bridge.

❦ GUNWALLOE

Gunwalloe is a picturesque country village by the sea. It has a church, church room, pub and a village hall. In years gone by it also had a Methodist chapel. The chapel Sunday school room is now the village hall. The chapel congregation dwindled, the chapel was closed, and has recently been altered into living accommodation. We now have a playing field, swings and a football pitch.

The village of Gunwalloe was at one time owned by the Penrose family and was part of the Penrose estate. Estate workers and local farm workers lived in tied cottages in the village but crippling death duties forced the family to sell. Most of the village was sold to sitting tenants and part was sold to the National Trust.

When Penrose owned the area the local farmers had permission to collect sand and seaweed from the beach at Church Cove. When the National Trust took over from Penrose these rights were questioned and the farmers had to go to court to fight for them. Only three decided it was worth the trouble and expense but these three won their case and now have Sanding Rights.

Being close to the sea, many people in the area fished to supplement their income. The shingle beach is called Fishing Cove and this beach still has a winch which was always used to haul the boats above high tide. Seine fishing was also done close to the beach and a huer would be on the look-out for shoals of fish close to the shore. When the cry of 'Hevva, Hevva' rang out everyone from the village would rush to the beach to help with the seine nets. Recently fishing has largely died out and the shingle from Fishing Cove is used in building.

The dangerous nature of the cliffs and sea-shore lent itself naturally to smuggling and wrecking and many stories are told, especially connected with the Halzephron inn which was formerly known as 'The Ship'. This was the headquarters of many smugglers over the years. One innkeeper, Rev Jan Peters, was the head of a smuggling gang. He was said to be a good man who looked after the poor. Between the bars in the inn there is an eight foot wall which houses a shaft that leads to a tunnel from the pub to Fishing Cove.

Lamps were said to be stored at the inn to use on the cliff called Halzephron to bring the passing ships on to the rocks so that the locals could plunder the wrecks. Halzephron is the old Cornish word for 'Hell's cliff' and anyone who has seen the cliffs will realise why they are so called. The inn was also used as a sort of trading centre. Horse-drawn waggons from Porthleven, which used the old track across Loe Bar bringing all sorts of goods to Gunwalloe and Mullion, stopped off at the Ship and then the bartering began – brandy in exchange for whatever was needed. This trading went on until the start of the First World War.

The church at Gunwalloe is believed to have been built in the 13th century. Services are still held in the church and it is open all the year round. The bell tower is separate from the church itself. The story is told of two sisters aboard a boat one wild stormy night, fearful for their lives, praying that they would reach land safely. They agreed that if they did reach land they would build a church on the spot where they landed, to thank God for their deliverance. Their boat was thrown up on the sands at Gunwalloe and the sisters kept their word and set about building the church. Unfortunately they fell out. They could not agree on a site and settled their differences by one choosing the place for the bell tower and the other the spot where the nave and chancel should stand. In recent years it was feared that cliff erosion would leave the church on an island so a great deal of money was spent putting granite slabs down the cliff face to stop further erosion.

Carminowe Farm and woods were once a manor and the buildings included a mansion and a beautiful chapel surrounded by a moat. The chapel was thought to have been built about 1308, and it is said that there was once a monastery on the site. Today some of the farm buildings are listed as they include windows and stones thought to be from the original chapel.

🍁 GWEEK

Gweek is situated at the upper tidal limit of the Helford river, which is a 'drowned' river valley system and formed thousands of years ago when the land sank and the valleys were flooded by the sea. The name derives from the Cornish word 'wyk' meaning creek.

A settlement grew up here in ancient times as it is situated in the centre of the Lizard peninsula at the highest fordable point on the river, and it became the centre of communication both by land and sea.

The streams which run into the river flow through the inland tin bearing areas and their valleys became an early source of alluvial tin which made the area important from Bronze Age times. An ancient tradition holds that Phoenician merchants came here from the eastern Mediterranean to trade for tin and there was, certainly, much commerce with the continent.

After the silting up of the Loe Bar sometime before the 14th century, Gweek was incorporated into the port of Helston by Royal Charter and remained a free port with no dues being payable to the Duchy of Cornwall. Large quantities of charcoal for tin smelting were imported and were also produced from the oak woods on the river banks which were coppiced at 30 year intervals.

In the 19th century, the port was very busy with the import of coal and timber for the mines – the timber arriving in logs from Norway and being floated up to Gweek to season in the creek before being used as props in the mines. Coal imports continued until the 1980s but timber imports ceased with the Second World War, after which the large saw mill was little used and, eventually, was removed. The timber yards have now become a boat yard where a large number of boats are laid up in winter and where repairs and some new construction are carried out.

The coal quays have been purchased by a company operating and constructing drilling rigs who have drill ships and teams operating worldwide, and some of their traffic is from the sea. Nearby, a local company builds catamarans which have achieved an international reputation. This carries on an old tradition as ships were built at Gweek throughout the centuries, the last being a 70 ton schooner finished at the end of the 19th century.

Other commercial activities include the seal sanctuary on the riverside which attracts thousands of tourists in the summer, a noted specialist plant nursery on the village outskirts, a garage and several small workshops and building firms.

The village is divided physically between the old settlement with its post office and stores, village pub, two restaurants and its rows of traditional cottages, and the large modern development of bungalows and houses built on a hillside overlooking the river. The population includes a large number of people from other parts of the country attracted here by the beautiful countryside and milder climate. There is an increasing consciousness throughout the community that the peace and beauty must not be threatened further by too much development.

Up to the last decade, Gweek was divided in local government terms between the three parishes of Constantine, Mawgan and Wendron but, at the last boundary revision, a Gweek parish was formed with a parish council and a population of some 500 people.

Gweek has always enjoyed a very active community life with many organisations flourishing despite its small population. Possibly the oldest of these is the Gweek Silver Band which was formed in 1926 and has provided a focal point in village life ever since and a great interest for its members and particularly the scores of young people who have learned to make music in its ranks.

This is a flourishing community where many of the new residents have integrated well into village life and where village facilities are well supported. It is a busy community but close by are the peace and tranquillity of the tidal river with its ancient oak woods rising from the water's edge. This is an ancient settlement which has greatly changed in the past 50 years but still preserves interest and charm, and a good background for life.

❧ GWINEAR

Gwinear parish is the most easterly parish in Penwith district. It is possible to see the Atlantic and the English Channel from the highest point, 240 ft.

The parish covers 4,618 acres, with 250 acres of waste mining land. The 2,000 population live in various hamlets, farmhouses and cottages. Since 1968 300 to 400 new houses have been built, due to mains water and sewers being laid on. There are three caravan parks, in delightful rural surroundings. Many cottages and flats are summer-lets for tourists.

The name Reawla means Royal Place. A Cornwall Archaeological Unit 'dig' in 1987 revealed a 2nd century defended farmstead, expanding to two and a half acres in the 4th century. Farmers grew corn, wheat and kept sheep. Finds included a spindle for hand weaving, a 3rd century small stone handmill and a lead ingot, a sign of industrial workings.

Among many mines, Rosewarne and Herland produced silver, Wheal Alfred and Relistian copper. One of the first steam engines in the world, with a 70 inch cylinder, was erected at Herland Mine in 1758, perhaps even earlier ones in 1740-1747 were erected in Gwinear. Roseworthy Hammer Mills Company made shovels, chains and boilers etc for the mines and was still in business in the 1940s with lakes to work the waterwheel.

Mr Hamblim, the blacksmith's son, invented a pile cutter for velvet, making velveteen in Victorian times. The first horseshoe his father made is still at the blacksmith's shop in Carnhell Green.

The parish takes its name from St Gwinear (Gwynnyer), son of a King of Ireland. After being converted to Christianity he sailed to Brittany and set sail for Cornwall around the year AD 460. He landed at Hayle at the head of 777 Christian missionaries, among them seven Bishops.

In 1311 Gwinear church was endowed and Drannack land was given to help twelve scholars at Oxford University. The Bishop of Exeter founded Exeter College with the great tithe in 1318. The tower is one of six towers in West Cornwall, where fires were lit as a signal to seafarers in earlier times. The victims of the last cholera epidemic were buried together and fir trees were planted. There is a Charles II letter in Cornish, written in appreciation for help given during the Civil War. The Pilgrim Way brought George Fox, the Quaker, and John Wesley to Wall. John Wesley came to preach at Wall in 1747 and Gwinear chapel was in existence in 1767.

Gwinear Road became a main line station in 1843; the sidings loaded cattle, pigs and vegetables and it was the branch line for Helston. The level crossing gates were the longest in the county, if not the country, replaced in 1965 by automatic half-barrier gates. Everything goes by lorry now.

There was an air landing ground at Polkinghorne in the 1930s, near the Roman road, where there are two old milestones; Roman coins have been found in the parish on two different farms.

There is plenty to do with a pick-your-own fruit farm, a restaurant, two public houses and, during the year, Gwinear Agricultural Show and Wall Music Festival.

❦ GWITHIAN

Gwithian is a picturesque village on the north coast. It is situated about three miles north-east of Hayle and seven west of Portreath.

Its patron saint is St Gothian, who was by tradition an Irish missionary martyred in the area, and its present name dates from the 16th century. The church at Gwithian honours St Gothian, whose feast falls on the Sunday nearest to 1st November. Today this church is thriving after having been in recession over the years and facing possible closure. It now attracts good numbers throughout the year and is well maintained and cared for. It is believed that the first St Gothian's chapel could have been a tiny oratory made of wood. In the 14th century a stone chapel was built and remains of this exist near the Red river. It is known to be about 50 ft long and 20 ft wide and was revealed in the 19th century by the shifting sand but is now covered by sand once again.

There were several mines around Gwithian – Wheal Emily, Nanterrow, Wheal Connerton and Wheal Prosper or Wheal Liverpool, the scene of Richard Trevithick's first great condensing engine, but agriculture was the main occupation with sheep being the commonest livestock. There is a village green with a banked circular enclosure which until the 18th century was used to impound stray cattle, which would later be released on the payment of a fine.

Probably the most famous building in Gwithian is the Methodist chapel, which was built in 1810. It is of rectangular shape with a thatched roof and is now a listed building. It is still used for worship on Sundays and has undergone extensive restoration over the years but fortunately it has retained much of its original character.

The first post office in the village was in a shed in the garden of Glencoe. Some years later it transferred to the home of Mrs May Johns who used her front room as a shop. Mrs Johns was postmistress for over 40 years until 1989 when she retired. Summer visitors were fascinated by this quaint little shop and many returned year after year.

Between Gwithian and the sea there is half a mile of towans which extend from Hayle to Godrevy point. There are many chalets and bungalows on the towans, some of which are let only during the summer months and others are lived in all the year around. There are two shops on the towans, one of which is an unusual shape being almost round in appearance and known as The Jam Pot. It was originally a look-out during the First World War.

Godrevy Island is very close to Gwithian and after several ships were wrecked on the nearby rocks it was decided to build a lighthouse, which was first lit in 1859 and was manned until around 1940 when it was controlled electrically. Many birds now use this as their nesting ground as it is so peaceful and undisturbed.

There has been very little building and development in the village and today there are still less than 40 houses. There is a public house known as the Pendarves Arms and there are also two residential homes but no shop or post office. In the winter months it is relatively quiet but during the summer hundreds of holidaymakers spend their holidays in and around Gwithian on the various camp sites and chalet parks. The beach attracts many locals as well as visitors and now has a new car park which holds a large number of cars. The beach is patrolled by lifeguards during the summer months and has a good access.

🍁 Harrowbarrow & Metherell

In 1989, a couple in Harrowbarrow building an extension to their home uncovered a Bronze Age cist, complete with decorated pot. Experts believe it was the burial place of a child. The pot is made of local clay and probably dates from around 2000 BC.

The two villages of Harrowbarrow and Metherell lie on the extreme edge of Hingston Down. In the year AD836, Egbert, King of the West Saxons routed a combined force of West Britons and Danes at the battle of Hingston Down. The area was a settled agricultural community in Saxon and Norman times under the manorial system. Aerial photography and maps of Harrowbarrow reveal the large open field system with strip fields within (which were enclosed with hedges at a later date).

In 1337, Edward III established the Duchy of Cornwall by appropriating 17 manors, of which Calstock was one and of which Harrowbarrow and Metherell formed a part. The name Harrowbarrow derives from the Old English Harebere, meaning either boundary wood or hare's wood. Metherell, in the 13th century spelt Meddelhille, simply means middle hill.

Open cast mining and streaming for tin had been practised for centuries on the down, but from the 1800s Harrowbarrow was one of the centres of the mining boom of the Tamar valley. Copper, tin, arsenic, silver and lead were all mined at Harrowbarrow. Mines opened, closed and reopened with changing fortunes. Wheal Duchy, later renamed Wheal Brothers, began mining silver in good quantity in 1810. The *Royal Cornwall Gazette* reported in 1812 that the Prince Regent had been 'graciously pleased to receive an elegant snuff box made of Harrowbarrow silver'.

As the 19th century progressed the population of the two villages exploded. Although new terraces of cottages were built for the influx of miners and their families, there was much overcrowding. Three chapels were built – the Bible Christians (to become Methodist later) at Harrowbarrow and Metherell, and the Baptist at Lower Metherell. All Saints church was built at Harrowbarrow in 1870 and was used as a day school from 1872. A school attendance census of 1876 showed a total of 226 children under the age of twelve in the two villages, 164 of whom were on the roll of the church school. Land was purchased from the lord of the manor to build a new school in Harrowbarrow which opened in 1879 and still continues.

Alongside the mining, market gardening flourished. Fields of daffodils and anemones bloomed, followed by strawberries, and there were acres of apple and cherry orchards. Sadly the industry has disappeared in Harrowbarrow and Metherell. It is only recently that Metherell's last 'gardener' retired from

The Post Office, Harrowbarrow

working on the steep slopes by Comfort Woods, to the south of Metherell, which were once a hive of activity. The area has now been planted with coniferous trees.

Mining declined rapidly at the turn of the 20th century. Many people emigrated or sought work in other parts of the country. Once again agriculture was the main occupation. Social life still revolved round church activities and festivals. There was a silver band, a men's institute, two football teams and a cricket XI. There was much sporting rivalry between the local villages; a rhyme chanted by Churchtown, St Dominick youngsters went:

> Harrowbarrow Flinkers,
> 'Etherick* Brags,
> The little boys of Churchtown,
> Beat 'em all to rags.   *Boetherick

Coombe Mine ended its days as Coombe Arsenic Works, mundic being brought from other mines to be treated. The ovens and flues stopped working in the 1920s, but remained visible until the 1970s when the area was landscaped. For a brief period in the 1970s the long closed Prince of Wales mine was assessed for the possibility of reworking.

After the Second World War the number of children at the school dropped so dramatically that it was under threat of closure. However, over the last 20 years numbers have steadily increased. The School House was developed and extended along with a playing field and car parking area. Plans are afoot to extend the building further. Families from all over the Tamar Valley attend the school and it has become a highly sought after centre of education.

The region of East Cornwall began to thrive when the Tamar road bridge was opened in 1961 linking it by road to Plymouth. New extensions to the road bridge will make travel to the area viable for industries both large and small. Harrowbarrow and Metherell have prospered over the last 40 years and the villages have become popular places to live and work. There is a manufacturer of portable buildings, an egg farm, a car body repair shop, a haulier, a bus company, a post office, a restaurant, a pub, a plant centre, a holiday caravan park, several self-employed builders, plumbers, decorators, carpenters and joiners, craftsmen and women, a florist, gardeners, landscapers and electricians, and of course farmers and nurserymen. With the advance in Information and Communication Technology many are connected to the internet and much commerce is conducted over the world wide web from the comfort of village homes.

The village hall, which serves both villages, was completed in 1995. It was the culmination of the efforts of the Harrowbarrow and Metherell Community Association, which had worked hard and long to secure a future for the community. Many voluntary groups meet regularly including the WI and a thriving committee run pre-school. The Community Association keeps almost 700 households in touch through its publication – Hamlet.

🍁 HEAMOOR

Heamoor is a village two miles from Penzance. In 1934 the borough of Penzance was enlarged for the first and only time after it received its charter in 1614, so as to include several surrounding villages, including Heamoor.

The most interesting building is the Wesley Rock chapel, so called because the pulpit stands on a rock brought from a common nearby on which Wesley preached from 1743-1760. John Wesley came to a small hamlet called Hea which consisted of a few farms and cottages. He preached, standing on a rock, in the field owned by a farmer called Richard Pengelly, who was converted by

Wesley and gave the ground for the first chapel, which is now the Sunday school. Miss Pengelly, his daughter, gave the ground for the present chapel. The church (St Thomas's), which started as a mission church, is always well attended.

Heamoor has recently had a very modern new school built to accommodate 330 children. The old school is a much smaller, granite building, which served as Heamoor county primary school for over a century, until the growth of the village meant a population explosion and a bigger school was needed. The original building was opened in 1887 in the lower part of the village and at that time accommodated 60 children.

Many new houses have been built in this area and building is still going on. However, the very old, original part of the village is still the most picturesque. Basket making (mainly to serve market gardening) took place in Heamoor in years gone by. 'Treneere Barton' was once an old mill.

🍁 HELFORD

Helford is a picturesque village on the south side of the Helford river. The pedestrian ferry is a very ancient one, mentioned in the Domesday Book but under another name. In 1536 John Thomas held the passage and paid 22 shillings annually, quite a sum in those days. There is some evidence that Treath (Cornish for ferry or passage) was the original landing place on the Meneage side. The ferry has not always been purely a passenger ferry – there used to be a flat-bottomed boat in which cattle etc were conveyed. A horse bus was used to run from Manaccan to Falmouth and was taken across the river. Women from Meneage used to cross with their produce for Falmouth market.

The Helford river is well known for its oyster beds owned by the Duchy of Cornwall. Several fishing boats work out of the village, crabbing, long lining and netting. Trigging (cockle picking) is a traditional occupation for local people on Good Friday. The thatched cottages once occupied by local people are now mostly holiday lets. The Shipwrights Arms, on the edge of the creek with a waterside terrace, is very popular with visitors. There is an excellent general store with post office and gift shop. The Riverside Restaurant provides evening meals.

There was a mission church, built by the Vivian family, which housed the bell from the *Bay of Panama* wrecked in the Great Blizzard of 1891. The large car park beside it is provided for visitors to avoid congestion in the narrow village street, there being no through road.

During the Second World War there were French fishing boats based in the river for use of the naval secret service. Soldiers left the river embarking on the D-Day landings. A boom was in place across the mouth of the river, with a space open during the day for access and closed at night. At the end of the war sections of the Mulberry Harbour were brought back from the landing beaches to be later towed away.

Frenchman's Creek has been immortalised by authors Quiller-Couch and Daphne du Maurier. The Helford River Sailing Club is well known and very popular. A cross channel race between HRSC and L'Aberwrac'h in Brittany takes place annually. There is also a village regatta in August.

🍁 HESSENFORD

Hessenford is a pretty little cluster of late 17th – early 18th century cottages lying on the main road from Plymouth to Looe at the foot of a well wooded valley crossing the Seaton river; a village nearly in a time warp as there has been very little building expansion. Unless the motorist stops here, this attractive little place has been and gone in a flash of non-seeing non-stop summer holiday traffic.

The village has been here a very long time; one of its earliest records being of a mill in 1286. Originally called Hestonford, believed to mean the witches' ford/place in the woods, it belonged to the Duke of Cornwall to the west of the river and on the east side to the Bake estate which used to belong to the Copley family, absentee landlords with properties in London and Yorkshire.

Long ago there were two pubs, now one, the Copley Arms attractive and welcoming where families are able to relax beside the river with a very sturdy play area for the children. Hessenford was a thriving crossing place on the Plymouth south coast route, with an annual cattle fair held in its street between the cottages, its own school, village shop, shoemaker, postman, taxi service and resident policeman, whose station is now called Peel Cottage, still with its village lockup, cobble-floored, slate-roofed and with no window, in the back garden. Small cottages were occupied by families with up to 14 children. It has now become a community of mainly retired people and a few commuting daily to Plymouth. Now most of the cottages (39 houses in all) are privately owned having been converted and tastefully modernised.

The two mills used to be in working order, the larger for local farmers to bring their corn to by horse and cart for milling. It is now a private house and holiday flats. The smaller mill, also worked by a water wheel, was used to make joinery for the local cottages and farms, the last time being to make new windows and doors for St Anne's in the village in the late 1940s when Mr

Paynter was the Bake estate's foreman and in charge of the mill. The fields around the village were much smaller and a living could be made from growing potatoes and taking them to Plymouth market by horse and trap via the Torpoint ferry. The loaded vehicles would be taken to the top of the steep hill to Carracawn Cross where they would be unhitched and left overnight; that hill which was once so much steeper with its bad narrow bend out of the village, has been long since widened and made easier for the car age. The horses would return to the village to rest before leaving early the following morning to continue the downhill and gentler journey to Plymouth, 15 miles away. The Methodist chapel and post office have closed and the village now has a garage, the working men's institute, a handicraft group, the church and village hall. Sadly the village football team and young people's club have wound up for lack of youngsters in the village but there are billiards, snooker and darts teams, an active and a regular fare of whist and skittles.

J. Polsue writing in Lake's *Parochial History of Cornwall* in 1868 says 'There was an ancient chapel situated in a wood at Hessenford, dedicated to St Anne, some distinctive remains of which are yet to be seen'. However, now St Anne's church, surmounted by its handsome golden cock, well loved and cared for, lies up the hill past the clearly visible parish pump, overlooking the village from its new-surrounded churchyard covered in springtime daffodils and primroses. Originally a very small chapel of ease built in 1833, it was not until 1871 that permission was given to rebuild as it now appears, an attractive little church in Early English style with a fine barrel-vaulted roof. As the original building had no bell there grew a tradition of Hessenford Shotgun Weddings for local girls, and a volley of shots is still fired in lieu of a peal of bells.

🍁 JACOBSTOW

The name Jacobstow is derived from either Jacob's dwelling or, as some reference books state, Jacob's holy place. With a population of around 450, it has an acreage of 4,471.

Being mainly agricultural land the majority of the men are connected with farming. The remainder are tradesmen or travel to nearby towns to work in shops or factories. A blacksmith's shop which had been run by three generations of the Parsons family was closed down about 40 years ago when working horses were replaced with tractors and other modern machinery. Many years ago the inhabitants of each local parish were known by a collective nickname, such as St Gennys 'wreckers', Poundstock 'owls' and Jacobstow 'gentlemen'. Three of the oldest cottages in the village date back to around 1750. One of these is reputed to have a ghost who still makes her presence felt by leaving a distinctive 'fishy' smell.

At the north end of the parish can be seen the remains of a large moated manor house. This house at Bury Court was excavated, and protective wire attached to the walls between 1968 and 1973. There is now no trace of Penhallam manor in the same area, which was once owned by a member of the Acland family.

The church dedicated to St James was built in the latter half of the 15th century. A complete list of vicars dating from 1270 suggests there was a place of worship on the site long before the present church was built. There are a number of interesting features in the church, one of which is the granite slab which is used as it originally was, as an altar in the Lady Chapel. For many years this slab was used as a bridge across the stream, before it was brought back into the church through the efforts of Rev Michael Pearce and a band of helpers. Ancient bench-ends depicting the Passion of Christ have been incorporated into the pulpit and an Elizabethan chalice deposited at a bank is dated 1577. The headstones, many over 200 years old, bear some interesting inscriptions. Three little pigs carved on one headstone suggest that this person may have been a pig farmer. One of the best loved and respected rectors who has served the parish was Rev John Allsopp, who came in 1917 and stayed for 40 years until his retirement.

There have been a variety of schools in the parish, the earliest being a dame school at Pear Tree Cottage run by Miss Betsy Hockaday in the early 1800s. The foundation stone of the present school was laid in November 1971, and it serves the parishes of Poundstock, St Gennys, Week St Mary and Jacobstow.

With around 40 new dwellings built in the last 20 years, the parish has so far not been spoilt by over-development.

🍁 KELLY BRAY

Kelly Bray, in the Cornish language, means 'Wood on the Hill' – the hill being Kit Hill, a very well-known landmark. Kit Hill was given to the County of Cornwall by HRH Prince Charles, Duke of Cornwall to commemorate the birth of his son Prince William. The former granite quarry on the hill supplied rock for many famous buildings and structures. The area is being used as a Country Park without commercialism, with many pleasant walks around the summit, and is in walking distance of Kelly Bray. Another locality owned by the Duchy of Cornwall was cleared for a picnic area at the edge of the village and adjoining Kelly Bray woods, where it is possible to explore. The altitude of the village gives glorious panoramic views of the Cornish hills toward the south and Dartmoor northwards; in any direction the scenery gives a marvellous backdrop.

Smallholdings dotted the land before the middle of the 19th century. Three mines operated around the village and cottages were built at this time for miners and their families. One mine – Redmoor – was reopened during the Second World War for the excavation of minerals to use for the war effort.

By 1908 the railway was established in Kelly Bray, although called the Callington Road station. Trains leaving the terminus were renowned for their flexibility, the station staff would await a regular passenger's arrival or telephone to check if they were coming before signalling the train to depart! A very busy freight trade was centred at the station with coal, agriculture and transport businesses served and their premises occupied the surrounding area. When the line was axed during the Beeching cutbacks in 1966 the last train left the station with a wreath tied to the engine and a placard reading 'Callington – Gunnislake Line 1982, 1908-1966 Farewell'.

Also in 1908 a new Methodist church was built with adjoining schoolroom and classrooms above. This is still busy with a thriving Sunday school and a weekly night guild meeting.

The busy A388 south to north coast road runs through the centre of the village. Alongside this road a piece of land was given for a mission church but this has never been built and remains an area where wildlife can live unmolested.

Two small estates were built during the last 25 years and three more larger estates are planned for the near future. Many small businesses are run in various buildings in the village and a small area of factory units has been established for several years. A new larger business park was opened in 1990 on the old station yard, this has several units operating a variety of businesses. An agricultural engineer's and farm implement distributors are sited in the middle of the village on the land of an old sawmill which operated until the middle of this century.

A busy post office with stationery and gifts is open daily also a well-stocked grocery shop and a very popular family baker's. The Swingletree pub, one of the oldest buildings in the village, is a hive of activity with its own football team, also darts, pool and euchre teams. Two garages are open long hours with repair and accessory shops always doing a brisk trade. People also commute to Plymouth and other areas for their work.

Kelly Bray, although a small village, is a thriving area and has friendly people and organisations. It is a very pleasant place to live, especially in summer when traders and organisations plant flowers in abundance.

🍁 Kestle Mill

Kestle Mill is situated in a peaceful valley between Summercourt and Newquay, Quintrell Downs is just up the hill and it is surrounded by Trethiggey, Tresillian and Kestle farms where the Eustice, Davey and Rundle families have lived and farmed for generations.

Many years ago Tresillian Barton was a mixed farm with a herd of about 30 cows. In 1975 it was the first farm of its kind in the UK to diversify. Now known as 'DairyLand', this 550 acre farm is a nationally awarded tourist attraction. Winding through these farms and the small village is a river making its way to the Gannel in Newquay.

The lanes around Kestle Mill provide lovely country walks, one leading to the beautiful Elizabethan Trerice Manor and gardens which became the property of the National Trust in 1953. Trerice belonged for over four centuries to the Arundells, one of the great families of Cornwall. The house was rebuilt by Sir John Arundell in 1572. When looking around this magnificent manor the guides may tell of the ghost which goes along the corridor leading to the musicians' gallery, but the local people know the real ghost of Trerice is a headless horse rider. At midnight he rides across the courtyard with his head under his arm and has been seen in the moonlight on a number of occasions.

The small chapel and Sunday school, once filled and renowned for its harvest festivals (ably organised by Mrs Ruth Rundle and decorated with beautiful flowers from the Mays' garden across the road) is now closed and made into a charming home.

In the past many children attended the Sunday school, the highlight of the year being the tea treat where large saffron buns were enjoyed, eaten in a meadow under the trees. Then it was the custom to march from Kestle Mill to Tresillian House where everyone would go around the grounds before returning to the village.

During the Second World War most homes accommodated evacuee children from London, Plymouth etc. This caused the St Columb Minor school to be bursting at its seams so the Kestle Mill Sunday school was used as a classroom. The children living at Trerice enjoyed this as they usually walked the two and a half miles to school in all winds and weather. At this time the American army had a water purification plant situated at Kestle Mill which took the water from the river to be stored in large, round canvas tanks. At the end of the day the children would leave their temporary classroom and spend time in the Americans' tent listening to their stories and would be given candy, tins of coffee and cocoa powder.

The changes are vast in this small village. The shop and post office, once run by Mr Wallace Tremain, is now the kitchen of The Willows, a licensed restaurant. The mill where farmers once brought their corn has become a large warehouse, making and selling pine furniture. Situated across the way at the end of Kestle Farm cottages was another mill from which this village acquired its name.

The biggest change of all was made when the pretty narrow road was replaced by a new, wide one. Hopefully this doesn't cause drivers to travel through too quickly and miss seeing this picturesque little village.

🍁 KILKHAMPTON

Nearly 600 ft above sea level and astride the A39, Kilkhampton is Cornwall's most northerly village. The Chilcheton of the Domesday Book of 1086 and the Kilketon of possible Saxon origin is only two miles from the river Tamar, the border with Devon, which rises in nearby Morwenstow. Visitors may not realise that they are using the ancient Ridgeway along which monks travelled to visit their grange at Aldercombe or their land and cells at Launcells, coming all the way from Hartland Abbey. The Romans incorporated it in their road building schemes and had a rest camp at Abbury, just east of the main road. The first Granville came along it, having been awarded the manor in 1088 after Oddo's revolt. Later, Royalists bore the body of their hero, Sir Richard Grenville of Stamford Hill fame, along it for burial in Kilkhampton church after his death from many wounds at Landsdowne.

Once a market town, some locals still refer to the Lower Square as the Bull Ring. Local field names reflect the history of the village too. Gallows and Gibbet Moor bear witness to stern justice. Bear Park and Tumblers Field recall happier occasions when entertainers came for three fairs held annually.

The arrangement of many fields and gardens in long strips dates back to the days of the Saxon 'hundreds' and there are the remains of a motte and bailey castle to climb, affording excellent views of the sea and surrounding countryside. The monks of Tewkesbury Abbey are believed to have built the parish church of St James the Great. This church is on the Pilgrim's Path of St James of Compostella. A recent entry in the Visitor's Book records the visit of a true pilgrim from the USA following this path. His night's vigil was spent in one of the finest churches in Cornwall with its Norman porch and 14th century individually carved bench ends. The vibrant faith of the village today is truly represented in the ecumenical co-operation between the parish church, the Methodist church and the Christian Fellowship centre. Kilkhampton has a thriving primary school and the village hall aptly named the Grenville Rooms is home to the Pre-School and Mother & Toddler groups.

Although it has lost many of its former trades such as tanning, boot-making, cobbling and saddlery, Kilkhampton still takes a great pride in all it does. 'There is a thing of all sorts and all sorts of things in Kilk when you do go looking' proves to be a true quotation when a survey of all amenities in the village is carried out. Shops range from an outfitter's and draper's shop established in 1807 to two modern self-service grocers and fruiterers. There is also a butcher, a baker, a post office and newsagent, an electrical goods sales and service concern, a pine furniture outlet and a gift shop. Refreshment is available in the two ancient pubs, one an old coaching inn, the tea rooms and the fish and chip shop. There are two builders/agricultural merchants, a service garage, and a petrol station, next to which five small rural workshops are being built. For relaxation there is a fun park, the riding stables, a nine-hole golf course with driving range, a sports and leisure centre, the sports field and the children's play area. Next to the parish church are the public toilets and the free car park, an ideal starting point for the network of beautiful circular country walks.

Penstowe Manor was once the home of Mrs Thynne. As a magistrate she penalised any Kilkhampton offender brought before her much more harshly than people from elsewhere. Present day motorists have this formidable lady to thank for the easier gradient on the hilly road from Stratton. Having quarrelled with the Vicar of St James she began attending services in Stratton. In bad weather her horses were unable to negotiate the steep slopes of the narrow road through Ivyleaf Combe, so Mrs Thynne had the wider, safer road carved from the hillside beside Tiscott Wood along which her carriage – and later her Rolls Royce – swept majestically.

Tourism and farming are the main sources of income though there is now only one farm within the actual village where once there were several. A warm welcome awaits all who visit Kilkhampton, gatekeepers of the northern holiday route into Cornwall. Contrary to local jokes, the only 'passport' you will need to enter this lovely part of the country is an answering smile to the welcoming one you will receive.

🍁 KINGSAND & CAWSAND

This collection of villages and hamlets was brought together by historical and accidental events to form the parish of Maker with Rame on an unspoilt peninsula of south-east Cornwall.

The twin villages of Kingsand and Cawsand owe their existence mainly to the fishing industry and smuggling, and until 1844 were in different counties being separated between Devon and Cornwall by the little stream which runs

Cawsand from Minnadhu

between them. The boundary is recorded on the house called Devon-Corn opposite the Halfway House inn. They were further drawn together by joining the parishes of Maker and Rame in 1943.

Into this lovely area in the 15th century moved the Edgcumbe family from Milton Abbot via Cotehele, and Mount Edgcumbe Park was created, now the finest country park in England. This may be approached by road or by Cremyll ferry. Cremyll is part of the parish and a 'Gateway to Cornwall' and it owes its being to the ferry, the park and to a flourishing boatyard from whence many famous transatlantic and round the world yachtsmen have departed. Lower Anderton, the fourth member of the union, resulted from its navigable waters where ships of the Fleet were once laid up.

The area is dotted with quaint little chapel-like buildings and 'ruins', some of the latter built as such! Halfway between Cremyll and Maker church is a Cornish well chapel six ft square known as St Julian's Well. Some of these buildings, including the churches at Maker and Rame, were used for many years as lookout stations and provided sound shoremarks for maritime navigation.

Lovely aged farms in local stone abound which have mostly escaped the developers' depredations but some of the forts of Palmerston's days which guard the peninsula have not been so lucky. Remains of the pilchard fish cellars may be found all around the coasts, a reminder of more flourishing times.

Violent storms occasionally hit the bay. Stories of past wrecks and disasters are many. In the season the bay is filled with boats reminiscent of the days of sail when ships found safe anchorage before the breakwater was built, the twin villages providing entertainment for the seafarers as they do now.

Edgcumbe ladies provide two stories from the past. An obelisk at Cremyll is supposed to commemorate a pig kept by one countess as a pet. Another countess, awaiting burial, was in the process of being robbed of her rings when she was revived by the pain and to the surprise of the robber left the church at Maker and returned to Mount Edgcumbe House to survive. The robber leapt off a nearby cliff!

A watchman in the church tower was murdered for his silver watch and buckles and a man from Saltash later convicted of the crime was hanged at Exeter. It is, however, a benign peninsula as far as its ghosts are concerned. Apart from notable exceptions, one at Anderton where a ghostly lady became very upset that her treasure might be found and taken during quite recent renovations and a poltergeist at Rame long departed, the ghosts are a tranquil breed!

A candlelit carol service is held in Rame church at Christmas and at Rame Head in the little St Michael's chapel a service is held on Whit Sunday followed by a parish picnic. Songs of praise are sung annually in the open air on the Cleave, Kingsand.

There are traces of Iron Age fortifications at Rame Head and an earlier round barrow in Mount Edgcumbe Park. Many intriguing 'lumps and bumps' can be seen and are worth investigation. Mount Edgcumbe has long claimed the distinction as 'the haven' where the Duke of Medina Sidonia of Armada fame aimed to be, following his anticipated victory. He was defeated and happily for us there are now 865 acres of lovely parkland in which to roam.

In 1991 and 1992 the twin villages won the Best Kept Village Award from CPRE and more recently in 1998 and 1999 were the proud winners of the Caradon in Bloom competition.

🍁 LADOCK

Ladock is a village on the A39, lying between the A30 Bodmin-Penzance road and the A390 St Austell-Truro road. Up until about 1840 the old toll road from Bodmin to Truro went through the centre of Ladock and parts of it can still be seen across the fields and over the river. One of the tollgate posts is still standing. One of the local inhabitants tells the story of his great-great grandfather who regularly jumped the gate on his horse to avoid payment of toll.

As in most Cornish villages, the church is the outstanding feature and can be seen towering over the village from several miles away. The church of St Ladoca has stood since Saxon times but was largely rebuilt in the 19th century. Originally the church had three bells dating back to the Civil War but these were replaced in 1883. One of the present day Ladock ringers claims to have met the Ladock ghost who appears in the church only when the bells are being rung. In 1988 Ladock joined in the ringing of church bells throughout Cornwall to celebrate the tricentenary of the release of Bishop Trelawney from the Tower of London.

Ladock takes its name from the legendary St Ladoca who is supposed to have sailed across the Irish Sea in a coracle with St Piran and St Probus. St Piran remained near Perranporth but the others walked on towards central Cornwall. St Ladoca settled in the wooded Ladock valley at Fentonladock where there is a record of a chapel and a well being discovered (fenton is Cornish for spring). St Probus went on to the next valley and the two saints worked together to bring Christianity to the people, until they decided that a boundary should be settled between the two parishes. They agreed to rise at dawn and walk towards each other, the boundary to be drawn at the spot where they met. St Probus, being a man, set off at sunrise but St Ladoca was very beautiful, with long copper-coloured hair of which she was very proud. Legend has it that on the morning of the boundary marking she spent so long combing her hair that St Probus had almost reached Ladock before St Ladoca had set out. To this day the boundary between the two parishes is two miles from Probus but only a few hundred yards from the centre of Ladock. The banner of the Ladock WI shows this legend together with the discovery in 1802 in the Ladock river of the largest gold nugget found in Cornwall. This can now be seen in Truro museum.

The oldest house in the village is dated about 1380 and it is outside this house that the old tollhouse was built. Next to it is the old blacksmith's shop, now closed. Many local residents remember when the smithy was in constant use; one farmer bringing 13 horses to be shod on a rainy day. The smith worked in conjunction with the carpenter in making coffins – the pitch to line the coffins being warmed in the blacksmith's shop. The coffins, when required, were delivered to the house in the butcher's van. Bissick Mill, which dates back to the Middle Ages, was a working mill for corn-grinding until 1950, and its two huge water wheels were always a source of great fascination to the children of the village. The mill is now a guest house.

Today the village has one shop cum post office, but within the memory of many people is the time when there were four shops. The Ladock reading room (now the Oddfellows Hall) is called the Stamford Raffles Room in honour of the local links between Ladock and the founder of Singapore. Indeed, one of the local gardens contains one of the only two specimens of marsh spruce to be

found in Cornwall. This was grown from seed brought back from Singapore by
Stamford Raffles himself.

 LAMORNA

Lamorna is a village in a valley, a lane running parallel with a stream
downwards through woodland, for a mile to the sea. Passing artists' studios,
the village hall, public house, hotel, mill and cottages, it gets more narrow and
steep as it reaches the harbour and the shore of granite boulders. The stream
divides the village into the two parishes of Paul and St Buryan, situated about
halfway between Penzance and Land's End.

Beneath the lush growth of trees and ferns the valley's industrial past is still
evident. At some time in the past tin streamers operated the whole valley, and
traces of their workings can be seen in the banks and gullies.

A Captain Owen came to Lamorna in the middle of the 19th century to quarry
granite on the right hand side of the cove. He built the quay, cottages for his
workers and a house for himself, which is now the Lamorna Cove Hotel.

However, the quality of his granite was poor and eventually his enterprise
made him bankrupt. Then a company, Freemans of Falmouth, opened a quarry
on the other side of the cove where the granite was of very good quality. It was
used in building London's Victoria Embankment, the Houses of Parliament and
the Wolf Rock Lighthouse, in addition to many local public buildings. An
obelisk 22 ft high was exhibited at the Great Exhibition, Crystal Palace in 1851.
A cut granite sample still stands in the cove.

The old mill, known as Kemyel Mill, ground corn for local farmers. The
lower mill ground wheat and barley for human consumption, and the upper
mill, corn for cattle food. The property has been occupied by the Hosking family
since the early part of the 14th century, probably longer, there being no record
of the occupants before that time.

Mixed farming in the area was followed early last century by flower growing
for the wholesale markets. Daffodils, violets and anemones were grown to some
degree by almost every household. The cliff land was divided into pockets of
shelter by hedges of fuchsia and privet for growing early potatoes and flowers.
Nowadays this method of cultivation is no longer a viable proposition, and most
of the meadows have gone back to the wild, although daffodils are still grown
in more suitable areas of the valley.

Lamorna has a history of legends and ancient stones. There is a mermaid
rock on the headland, where a mermaid is said to show herself with comb and
glass in her hand, singing plaintively before a wreck. Young men have swum

off to the rock lured by her song, never to return. The circle of stones at the head of the valley, known as the Merry Maidens, were maidens carelessly dancing on the sabbath. As the music and dancing became more excited there was a flash of lightning and the maidens were turned to stone. Their two pipers, as they ran in terror, were transfixed to stone two fields away.

The Wink public house has over the years been the meeting place of many famous actors, writers and artists. Several artists of the Newlyn School built homes and studios in the valley.

The village was originally called Nantewas, the summering place', and the cove Lamorna, but now it is all known as Lamorna.

Many of the cottages are now holiday homes and lets, and apart from a little market gardening and farming, the main income of the residents comes from tourism. There is one pottery, studios selling paintings, and the old corn mill is a craft and gift shop. The Cove and Wink cater for tourists, and Lamorna Pottery, which was the old milk factory, also has a restaurant.

LAND'S END

The village of Sennen consists of two parts, Churchtown and the Cove. The church of St Sennen which dates from the 5th century and the chapel are well attended. The road which brings Churchtown and the Cove together was built by the Western Union Cable Company, which used huge cables spread across the beach and under the sea to America. These have been superseded by the age of the satellite. The well built Trinity houses standing out on the cliff no longer house the families of the men working on the Longships lighthouse, which is now worked by automation.

The large Sennen fishing boats go out from Newlyn, the smaller boats remaining fish for mackerel, pollock, some flat fish, crabs, lobsters and crayfish. The big mullet seine boats and nets have long fallen into disuse as the large shoals of mullet no longer appear.

Exhilarating walks along the cliff path from the Cove to Land's End, or to Cape Cornwall across the wide stretch of white sands may be taken. The beach now has the blue flag representing the EEC standards of cleanliness.

Fund raising days for the lifeboat are enjoyed by all; locals and visitors join in the fun, be it trips in the lifeboat or shopping at the many stalls and sampling the cream teas which are served by the ladies of the Guild, dressed in costume of days gone by. Nearby the Round House, a listed building originally used as a winch-house and net store, is now a well preserved and presented gallery for the arts and crafts of Cornwall.

Gig racing from the Cove has now become popular. Used in the old days as pilot boats in Scilly, these long narrow boats manned by many oars provide healthy outdoor exercise and excitement for young people around the area. The most popular sports are surfing and canoeing and diving with bottled oxygen. These seas often provide the breakers loved by the bass fishermen and from dawn to sunset the breakwater is peopled by fishermen looking for pollock and rock wrasse which are good sport and always happily accepted by the crabbers for bait.

There are several shops, cafes, an hotel and plenty of accommodation in the cottages for the visitors. Sennen primary school at the top of the hill was built in 1880, serving the children of the village still today. Behind the school is the recently built community hall, providing extra room for the school children as well as a doctor's surgery.

Land's End, which is in the parish of Sennen, is a mecca for most people when coming to Cornwall. One of the highlights before the Second World War was the Motor Trial Race when cars of all sorts starting off from John O'Groats arrived at Land's End on Easter Monday. One of the early walkers who made news was Dr Barbara Moore in the early 1960s, followed by Wendy Lewis a month or so later. These days a sponsored walk to Land's End is almost a weekly occurrence. Land's End Hotel, the State House, the First and Last House, sitting on the point, are all well known, as is the First and Last inn just a mile along the road.

The outer perimeter of the village consists of working farms growing early potatoes, cabbages, broccoli and flowers for the up country markets; farmers' wives often take in visitors in the summer months. Mentioned in the Domesday Book is Penrose Farm. Tourism is much a part of the village; hotels, guesthouses, as well as bed and breakfast accommodation, caravan and campsites, and self catering are all well booked up. The post office, small supermarket and garage are all well used the whole year and are even busier in the summer.

The village and peninsula are wind swept, therefore not a place for gardens or tall trees, but the true beauty lies in the splendid cliffs, wide open areas of gorse and heather and spectacular sea views. Hedges of fuchsia, escalonia and tamarisk frame the cottages, honeysuckle and wild flowers in the country lanes and sea pinks, squills and sea holly adorn the dunes – in all, a good place to live.

🍁 LANHYDROCK

No school, no pub, no shop (except the National Trust shop in summer months), no public transport. So what attracts more than 148,000 folk of all nationalities to the parish of Lanhydrock every year, mainly between 1st April and 31st October? It is the majestic Lanhydrock House, one of the finest stately homes in Cornwall, and 900 acres of formal and woodland gardens with parkland which contains many rare trees and shrubs. The National Trust has owned the property since 1953.

About two miles from the centre of Cornwall, a house was built between 1642 and 1644 on the site of a monastery which had belonged to St Petroc's Priory in Bodmin until the Dissolution of the Monasteries. The builder was Baron Thomas Robartes – formerly Roberts – a Truro businessman who bought his peerage for £10,000. The house was built originally in the form of a quadrangle surrounding a courtyard but the east wing was removed in 1780 to open the rooms to the sunlight.

During the Civil War Robartes, a Puritan Parliamentarian, then Lord Lieutenant of Cornwall and a Field Marshal, made his headquarters at Lanhydrock House so there would have been much military activity in the parish. However, Baron Robartes did not agree with Cromwell's principles and returned to live at Lanhydrock. He planted the beautiful avenue of sycamore trees in 1648 and beeches in 1651 which line the road leading from the gate house to the river Fowey.

Over a hundred years ago the house was rebuilt of local stone and timber from the estate under the directorship of Richard Coad. This followed the disastrous fire on 4th April 1881 which destroyed all but the North wing. Folk talked about the fire for years afterwards. The horror of it caused the death of Lady Juliana Agar-Robartes four days after the event. Her husband, Lord Thomas Robartes, died the following year.

In those days nearly every parishioner over 13 was either a servant in the big house or a tenant – village life revolved around the Robartes family. Single servants lived in their own quarters in the house. When the National Trust took over it was thought there were about 40 rooms but in all 100 were counted – many of these were servants' quarters. Married servants, coachmen, grooms etc were given tenancy of estate houses in the grounds or very close by. The village school, built in 1840, had to be enlarged to take 100 pupils with one certificated teacher and a pupil-teacher. A familiar sight in the deer park would have been a coach and horses taking members of the Robartes/Clifden family along the two mile track to the nearest main line station at Bodmin Road.

The vicar of St Hydroc's church (built in Perpendicular style a few yards to the rear of the big house) lived nearby in the vicarage with his wife, four children and a live-in staff of a cook, nurse, under-nurse/domestic, lady's maid, parlour maid and groom!

Sunday school was often held in the great Long Gallery of the house where the 24 enriched plaster barrel panels on the ceiling depicting incidents of Old Testament history provided the subject matter for lessons. The girls were taught by the ladies of the house, the boys by Lord Robartes. The Robartes family made it their business to know everyone in the parish. If anyone fell upon hard times they would be first to help.

There have been a number of developments since 1945. Four private homes and five council houses have been built in the parish. Part of Lanhydrock Golf Club is in the parish and here, plans for seven executive-style houses have been passed. Throughout the parish many barns and outhouses have been converted. These are used mainly for holiday accommodation. Some of the rooms in the big house have been turned into flats for private occupation. The former stables and coach houses, set in a corner of the park, now accommodate the headquarters of the National Trust in Cornwall which employs many people. The village school known as Cutmadoc, which was using buckets for toilets as late as 1948, closed in the early sixties and is now a private residence. The parish extends to about 1,740 acres and has 135 persons on the electoral register.

Descendants of Lord Clifden's family have taken previously tenanted farms in hand. In a set of new, modern buildings at Tredinnick a dairy complex has been established in the name of Lanhydrock Farms. The aim is to build up a herd of 500 milking cows plus other cattle. Plans for the renovation of the dilapidated forge, a listed building, have been passed.

Sons of the big house lost their lives in the 1914-18 war and their father built the present War Memorial Hall as a tribute to them and others from the parish who died. With its large car park and excellent facilities, this is one of the centres of social life. Dances, the annual harvest supper, Christmas parties, dog training courses, a gardening show, the WI and many other events keep the hall well booked.

The beautiful park running down from the house to the river Fowey is a favourite venue for annual events such as the British Horse Society trials, village fete, craft fairs, jazz festival, dog show, outdoor theatre and, in 1990, the Cornwall Spring Garden Festival.The popular cricket club enjoys a pitch in the most beautiful setting on the edge of the park. The river Fowey provides a mile of excellent fishing on which special platforms have been built to accommodate anglers in wheelchairs.

🍁 LANIVET

Lanivet, with a population of around 1,500, is at the geographical centre of Cornwall and a large stone in Lanivet churchyard bears testimony to this fact. Originally the 'Enclosure of St Nevet', Lanivet compares with Lannevet in Brittany. Once situated on Cornwall's main artery, the A30 trunk road, Lanivet suffered very heavy traffic problems, but since the building of the Bodmin bypass the village has obtained the peace it deserved, though today the Old Coach Road takes the traveller from Bodmin, through the northern edge of the village, to join the A30 further along its westward route, cutting the journey from Bodmin by several miles.

Along the Old Coach Road, on the edge of Lanivet parish, is now a highly modern holiday complex providing fishing, sporting and leisure facilities for both local and holiday people, together with unusual 'A' frame cabin accommodation. Lanivet is also on the Saint's Way, the route followed by the early Christian saints on their journey from Padstow to Fowey en route from Ireland to France.

This busy village, with a new development of detached houses being built at its centre, has a school, a playgroup, two churches, car sales, a village store, a post office, a fish and chip shop which is famous for miles around and a public house which displays a panda on its sign. This is in honour of the zoo pandas who were at one time fed with bamboo shoots supplied from Lanivet, where the growing and marketing of bamboo cane provided much employment.

A stream runs through the village to join the river Camel some distance away and on its way it passes St Benet's Abbey, a 14th century building which was once a hospital under the patronage of the Courtenay family. The building is now an hotel and restaurant, but the old tower which was St Benedict's chapel has so far not been renovated.

One of the oldest and best preserved ancient monuments in the west exists at the southern edge of the parish. This is an ancient henge dating from the Neolithic period.

During the period of mining in Cornwall, Lanivet was very prosperous, having eleven copper mines. Lanivet Consols and Tretoil produced between them 20,000 tons of copper, earning £40,000 for Lanivet.

The parish church dates back to the 12th century and records in the vestry go back as far back as Elizabeth I. Although the church has no patron saint, it has been a place of worship for many years as the two huge Celtic crosses in the churchyard show, and inside the church is a slate carving dedicated to the ancient Courtenay family, landowners in the district in the 14th century.

As recently as 1965 permission was granted for a geo-chemical survey and test drilling for gold to take place. Nothing seems to have been found at that time, but with the present interest in gold drilling, maybe Lanivet will again become as prosperous as it was with copper mining.

🍁 LANLIVERY

Lanlivery is a large parish situated to the west of the A390 Lostwithiel to St Blazey road. In spite of its size it only has about 300 inhabitants with a nucleus of houses at one end known as Lanlivery Village and another about two miles away known as Sweetshouse. Redmoor 'straggles' in between the two and there are many farms all around.

The church at Lanlivery was built in the 15th century and was the mother church to Lostwithiel and Luxulyan. Since the 1950s Luxulyan and Lanlivery parishes have again shared the same vicar but each keeps its own identity. Over the past decade the church has undergone a major restoration. The Kendall family of Pelyn were responsible for building the church, and were always very active in church affairs. The school, now 123 years old is still thriving and has just opened its own pre-school.

In the Dark Ages the Saints' Way, used by pilgrims from Ireland, passed through Lanlivery on their way to France. This walk from Padstow to Fowey was re-enacted in 1990 with parishioners taking the part of the saints. After a ceremony on Helman Tor, a pageant showing life from the Neolithic Age, through Norman times to the present days was held in the village with almost everyone taking part.

Farming, once the main industry in Lanlivery, has changed. The majority of the farms, once owned by either Lanhydrock or Pelyn estates, have been divided into small 'lots' and sold to adjoining farms, while the houses and buildings have been modernised and sold to buyers mostly from out of the county. Today most people travel out of the area to work, some going as far as Plymouth. New local industries include a used car garage, caravan and camp sites, a fish farm and a nursery.

Once known as the reading room, and in the middle of the 19th century used as a school, the building at the bottom of the churchyard became in need of repair so it was leased to a newly formed village hall management committee. With various grants and help from all the parish, a mammoth restoration job gave us the village hall as it is today.

The Crown inn, another old building, was built in the 12th century. It allowed its licence to lapse just before 1930 for both local folk and visitors.

One of the most ambitious projects in recent times, and one which really put

Lanlivery on the map, was the conversion of the Churchtown farm buildings to Churchtown Farm Field Studies Centre, which provides recreational activities for disabled people from all over the world.

The remains of Jinny Gerry's cottage still stand at Redmoor Bridge. Legend says she was a witch but there is no confirmation of this.

Lanlivery was designated a green belt area by the council but after some persuasion a few extra dwellings were allowed to be built. These included six houses built by the Cornwall Rural Housing Association for rent to local people. This small estate is known as Thomas Bullock Close.

Thomas Bullock, a bachelor, was born in 1649 and when he died he left £110 to the elders of the parish to purchase land, the rent to be distributed between the widows and fatherless children of the parish. They bought a farm in the parish of St Wenn. A few years ago this was sold and the money invested. The charity is now controlled by the specially formed Thomas Bullock Charity Trust.

This is a very friendly village, where there is always something going on and everyone is made to feel very welcome.

🍁 LANNER

Lanner means simply 'a clearing', and before the advent of the bustling village of the 19th and 20th centuries, it is said to have contained only six cottages and a chapelry.

The village does not immediately strike the visitor as picturesque, dominated a it is by the A394 Redruth/Falmouth road. Largely rural in character, its charms are well hidden. It is up the tiny lanes, which lead off to right and left of the busy main road, that Lanner comes into its own. It sprawls up the long slopes of a wide valley and is shielded by welcoming hills from the prevailing wind and sea-borne rain that runs before it.

Lanner is part of the rich history of Cornish tin and copper mining and its roots lie in the old mining area known as 'golden mile'. Standing on the lower slopes of Carn Marth, the fine engine house of Pennance Consols has recently been preserved from further decay. It is one of the most visible in Cornwall and Lanner's most recognisable landmark. Locally dubbed 'Wheal Bloody Nose', the reason why has been lost in time. On the north side of the valley, running from the top of Lanner Hill across Pennance and out to Carharrack, the track of the historic four foot gauge Redruth to Chacewater mineral railway line can still be traced. On the south side a branch line linked Tresavean mine to the old Cornwall Railway. When Tresavean closed in 1928 it had reached a depth of 2,660 ft, making it the second deepest mine in Cornwall.

In the heyday of mining, the village working day rang with the sound of men tramping to the mines in their heavy nailed boots and the clop of horses' hoofs as steady teams of four pulled ore-laden carts to the top of Lanner Hill, and on to the smelting works. Whistles blasting out the change of shifts and the roar of surface stamps crushing ore could be heard all over the valley. It was known that if, during a shift, the stamps went quiet an accident had probably occurred at the mine.

Butchers and blacksmiths, the bakery with its coal ovens, the cobbler and the corset shop, a post office and a high class provision store were open all hours. Three public houses helped the miners forget the dangers of their subterranean existence and twice on Sundays three packed chapels and a church resounded to accomplished choirs. It was a self sufficient and independent village, albeit a noisy one.

Modern facilities were slow in coming but eventually 'Figgy Dowdie's' well on Pennance and other communal drinking wells were superseded by piped water and one of the houses was fitted with a bath. All great cause for excitement as the pace of life quickened.

The village is alive with social and sporting activities for all ages, outside events usually accompanied by the Lanner silver band. In the summer of 1989 villagers joined together in a day of glorious celebration to honour the birthday of their oldest inhabitant. Born in Lanner in 1889, she was a farmer's daughter who married a miner.

On the hills, where foxes bark and buzzards wheel, new life of a different kind is rising from dereliction as abandoned and neglected areas become local assets. The landscaped Tresavean has a football field and will soon boast a sports hall. The old railway tracks have been preserved and made into walkways for those interested in Cornwall's industrial past. A disused granite quarry on Carn Marth has become an open-air theatre, its sheer walls a natural back-drop for the performers and from the top of those granite walls the view towards the north and south coasts of the peninsula is breathtaking.

The miners have gone now and most folk live in Lanner but work in the towns which encircle it, Truro and Redruth, Falmouth or Helston. Large housing estates springing up on either side of Lanner Hill, mean that Lanner is no longer separated from Redruth, and is in danger of losing its own unique identity.

🍁 LAWHITTON

Lawhitton is a pretty village, just off the beaten track. There are beautiful views all round and Dartmoor can be seen in the distance. Originally called Languiton, or Landwithan, it dates from before the ancient Britons. It became known under its present name 150 years before the Norman Conquest. An interesting relic of the Bronze Age was discovered in a local field. A farmhand, wielding a scythe, struck what is known as a celt, a weapon of war of the early British. This specimen weighs over a pound and stands over five inches high, and is composed entirely of bronze.

In AD 909 the parish was granted to Eadulph, the Saxon Bishop of Crediton, so that he might 'every year visit the Cornish race to extirpate their errors'. In 1046 the parish came to Leofric, the first Bishop of Exeter. In 1153 William Warlest, then Bishop of Exeter, was resident in Lawhitton. The Bishops used to travel from Devon, and cross a chain bridge over the river Tamar, which sadly is no longer in being, although we can see just where it was positioned. There was a bishop's palace in Lawhitton, but this fell into ruins. In the 19th century it was rebuilt as a private house, and the bishop's mitre can still be seen at one end of it.

There is no shop or inn in the village, although there used to be an inn called the Bennett's Arms, but this also is now a private house.

In medieval times there was a flourishing market in the village, but this ceased as the years went on and farmers used the larger market in Launceston.

On one of the farms there is the site of a holy well, unfortunately now trampled by cattle. The church of St Michael dates from Norman times. Parts of the foundation are Norman, and the font is typically Norman with carved heads which are beardless.

Because it is such a small village, people are all friendly and companionable. Being off the beaten track, we seldom get people coming into the village unless they are visiting friends or families, or or course, delivering items to the residents.

The population is quite varied. Whilst there a number of retired people, the village has a fair share of young people, mostly working in nearby Launceston, which is just two miles away. However, there is a petrol station and repair garage, which is more than useful, for although there is a school bus for the children there is no public transport as such. There is a village hall, which is organised by a committee of residents, and also an enthusiastic group of bell-ringers.

🍁 LEEDSTOWN

The village of Leedstown, as its English name suggests, developed comparatively late, in the first quarter of the 19th century. It grew from small settlements at Carsize, Carloose, Binner Downs etc, which all had Cornish names. It is part of the ancient parish of Crowan. The village owes its name to the Godolphins from the neighbouring parish, who owned most of the land in the area, whose last surviving heirs were the Dukes of Leeds. The arms of the two families can still be seen on the Duke of Leeds inn sign in the centre of the village.

There are few old buildings, though there are some cottages built of clay or 'cob' dug from the surrounding land, which have been much altered. These used to be leased on three lives, as was the custom in Cornwall. However, the ancient manor of Binnerton still remains on the outskirts of the village. It is run as a farm. The manor of Binner was mentioned in the Domesday records. At one time, there was a chapel there dedicated to St Augustine and one of the fields is still called Chapel Field. One of its famous visitors was John Wesley, who preached from the porch to a crowd waiting outside.

Leedstown developed because of the mines springing up in the early 19th century. In 1835, there were twelve in the parish. At Wheal Abraham, Horsedowns, on 21st August 1806, there was a terrible disaster, when a flood, caused possibly by a water-spout on the high hills above Crowan, poured into the mine. Within 15 minutes Wheal Abraham was filled with 50 fathoms of water. Seven were drowned, but about 50 men escaped with great difficulty.

The village continued to grow during the rest of the 19th century. Chapels were built in 1837 and 1863. In 1878 the village school was built, which is still a centre for education in the village. By 1884 there were several shops and an inn, providing for the inhabitants' daily wants as well as servicing equipment for the mines. By 1885 there were 233 pupils at the village school. Today, there are under 40!

As the mines began to fail towards the end of the century, many travelled to Canada, America, Australia and South Africa, taking their families with them. The Boer War and the First World War took more from their homes. In 1921, the Duke of Leeds sold the freehold of all the properties, which led to the break-up of the old system of landlord and tenant. The Second World War increased the rate of change. Finally, 20th century technology completed the process. With the development of transport and communication, the movement out of Cornwall for further education and the movement in of those who seek a quiet place to retire, changes have been rapid.

Today, the village is nevertheless still a thriving community with its large Methodist chapel, the village school, and the mission church of St James. The

Duke of Leeds is still open, the cricket club plays with fervour, there is a large village hall where events can be held, and the men's institute and the WI have many active members. There is an Over Fifties Club for the less energetic and a play group. At Catloose, there is a very large camp and caravan site which has won several international awards. Much of the area is still farmed, with major crops being potatoes and cauliflowers with some flower farming, cattle and poultry, and now a vegetable processing plant. There is a flourishing post office and stores in the centre of the village, catering for locals and passing trade, an antiques shop, a corner shop and bakery, and a large garage serving the agricultural community over a wide area.

Despite its insignificant appearance, Leedstown has nurtured several 'characters', among them R.R. Blewett, bard of the Cornish Gorsedd, a pupil at the village school, who became one of the best-known local historians for Leedstown and Cornish history generally. At the age of 88, he was given an honorary MA for his research into Cornish surnames. It is also home to Ann Trevenen-Jenkin, the first Cornishwoman to become Grand Bard. Then there was John Rapson, coal-man, who could move school benches single-handed. His great strength took him into the Guinness Book of Records, when on 4th April 1953 he carried one cwt of household coal in an open bag 14 miles from Perranporth to Camborne in three hours 40 minutes. His record remained unbeaten for nearly 25 years until 1977.

🍁 LELANT

Lelant is a delightful village situated on the west bank of the Hayle estuary, three miles from St Ives.

In the 14th century Lelant was an important port when the Hayle estuary afforded deep water and before St Ives rose to prominence. The present church was consecrated in 1424, incorporating a Norman arch, the only remaining feature of the original church, which like the rest of the village had been engulfed by an enormous drift of sand at an earlier period.

Originally called Lannant, the definition of the modern name is 'Holy place of St Anta' and there is indeed a wishing well on the coastal footpath near the sand dunes. Part of the village known as Lower Lelant was formerly called Trendreath, the town on the Sand (or Beach), and it was this area that was most affected by the building of the branch railway line by the Great Western Railway in 1877. This scenic line runs from St Erth to St Ives, about three and a half miles, following the coast but passing through Lelant and Carbis Bay en route.

Before the Hayle Causeway was built in 1828, travellers wishing to go west had to ford the estuary at low tide and one or two of these crossing points can still be identified.

There are some interesting houses in the village and although there is no longer a squire, the manor house, Trevethoe, survives in its own beautiful parkland. It was the home of the Praed family whose name is associated with the Grand Union Canal and Praed Street in London. The property passed through marriage to the Tyringham family whose estates were in Buckinghamshire and since 1958 Trevethoe has been a photographic laboratory, the original house surviving in all its former glory. The houses of both estates are depicted in the east window of the parish church.

Probably one of the oldest houses in the village is The Abbey. Owned by the priory on St Michael's Mount, it was used as a rest house by the monks and there is reputed to be a secret passage from the beach, running under the village to the abbey, probably used for smuggling. Today it is privately owned.

The original vicarage, no longer used by the clergy, is an imposing Georgian house built in 1834 and standing on high ground with views across the estuary. In the latter half of the 19th century the village inn, known as the Ship, was to be found in Church Road. It was situated at the top of a steep track, Brewery Hill, so called because the beer barrels which had arrived by sea were rolled up the hill to the inn.

Parson Tyacke, as he was known throughout the parish, was the incumbent of Lelant from 1869 to 1901 and was undoubtedly a good priest but his lasting memorial is the West Cornwall Golf Club which he founded in 1889.

The population has increased greatly in recent years but the village atmosphere remains and this is reflected in the support and enthusiasm given to the Produce Association and WI. Many residents are gifted artists and potters and in needlecraft, exemplified by the creation of a 42 panel tapestry depicting village life that was produced for the Millennium celebrations.

🍁 LERRYN

The name is said to derive from the Cornish word lerrion, meaning waters and it is thought the village was connected to the port of Lostwithiel. The village is divided by the river, the north-west side being mainly in the parish of St Winnow and the remainder in St Veep.

There was a corn mill here before 1346 and in the 16th century it was converted to ore-crushing. It reverted to a corn mill in the 18th century. Before road transport was mechanised, coal, limestone, fertilisers, grain, roadstone, sand and timber were brought to the village by boat. There was employment for several men as well as pilots to bring the boats from Fowey, about 200 tons cargo, plus men to unload. The quays were rarely without heaps of blue elvin roadstone, which would be carted to stone depots in the parish. 1918 saw the last of the boats bringing lime-stone. There were two limekilns, one of which can be seen opposite the village hall and is now being restored. The other has been converted to a dwelling.

In its hey-day Lerryn was the venue for annual regattas, likened to Henley. Spectators could view the events from both sides of the river. It was discontinued in 1968 for lack of support. There was also a village fete held in June with horse and athletic events. Concerts were held in the school room, local bands, talent and dancers. Nowadays there is the annual produce and flower show held in August. A race on the river takes place at the end of December known as the Sea-Gull Race. The river can be crossed by stepping stones at low-water but is normally crossed by road bridge.

A small water-wheel about five foot in diameter was installed down by the mill to pump spring water to the school, before this drinking water was fetched from the bottom of the hill in cans. The village pump is still to be seen by the lime kiln. There is now only one carpenter and one mason but several people have their own businesses. There are two guest houses and two shops. One is a post office and general store which it is to be hoped will continue to serve the village and surrounding area. In the old days mail was brought from Lostwithiel by a postman on a bicycle and three postmen would deliver on foot. There was a single telephone line from Lostwithiel to the only phone at the Lerryn post office. The postmistress on receiving a telegraph would go down by the river and blow a horn to call the telegraph boy who lived on the other side. On pheasant shooting days at Boconnoc this boy was kept busy cycling to and fro (six miles) for four pence per trip.

There is a legend concerning the so called 'Giants Hedge'. It is said:

'The Devil having nothing to do,
Built a great wall from Lerryn to Looe.'

Historians say that the 'hedge' is a giant fortification. Part of it is still visible and one resident has named his house after it.

🍁 LEWANNICK

Lewannick is a small village situated approximately six miles from Launceston, which was the ancient capital of the county. It is just off the main A30 trunk road to the south.

Unlike most villages in the area which are to be found in sheltered valley situations, Lewannick is a hill top settlement looking towards the moors, Fox Tor being the highest visible point.

The earliest buildings are around the church and the public house. It is not a village that is typical of this area. It has its heart at the crossroads whereas many Cornish villages have a sprawling ribbon development.

Lewannick church is particularly fine. There has been a church on this site since the 5th or 6th century. The present church of St Martin was given to Launceston Priory about 1230 by Richard, lord of Trelaske. About 200 years later it was rebuilt. The tower was built primarily in polyphant stone, quarried in the parish of Lewannick. This stone is also used extensively in other churches in the area and also many buildings in the nearby town of Launceston. It is a soft porous stone which is liable to weathering. It is no longer quarried commercially.

In 1890 the church was almost completely destroyed by fire. It is felt that more of the church interior might have been saved were it not for a sad happening. A messenger was dispatched to Launceston on horseback to raise the alarm and call the fire brigade. On arrival the firefighters found that their hoses were not long enough to reach from the well to the church. The building was all but destroyed. There remains in the church a Norman font and in the churchyard two Ogham stones inscribed in Latin and dating from the 5th or 6th century.

The village still consists of some very old cottages, some of which have been recently restored. The largest number of houses are post 1939 and are on the outskirts of the village, including one small modern estate. Many retired people live in the village and there is one residential home for the elderly, 'Pen-Inney'. There are three shops, including the post office. The latter has been housed in the same house, except for a short break after the last war, for over 100 years. The public house, the Archers Arms, was originally a temperance hotel and takes its name from the lords of the manor at Trelaske.

The 18th century saw the beginnings of Methodism, with the arrival of John Wesley, a frequent visitor to Cornwall. Many difficulties arose in Lewannick between the Anglicans and the Nonconformists.

In the first instance the Methodists of the village met in the house belonging to the shoemaker. This upset the local parson, one George Mangles, who then refused to patronise the cobbler and so the Methodists had to find other accommodation. After this they rented a room in a cottage that was being rented by a widow. This incensed George Mangles still further and he offered a higher rent. This was accepted and both the widow and the Methodists were homeless. After further hounding by Mangles, who by this time had engaged a lawyer to prove that alterations to their latest rented cottage were illegal, again the Methodists were evicted. Eventually they were able to rent a room at Ravadlock, the home of Grace and John Nanscawen Dawe. Mangles was still determined to get the better of them and insisted that the Methodists should pay tithes in kind rather than in cash. Mangles died very suddenly before any actual transaction had taken place. John Dawe was so delighted that out of gratitude he gave the Methodists a plot of land at Trevadlock Cross plus £10. Here they built their own chapel. This chapel is still open.

🍁 LEZANT

Time has stood almost still in the quiet and peaceful parish of Lezant over the past century and this adds to its attraction. Pockets of new developments have sprung up here and there, but on the whole the area has been prudently protected.

At the turn of the century, many of the menfolk worked in the antimony and red and yellow ochre mines at Trevullet and Larrick. Today, apart from farming and a small industrial estate at Treburley, there is little local employment. Most people work in businesses in Launceston or Plymouth.

The sprawling parish spans some six miles from one extremity to the other – Rezare to Larrick – taking in Lezant village housing the parish church of St Briocus and church room, the village shop and post office; Trebullet with a chapel; Trekenner with the village school; Treburley with the village pub and local garage and Tregada where there is another chapel.

Lezant is rich in history too, the most outstanding feature being Trecarrell Manor, a major medieval monument and former seat of the family of that name until the reign of Henry VIII. In the early 16th century, Sir Henry Trecarrell, the second lord of the manor, started to build a large mansion, but abruptly abandoned the project after the tragic death of his infant son and heir. At that time only the Great Hall and a Lady Chapel had been completed. The heartbroken Sir Henry instead devoted his wealth and time on the restoration of churches in the area and much of the wrought granite procured for the manor house was used for the building of St Mary Magdalene parish church in Launceston.

Trecarrell Great Hall, Lezant

A chapel was first licensed at Trecarrell in 1383 and dedicated to St Mary Magdalene. One of the many relics kept there today is the parish bier, still in almost mint condition, but no-one is sure when this was last used to convey a coffin to its final resting place. Other chapels were built at Greystone, Landue and St Lawrence.

Trecarrell was later acquired by the Manatons then the Coode family, until it was recently purchased by the present owners, Neil and Ruth Burden, whose family have lived there for four generations.

Lezant parish church was dedicated to St Briocus (or Breoke) on 25th September 1259, but there appears to be a certain amount of controversy about this because some claim it was dedicated to St Michael, the patron saint of Cornwall. Apart from the Norman font of polyphant stone, little remains of the old Norman church. A lychgate was erected in memory of John Tregoning who died in 1909. Nearby lies a holy well, the water from which was used for baptisms.

Other properties with a flavour of the past include Carthamartha, where the rivers Tamar and Inney meet, once part of the extensive estates of the Dukes of Bedford and where the well known Cornish artist, Arthur Bevan Collier, 1832-1908, lived. He was also responsible for erecting the crosses over the well at Rezare Green. Landue Mill was once a foundry belonging to the famous Pennington bell-founding family.

❧ LINKINHORNE

Linkinhorne parish lies in the manor of Rillaton, the premier manor in the Cornish Domesday Book when it was spelt Resleston (town by the ford). It is divided by the wooded Lynher valley – the eastern half largely agricultural while the west rises steeply to Bodmin Moor with extensive views.

Linkinhorne church contains medieval wall paintings and one of its vicars, Richard Peryn, was cruelly murdered in 1411 by 'Disciples of Satan'. Apart from the church other interesting buildings include St Melor's Well, dedicated to Melor, son of a Cornish king. Stara Bridge is an excellent specimen of a clapper bridge, built in the 16th century. The Phoenix Mine is probably the best known local mine and was visited by the Prince of Wales (later George V) in 1909 when a shaft was named in his honour.

The most famous character must surely be Daniel Gumb, an 18th century eccentric who, being averse to paying rent, rates and taxes, lived in a cave near the Cheesewring. There his children were born and from that spot he studied the stars. He was a stone cutter and cut the stone in the churchyard bearing the inscription:

> 'Here we lye without the wall
> Twas full within they made a brawl
> Here we lye no rent to pay
> And yet we lye as warm as they'.

There are several old and interesting houses in the area including Westcott, a small manor house built by Edward Kneebone in 1653. Darley Farm is best known for its oak tree, 'The Darley Oak'. It is upwards of 1,000 years old and measures 36 ft in circumference, the oldest living tree in Cornwall. Although hollow it still produces acorns. It is mentioned in Harvey's *History of Linkinhorne* 1727.

Linkinhorne contains its own mini 'Stonehenge' in the form of the Hurlers. This complex is believed to be part of a calculator used by early farmers to determine dates for planting. Not far away is 'Stowes Pound', an ancient hill fort, and the famous Cheesewring, a natural fungoid-shaped formation about 20 ft high. There are also many hut circles in this area. The Rillaton Gold Cup (now in the British Museum) was found in a burial mound near the Hurlers in 1837 along with a skeleton, dagger, jade beads and an arrowhead. The cup was sent to William IV and then disappeared for many years until rediscovered after the death of George V. The burial tomb can still be seen.

In the past people of this parish were wheelwrights, blacksmiths, farmers, miners, carpenters, etc. The Bartletts of Plushabridge specialised in making carts, waggons and gipsy vans. There are still farmers, but many people commute to Plymouth. However there is a cheese farm with visitors centre, an open air theatre, clay pigeon shooting and river fishing. There is an art gallery with tea rooms in an old cider house, also a specialist joiner/funeral director and three shop/post offices.

🍁 LUCKETT

The village of Luckett nestles at the foot of Kit Hill, a 1,091 ft high landmark from the top of which a large area of both Cornwall and Devon can be seen, in addition to being a guide for many miles out to sea.

It narrowly escapes being a Devonshire village – lying right on the banks of the River Tamar which divides the two counties, and is situated in a particularly beautiful part of the valley, surrounded by hills and steep woodlands. The natural beauty has been changed over the years by the slow spread of agriculture and the various mine workings, making the village of unique archaeological interest.

The earliest sign of the village settlement is a prehistoric 'round' just to the east, while the farm in the centre was first recorded as 'Beau Lieu' – beautiful place in Norman French! Luckett is part of the parish of Stoke Climsland, and this manor was part of the ancient possessions of the Duchy of Cornwall, of tenure hold until 1845. The tenants were not allowed to send their children to school, or to marry off their daughters without permission. Part of the manor, a royal deer park from c1215 anciently named Kerribullock, is so near Luckett as to be part of it. In about 1329 the park was replenished with 150 deer. Though dis-parked by Henry VIII in 1542, fragments still survive unchanged.

In the 19th century, as well as the fine Brethren chapel at Hampt, the centre of village life was the Methodist church built in 1877 and considered to be one of the finest in the district. Methodism in the village began in the kitchen of a tiny cottage, on the site of the present post office, where John Rapson held services.

Over the years the working of the mines here brought changes to the village. The earliest deep workings were at Broadgate in about 1754, following openworks in the 1500s. Streaming for tin by digging through alluvial deposits beside the Tamar and the stream that still flows through the valley was known from at least the Middle Ages; the sites of blowing and stamping mills are preserved today.

Known as 'New Consuls Mine' in 1755, 'Wheal Martha', and later 'New

Consuls', there are notes from November 1876 of a visit to this mine. It describes how, 'Standing on the hill, the village is seen to be filled with buildings, tramways and inclines.' One and a half miles of arsenic flues and stacks had been rapidly erected in what had been open fields. Cottages grew up for the miners and their families and others were sub-divided. One large building known as the 'Union' where 20 or so single male miners lodged under the care of the Rowe family, is now a unique survivor of its kind and well preserved to its original plan.

When the mine stopped working, the cottages were claimed by the people living in them, to whom the market gardens developing in the woods (now a nature reserve) were a boon. The latest working of the mine was in 1946 with a reprocessing plant using a brand new chemical flotation method of separation, leaving behind large areas of settling beds and sandy wastes.

Now once again the massive and majestic engine houses stand idle, and ivy is growing over the stonework, providing a haven for the birds to build their nests. Natural succession slowly colonising the bare spoil provides scarce habitats for rare insects and flowers. A Remembrance Garden fills the chapel area within the graveyard, while in the village the centre of activity has migrated down the hill to the social club which hosts an ever-widening range of activities for today's varied and thriving community.

🍁 Luxulyan

Luxulyan is set on an upland towards the head of a very beautiful valley, about five miles from the St Austell bay on the south coast an 16 miles from Newquay on the north coast.

It is thought that since the name is so near to the Breton place-name Lossulian, that the church was founded by St Sulian, one of the party of Welsh missionary monks who accompanied St Sampson to Brittany in the 6th century. It was a missionary journey and many of these people held services on sites with pre-Christian religious associations. In the village of Luxulyan there were two such sites – one where the church now stands and the holy well. The church was the daughter church of Lanlivery. The first recorded parish priest, in 1303, was Sir Ralph de Restyn; towards the end of the next century the church was almost wholly rebuilt in granite and became independent of Lanlivery in 1497. To the parish came John Wesley in 1755 and he revisited it several times, on the last meeting the infant William O'Bryan. He blessed the child, saying that he hoped he would take the word of God to the hundreds and thousands. This, of course, William O'Bryan did, forming the Bible Christians.

Luxulyan village is surrounded by granite quarries from which granite was taken to build Plymouth breakwater, London Bridge, Liverpool pier head and the docks at Genoa. There is only one quarry working, now known as Tregarden but many years ago it was known as Golden Point because of the superior quality stone. One must not, of course, forget the Luxulyanite known locally as 'shabby rock', a massive boulder at Trevanney Farm which was used for the sarcophagus of the Duke of Wellington. The boulder weighed 70 tons, was dressed locally, shipped to London and is now in the crypt of St Paul's Cathedral.

In the early part of this century up until the 1930s there was a butcher's shop, a blacksmith's shop, a cobbler, the village shop and post office, and a corn and coal merchant. Now there is only the post office and village store left. The butcher comes with a van and the coal is brought on a lorry.

There is an infants and primary school – the present building only 30 years old but there has been a school in Luxulyan village since approximately the middle of the 19th century. In recent years there has been quite a lot of building of houses in the village and this has naturally brought in many new families. A lot more building is being planned.

🍁 MADRON

The village of Madron is situated on a hill overlooking Penzance, commanding magnificent views of Mount's Bay and St Michael's Mount.

Although the origins of the village are lost in the mists of time, men roamed the ridges of the hills in the Bronze Age for they have left their burial tombs. Within walking distance of the village the Lanyon Cromlech stands, stark and bare, and a mile or so along the road the Men-an-Tol or holed stone is reached.

The name Madron is derived from the Celtic St Madern who is reputed to have come from Brittany in the 6th century. Landing on the shores of Mount's Bay he followed the stream from the beach to its source and there built a baptistry. Now roofless, it can still be visited, and the stone altar and circular basin through which the water flows are still there. St Madern's well became famous for its healing powers and even today rags are tied to the surrounding thorn bushes as votive offerings, following the tradition of the early pilgrims.

From earliest times Madron was well-known for its hospitality. The ancient domain of Landithy had passed to the Knights of St John, who used the house as a port of call for travellers and pilgrims on their way to Jerusalem. A house still stands on the site bordering the village green, although a modern housing estate has replaced the farmyard.

Madron General Stores

Opposite, and close to the church of St Madernus, is Madron Daniel School, endowed through the generosity of George Daniel for the children of Madron. The tomb of George's father in the churchyard has this inscription:

'Belgia me Birth, Britain me Breeding gave,
Cornwall a wife, ten children and a grave'.

The village has a pub, the King William IV, which serves good food and cheer. Across the road from the post office is the site of the old blacksmith's shop, now a garage. This has always been the meeting-place for the men and you can always find someone to have a chat with or just watch the world go by. There is also a thriving cricket club which has the distinctive initials MCC!

Inhabitants of Madron work mostly in Penzance, but a small proportion are employed at Madron Meat Company which is an abattoir and meat supplier, and Kismet, a fish-packing plant, sending fish in huge refrigerated lorries to the Continent. The site where these buildings now are used to be the parish workhouse.

One famous inhabitant of Madron was Sydney Graham, a well-known modern poet. His book *Implements in their Place* speaks of village characters. Another was Arnold Wallace, a primitive artist whose work is now recognised. He used to beg pieces of cardboard from the village shop on which to paint his pictures.

Old customs are still honoured in Madron, including the Midsummer

Bonfire. Each year also, on the Sunday nearest 21st October, a service is held at the church to commemorate Trafalgar Day. News of the great victory was first brought to England by a Penzance fisherman, and as St Madernus was then the parish church of Penzance, a thanksgiving service was held there. Today one of Her Majesty's Ships sends naval personnel to attend and there is a procession round the village behind the old Nelson Banner.

Madron today is a thriving rural community, holding its own in this modern world, but still maintaining its links with the past.

🍁 MANACCAN

Manaccan, originally Minster (the Monks' Church), is situated in Meneage (the Monks' Land) about ten miles from Helston. There were ancient chapels and wells in the area. Kestle Barton and Tregithew are old farmhouses from around the 17th century. The church has a Norman door and a 200 year old fig tree growing from the south wall.

Manaccanite, now known as titanium, was discovered in the parish in the stream of Tregonwell Mill in 1791 by William Gregor. On the Durra river, running through Manaccan to Carne Creek, there used to be five water mills, two of which were tucking mills.

The vicarage, still used as such, dates from the mid 17th century. A former incumbent, Rev R. Polwhele, was a Cornish historian who corresponded with Sir Walter Scott and entertained Captain Bligh of the *Bounty*. Captain Bligh was arrested whilst surveying the Helford river and was held captive in the vicarage for several hours.

Agriculture and tourism are the main occupations. The farmland in the area is of high quality and supports prize winning herds of dairy cattle as well as good beef bullocks. In more recent years several acres of flowers have been grown.

The well in the village square was restored to commemorate the Queen's Silver Jubilee in 1977. The thatched New inn and the village hall (formerly the school) stand opposite. There is an excellent village shop with post office. In the past there were two shops and a tea rooms. The former blacksmith's shop now houses a car repair workshop next door to a marine mechanic's business.

The Manaccan Sweet is an excellent apple and there is also a Manaccan Plum.

🍁 MARHAMCHURCH

Marhamchurch is a village in North Cornwall just off the A39 and within sight of the sea at Widemouth Bay. The population is fast approaching 700, with new houses being added all the time.

The 'Square' is dominated by St Marwenna's church, the Bray Institute, the Bullers Arms Hotel, Court Farm and the village store and post office, with several large and small houses. The church, mainly 14th and 15th century, stands on the site where St Marwenna, a daughter of King Brychan of Wales, had her cell and stayed as an anchorite in the late 5th century. The Bray Church of England Institute was given to the village in 1913 by a family of that name. It is said that among their effects was a piece of tapestry connected with Hampton Court, and the sale of this paid for the building, which is today used by the school as an overflow classroom, by the men's club and all the village organisations, and is famous for its prolific jumble sales. Court Farm is one of the many farms in the area, mainly for cattle and sheep.

During the early part of the 20th century Marhamchurch was self-contained with its own butcher, baker, shoemaker, blacksmith, carpenter and grocery. Milk was collected from the farms and drinking water from several pumps. There was also a foundry producing cooking stoves, all marked Box's Foundry. Now the post office stores is the only shop, apart from one farm shop, but there are regular deliveries of meat, fish, milk and bread from Bude and surrounding areas.

Marhamchurch's one claim to historical fame was its 'inclined plane'. From 1819 sea-sand and lime were brought from Bude by canal to be used as fertiliser by local farms. The canal used to run from Bude through Marhamchurch to Druxton near Launceston and to Holsworthy. At Helebridge in Marhamchurch the tugboats were winched up the inclined plane by a water wheel at the wharf, where there was an engineer's house. The rails for this were made at Box's Foundry. This lasted until 1888 when the railways took over the carriage of materials. The railway was finally closed in 1968. The towpath alongside the canal makes a very pleasant walk into Bude – about two miles.

It is in August that the village really comes into its own with the Marhamchurch Revel. August 12th is celebrated as St Marwenna's Day and the Revel takes place on the Monday following. The villagers, of whom a large proportion are retired, are mostly occupied with farming matters, though several commute to Bude and Holsworthy for their work. The Bullers Arms Hotel and Court Farm offer accommodation for visitors, and many people take in guests for bed and breakfast during the summer, with some selfcatering holiday cottages.

🍁 Marshgate & Tresparrett

Marshgate and Tresparrett are the two centres of population in St Juliot parish, an area that goes from the sea at Beeny to a marshy area just short of the A39 road. Marshgate is mainly new bungalows along what used to be the A39 until 1986. There is a post office/general store, and a primary school which is in Otterham parish. Old records show an active and fairly self-sufficient community with the carpenter, blacksmith and tailor.

Tresparrett also had two blacksmiths, the last within living memory. It now has only a pub. The old manor house at Tresparrett was of interesting construction with alternate courses of white spar and grey stone, but it was allowed to become derelict and was demolished to build four new houses. The Methodist church at Tresparrett is functional rather than of architectural interest.

St Juliot church is some way from any building and is largely 15th century granite. Thomas Hardy, while employed as an architect, came to St Juliot to supervise its restoration and partial rebuilding. While there he met his future first wife at the rectory (now a private house). There are some interesting Hardy memorial tablets in the church, as well as his drawings.

The house at Hennett, a working farm near the church, is very ancient and it was on this farm that the gold lunea in Truro museum was dug up. The farm hand who found it is supposed to have thought it was a sheep collar and traded it in the local pub for a pint.

There is a very beautiful walk from St Juliot church to Boscastle down the Valency valley. Most of the area is farm land and the sea at Beeny is inaccessible, which accounts for the fact that seals breed at the foot of the cliff.

🍁 Mawgan

The village of Mawgan is a farming community some four miles from Helston. It lies between the undulating slopes of the Helford river, the mysterious Loe Pool with its undertones of King Arthur's Excalibur, and the almost Flemish landscape of Goonhilly.

The 13th century church of St Mawgan is one of the most beautiful churches in Cornwall in the Decorated and Perpendicular style, lovingly cared for by a dedicated if somewhat declining congregation. Of the two chapels in the village only one remains in use, and although the congregation is small their love and faith shines through.

The ancient manor of Trelowarren some one and a half miles from the village has been the home of the Vyvyan family since 1427. One of the mills has now become the Dower House of the Vyvyans and the other is now a part of Gweek and has been most tastefully converted into flats. The cobbler's shop has gone, as has the forge with its blacksmith who was kept busy shoeing farm, carriage and riding horses, and no doubt repairing farm and garden tools. The farrier now comes on domiciliary visits by car, with the portable forge and anvil. However, many other small businesses have taken over. There are builders, decorators, dress-making, and a livery stable to name but a few. The village pub now serves good meals.

The ancient manor of Trelowarren is no longer the remote home of the lord of the manor, only visited annually for the distribution of 'goodies' at Christmas time. Part of the house has become an inter-denominational religious fellowship where retreats, quiet-days, healing sessions, and concerts are regularly held. This serves not only Cornwall but a greater part of England. People have found a serenity at Trelowarren which has helped them in many ways. The old coach-house has become a bistro, the stable a gallery of the Cornwall Crafts Association. A potter and a weaver are to be seen at work, and in the nursery one can purchase herbs, shrubs and herbaceous plants, whilst in the walled garden visitors enjoy camping where many amenities are provided.

The Goonhilly Downs Earth Satellite Station, with its giant saucers silhouetted against the sky, is indeed a monument to technology, and well worth a visit. At the other end of the parish the Royal Naval Air Station of Culdrose stands as a symbol of further technology. It is the largest helicopter training station in Europe and brings much business to the area.

🍁 MAWLA

Mawla is a little hamlet (many generations ago known as 'Mawle') and is situated approximately two miles from Mount Hawke. It consists of a cluster of cottages, Mawla Farm, Green Lane Farm, Forge Farm and a Methodist church and Sunday school.

Mawla has changed over the years; once there was a carpenter's shop and more cottages, now demolished. It was quite a secluded area with many trees but today it has been opened up and is clearly visible from surrounding areas, owing to the loss of most of the trees from Dutch elm disease. Mawla Farmhouse still has an old well in its courtyard.

The cottages are within the boundary of Mawla Farm and were originally occupied by the farm workers and their families. Two of these cottages have now been converted to holiday lettings and the others are still occupied by farm workers.

Green Lane Farm was purchased many years ago by the owner/occupier of Mawla Farm and today it is a mixed dairy and vegetable holding run as one unit. The old barns and buildings at Green Lane Farm have been converted to a luxury holiday complex which is very popular with visitors during the summer. The original Mawla Farm house has been sold and is now a private dwelling. Some houses have also been built on the surrounding farmland.

The Methodist church was built in 1908, the foundation stones laid by some local inhabitants. It is an attractive one storey building with arched stained glass windows and it seats about 120 people. The old Mawla chapel, which was unsafe to use, was demolished about 1960, and rebuilt as a new Sunday school.

Years ago the Sunday school tea treat was held in the adjoining field, with a full brass band parading with the children down through Mawla on the old tram road to Cambrose, where they were served with cold drinks and then marched back up again. Tea treat buns made of saffron were distributed to everyone for the tea and games in the field, which continued into the evening. Today the Sunday school have their annual tea treat outing to St Ives in July and it is an occasion enjoyed by all the children and their families and friends.

As Mawla has no shops or pubs and is not a busy thoroughfare for traffic, it is a very sheltered and peaceful little hamlet, tucked away into the Cornish countryside.

🍁 MAWNAN SMITH

In 1645 during the Civil War, Frances Coombe, 'the smith at Mawnan', paid Sir Richard Vyvyan £2 for iron from the old ship *The Creation* that had been broken up and used for fortifications at the Royalist camp on Dinas Head at the mouth of the Helford river.

Mawnan Smith takes its name from the smithy that was established in the centre of the parish where two ancient trackways met. One track led to the church of St Maunanus on the cliff; the other to the ferry at Helford Passage.

This ferry has linked the Lizard peninsula with Penryn and Truro since the 13th century and probably earlier. In the 19th century a horse-ferry ran from Manaccan on the south side, across the river and through Mawnan Smith to Falmouth.

The parish church of St Maunanus, a Celtic saint, stands within a 'round' high above the estuary, a magnificent but unusually conspicuous site. Today tourists come to visit the church and admire the extensive views. Above the lychgate a Cornish inscription 'Da thym nesse the Dhu' reminds them 'It is good to draw nigh to the Lord'. A request by coastguards in 1842 to whitewash the tower as a guide to mariners was fortunately never followed up!

In 1876 a second church, St Michael's, was built on a more convenient site in the centre of the village, next to the school. This had been established in 1833 on land provided by the rector, Rev John Rogers. Seven cottages were also built in the meadow and their rents used for the upkeep of the school and the teachers' salaries.

The Wesleyan chapel, opposite the school, was licensed for worship in 1815. The tithe map shows it standing in a field called Preaching Meadow where, it is said, John Wesley once preached. Mawnan's Roman Catholic church was built more recently in 1965. The focal point of the village has always been the picturesque Red Lion inn. It was a well established hostelry in 1717.

The local legend of Fine and Brave lane is set in the 18th century. The story goes that during the French wars the women of the village hurried down the narrow lane, pitchforks in hand, to repel an invasion from a French ship nearing Maenporth cove. Fortunately, glimpses of their red petticoats persuaded the French that a company of Redcoats was approaching and they sailed away. The men of Mawnan, proud of their women's initiative, declared 'it was a fine and brave thing to do'. And it is said that since then, the lane has been known as Fine and Brave. A more prosaic explanation is that the name may be a corruption of the Cornish 'Fyn an bre' – the boundary of the hill – for the lane lies below an impressive Iron Age earthwork known locally as the Round Field.

Large new residences with extensive gardens running down to the river were built in the 19th century bringing more employment and more people into the community. The glorious gardens created at Glendurgan and Trebah by Alfred and Charles Fox (of the influential Quaker family of Falmouth), and by the Rogers family at Carwinion and Bosloe, are now open to the public.

In June 1944 the village was closed to the outside world for several days when an endless stream of American military vehicles passed through to the river to embark for the Normandy beaches. Thanks to them, the road through the parish is no longer a narrow Cornish lane.

Today tourists from all parts of the world come to Mawnan to walk, to sail and to enjoy the gardens and unspoilt countryside. The village offers a post office and shop, doctor's surgery, part time bank, garage, restaurant, dress shop and hairdresser. Shops also sell local meat and game, antiques, gifts and gardening supplies. A bus service runs regularly to Falmouth, Truro and Helston.

Retired people have always come to live in Mawnan; today an excellent school attracts young families. Many residents now work in nearby towns, and the parish itself remains very rural. Newcomers soon become a part of village life for Mawnan Smith offers a wide variety of clubs, societies and sporting activities for all ages. Facilities have been upgraded in recent years; the sports pavilion was replaced by a community centre and the Memorial Hall modernised. A specially commissioned Celtic cross was erected to mark the Millennium celebrations.

❧ MEVAGISSEY

Men have always fished out of Mevagissey, at first when it was just a small hamlet on the east side of the inlet; there were just a few people here then in 1524. Trade grew and piers and wharves were constructed and cottages built into the cliff rock. The ground floor, for storing, was usually earthen, with living quarters above, and the entrance often in the roof. Walk along The Cliff today – they are still there. This is the oldest part of the village. The narrow alleyways behind the Fountain Inn gave cover to the fishermen escaping from the press gangs and also from the preventive officers, for smuggling was rife; brandy, salt and tea were brought in, tobacco and other items taken out, and as Mevagissey was a centre of this illegal traffic fast sailing luggers were built to take part. They went to Roscoff, unloaded, returning with the brandy. Coming in at night, the kegs were dropped overboard in the bay and collected by smaller fishing boats when the coast was clear. At its peak in the early 1800s the privateering and smuggling brought considerable wealth to Mevagissey, albeit in dubious ways, and the population rose accordingly, to 2,450 in 1820.

And what of women at this time? One of the country's historians, Polwhele, describes the fishwives of Mevagissey as 'boisterous females, ruder far than those who toil at Billingsgate'. They carried their fish from farm to farm for miles around, returning home to large families, without running water, sanitation or the conveniences belonging to this generation; life must have been very hard indeed.

There are countless legends, tales of smuggling and secret passages. Certainly there is a history here of a spirited people, but Mevagissey thrives still though in a different way. Probably only about one third of the people are Mevagissey born and bred. Of the 'up country' people, many are retired, but there are also young families who have settled here and enter wholeheartedly into its religious, social and sporting events. All in all, it is a pleasure to live here, not only for its beauty, but for the atmosphere that still pervades the narrow streets and winding alleys, and which continues to beckon many an exile.

🍁 MILLBROOK

Situated as it is at the end of an inlet of the river Tamar and between two hills, Millbrook is separated by that river from the city of Plymouth. The situation was probably chosen originally by the Stone Age community because it was impervious to attack. Proof of early habitation has been found. A stone axe-head was discovered when the gateway of Venton House was being built and this relic is now in Truro Museum.

During the reign of Elizabeth I Millbrook was a 'niche Fischar' town with its corporation, officials and seal. A large fleet of fishing vessels sailed from the creek and some 40 ships were sent to assist in repelling the Spanish Armada.

Millbrook was in the parish of Maker until 1869 when it became a separate ecclesiastical parish. Prior to this, in the 14th century services were held at Insworke manor chapel, the remains of which still stand. In 1826 a church was built at Dodbrook, which has since become a chapel of ease, surrounded by the churchyard. Later a new church of All Saints was built and consecrated on All Saints Day 1895. A Baptist church was opened in West Street in 1821 and demolished in the 1960s. The Methodist church was opened as a Wesleyan chapel in 1874 and is still open for services.

Because of the convenience of water transport, industries sprang up in the valley and goods were rowed and sailed to the ships and city beyond. Many industries thrived in Millbrook throughout the years. At Southdown a gunpowder works was in existence until 1870. There were three brickyards the first being at Foss Point, another at Pottery which produced 50,000 high quality bricks per day, and the third at Southdown. The latter commenced working in 1893, closing in 1948. Sailing barges came up to the mill where the bricks were loaded and taken to ports all over England. These works provided employment for a large number of men. Three slaughterhouses produced hides for the local tannery and bark from Penlee Woods was used for the tanning process. The hides were dried in a field where Molesworth Terrace now stands. A rope walk existed at Wood Park, Anderton, the old building still standing.

Millbrook was a lively village, especially at the time of the May Day Fair when stalls with fairings and knick-knacks were set up in King Street and West Street. Market days were very busy and it is noted that a fair and market were granted in 1319. One recently revived tradition was Garland Day when a replica of the ship sent to fight for the Black Prince's forces in the 14th century was rigged and garlanded. It was then carried shoulder high to Cremyll and taken by boat to Plymouth. The next day it was carried to Cawsand where it was set afloat.

🍁 MITCHELL

The village of Mitchell, formerly known as St Michael or Meideshol, is situated almost centrally in Cornwall on the main A30 road, with Truro seven miles to the west, Newquay seven miles to the north and St Austell 13 miles to the east. It is part of the parish of St Newlyn East.

Dating back to the 12th century, it was later known as a 'rotten borough'. In 1592 Sir Walter Raleigh was elected as Member of Parliament, in 1753 Robert Clive – Clive of India – became a Member of Parliament for the borough and in 1807 Sir Arthur Wellesley, who became the Duke of Wellington.

In the year 1239 the lord of the manor, Walter de Raleigh, secured a royal charter to hold an annual fair and a weekly market where cattle, ponies and poultry were sold by auction. The fair was held on St Francis's Day, the 17th October and the tradition continued until the 1940s.

A toll house was once situated at the east end of the village with a stop-gate at the west end. A meadow at the west end is still called Stop Gate. Another field in the area is named the Gallows, where it is reputed many hangings took place.

In the centre of the village is a terraced row of six houses originally built for the owners and managers of the East Wheal Rose Mine, where silver and lead were extracted until disaster struck on the 9th July 1846 when a cloud burst flooded the mine and drowned some 39 men and boys. The old mine stacks still remain as a reminder of the tragedy.

The chapel built in 1845 by men of the village was forced to close in 1989 owing to the lack of funds to renovate and refurbish the building. Unfortunately, with its closure many of the social events had to stop as the Sunday school attached to the chapel was used for parish meetings, children's parties, jumble sales, Women's Institute and Youth Club meetings.

The Plume of Feathers public house (closed 1999) at the west end of the village still features the balcony supported by two pillars from which Charles Wesley used to preach on his journeys through Cornwall, often met with much hostility. Wellesley House and Raleigh House still stand in the centre of the village and the Pillars Hotel, to the east end of the village, dating back to the 12th century, was once a killing house and butcher's shop. It is said that the Pillars Hotel is occasionally visited by a friendly ghost in the form of a tall gentleman wearing a black top hat.

On entering the village on the A30 from the east there is a thriving fruit farm which employs many young mothers of the village for the picking season. People from far and wide also visit the fruit farm to pick their own fruit from the many varieties available, and such visits often turn out to be a good family outing. Since the construction of the bypass the garage has become a vehicle recovery centre. About a dozen new houses have been built and in the near future a 48 house development will commence. Hopefully this will generate the need for a shop, a post office and the reopening of the Plume of Feathers.

Mitchell's linear shape with extensive tree coverage to the rear reflects the existence of the old field patterns following the ancient burbage plots, which were visible to the time of the bypass excavations.

🍁 MITHIAN

Seven miles from the city of Truro and two miles from the coastal villages of St Agnes and Perranporth lies the picturesque village of Mithian.

The railway came to Mithian in 1903 (one of the last branch lines to be opened in Cornwall) linking busy Chacewater station with Newquay. What busy places were the little 'halts' at Mithian, Goonbell, Goonhavern etc; a way of life to end in 1963 when the branch line was closed – a victim of Beeching's axe!

Most of the houses in the village were thatched but apart from a few, the thatch has now been replaced by slate. A high spirited rocket thrower on Bonfire Night was responsible for igniting the thatch and virtually burning a house down!

Mithian once boasted a bakery, a tailor, a shoemaker, three shops, a post office, a Methodist chapel, a church and a pub. Only the church, the post office and pub remain, the two former situated some distance from the village. The pub, the Miners Arms, is said to have been built in 1577. Two interesting features are a Penance cupboard and a decorative plaster ceiling incorporating the date 1577.

During the First World War Doris attended Buckshead school and well she remembers the children collecting 'eggs for the soldiers'. Each child wrote his or her name on an egg and it was duly dispatched to the serving men. 'At least one child received a reply from a soldier!' said Doris.

Standing in the peace, tranquillity and seclusion of its own wooded grounds is the magnificent Georgian house Rose-in-Vale, now a country house hotel offering excellent service and hospitality.

It is along the winding footpath through the woods that John Opie the famous painter wandered, finding inspiration and encouragement for his great talent. The paintmill in the woods probably provided him with his artists' materials. John Opie was born at humble Harmony Cottage but lies at rest with the eminent in the crypt of St Paul's Cathedral.

It is said that a tunnel ran underground from the Miners Arms to the manor house, but some years ago a villager reported that the middle section had collapsed and the tunnel was no longer accessible.

🍁 MORVAL

Set in rolling countryside, inland from the fishing port of Looe, is Morval – the name means 'Sea Valley'. The boundaries extend from Steppes Lodge, near Looe, to By-Lane-End and Jope's Mill, where the stream provides a natural border.

The scenic Looe Railway, sadly no longer steam, passes through Morval. It survived the Beeching axe and continues to provide links with the 'outside world'.

There was a time when jobs were plentiful. Local people were employed in agriculture; gardeners, carpenters, cobblers, forestry workers, butchers and blacksmiths could all find work, while the girls were employed on farms or in 'the big house' – Morval House. Now job opportunities are fewer, and young people must travel further afield to earn a living. The lucky ones snap up any opportunities which arise at the boatyard, garage and at the handful of industrial units which have been established at Widegates.

Sandplace, in the Looe valley, was once a hive of activity. Canal boats would come up the river with their cargoes of seaweed, collected by donkey and cart by farmers who would spread it on their fields as fertiliser. The boats would then return to Looe with lime from the kilns. In fact the lime kilns were a social meeting point in those days. Women would meet there to cook meals on the fires and old men would tell tales of days gone by as they warmed themselves.

The nearby inn, the Bullers Arms, was closed when a man was killed in a brawl. His murderer was later hanged. Today, the parish has two public houses-cum-hotels, one near the site of the old inn.

Morval House, home of the Buller and Kitson families down the years, is steeped in history. It was once a Roundhead stronghold and Oliver Cromwell is said to have quartered his troops there.

A stone's throw from the majestic house is the old forge, now converted to accommodation, and the lovely old church. Founded in the 6th century, it is dedicated to St Wenna. The cross on the west tower faces a different way from the others. It is said that the builders placed it correctly on a number of occasions, but it was always turned around come the morning … the work of piskies or the devil.

The 'Widegates Observatory' has become not only a landmark with its radio mast and aerials but has also established itself as one of the leading observation posts scanning the skies.

For sport and recreation, there are riding stables at Venton Vanes and a popular golf club at Bindown, designed by the legendary Harry Vardon, six times winner of the British Open between 1896-1914. Bindown is also the highest point in the parish, at 660 ft above sea level, and beacon fires have been lit there on ceremonious occasions in the past. Bindown, too, is the source of a number of well-loved folklore tales; older members can recount amusing stories of the days when the Home Guard trained there.

Once cart horses plodded the roads with their loads of vegetables, cream and butter, travelling to Devonport and Plymouth markets to sell their wares. Now bigger and still bigger lorries thunder through the parish. No blacksmith's hammer can be heard hitting the anvil; no aroma of leather in the cobbler's shop, just the smell of exhaust fumes as travellers speed through the parish, largely unaware of the community spirit which hides behind every hedgerow.

❦ MORWENSTOW

Morwenstow is the most northerly parish in Cornwall, and consists of six hamlets – Shop, Crosstown, Woodford, Gooseham, Eastcott and Woolley. The rivers Tamar and Torridge rise near Woolley Burrows. It is bound on the west coast by the Atlantic Ocean.

Crimp on the A39 is the second highest point in Cornwall at 734 ft. There are many cliffs and beautiful coombes, among them Hennacliffe, the second highest cliff to Beachy Head. It is believed that Morwenstow was named after St Morwenna, a Welsh missionary saint who came to Cornwall from Wales to convert the Cornish to Christianity. 'Stowe' means a holy place. Her holy well can be found on Vicarage Cliff.

Morwenstow is most famous for the incumbency of Rev Robert Stephen Hawker, who was the vicar here for 40 years from 1834 to 1875. He was a most eccentric person and many tales are told about him. Legend has it that Hawker at times was followed by ten cats to church, which entered the chancel and careered about during the service. One was excommunicated for having caught and killed a mouse on Sunday.

In past days farming was the most important industry. There were four smithies, but now none. Today farming has declined and many old barns have been converted to self-catering accommodation. Coombe Valley is still one of the beauty spots. In pre-war days there was a working mill with thatched cottages where during the summer months cream teas were served to visitors; it is now owned by the Landmark Trust as holiday accommodation. The old mill wheel is still in evidence.

In 1916 Mr Frank Heard established an agricultural merchant's with a few employees, a steam wagon and a Model T Ford truck. In 1946 he employed over 20 people with six trucks. Other local businesses include a garage, a riding stables at Gooseham Barton, a post office and stores, also builders, plumbers and painters. The Composite Signal Organisation Station, with its many large dishes, stands on the cliffs and employs some local inhabitants.

St John the Baptist's Day is celebrated annually on the 24th June. In years past this took the form of a procession of all the schoolchildren from Crosstown Green to the church for a service. They were preceded by Morwenstow Brass Band. The latter was founded by Mr John Cholwill in 1863 and was in operation for over 80 years.

The coast around Morwenstow is very rocky and many ships were wrecked here, one of the most famous being the *Caledonian*. Its figurehead is to be found in the churchyard where over 100 seamen, most unknown, had a Christian burial.

Morwenstow has several very important buildings. The 12th century Bush inn was partially destroyed by fire in November 1968 losing the entire thatched roof. The church made famous by Rev Hawker is partly Norman. St John's well stands in the vicarage garden and its waters to this day are always used for christening. Hawker's Hut can still be seen on the cliff edge. There he is reported to have written his poems and hymns.

Rev Hawker built St Mark's school in 1843. The school was extended and modernised in 1989. Hawker also built the beautiful vicarage, which has four remarkable chimneys, copies of the various church towers where he had worked.

Hawker had the bridge at Duckpool built, to which King William IV donated £20, and an inscription to that effect is on the bridge. Here on this bridge the poet Tennyson and Hawker shook hands and bade farewell after the former's visit to Morwenstow.

There are quite a number of old houses, the best preserved being Tonacombe Manor which dates from the early 16th century. Morwenstow boasts its own Men's and Women's Institute built in 1922. The Community Centre, opened in 1985 is used for Parish social and sporting events, a playgroup twice a week and a weekly doctor's surgery.

❦ MOUNT HAWKE

The village lies south of St Agnes and just inland from the sea, in north central Cornwall.

In 1965 the pace of development was for the most part one dwelling at a time, detached bungalows, often with Cornish hedges on their road frontages and only one dwelling deep. Then the big firms moved in and now there are bungalows by the acre. The present population is around 1,400 with many young families.

The name Mount Hawke has been traced back only to a document of 1820, relating to land for the building of a Methodist meeting house 'at a place called Mount Hawke'. There was a family of ropemakers called Hawke and there is still a lane called Ropewalk, though no Mount. The earlier name of Banns, said to mean hillsides, remains more appropriate.

The Methodist chapel, with alterations and updatings, still flourishes. In 1965 attendance was 'from eight to 30, according to the season'. Today it is from '18 to 30, according to the season and the preacher'. The parish church of St John the Baptist was achieved in the 1870s thanks largely to the perseverance of the Rev W.H. Allin. Previously services had been held in a building in a field 'little better than a barn'.

In 1852, while the church was still in the middle of the field, a strange event took place. An open-air service was held on the common nearby, where about 2,000 people gathered. Darkness came on and as many as could squeezed into the church – without permission – and the meeting continued day and night for a total of eight days. The vicar was not amused, but could do nothing. Now there is only a Sunday morning service at both the church and chapel.

In the 1870s a flat field adjacent to the church was consecrated as a burial ground. The village school built in 1874 was replaced by a new building in 1980. The old school is now licensed as 'The Old School Pub'. There are activities to suit all tastes and abilities having a Village Community Association to 'keep an eye on' the village as a whole. The WI hall is used as the community hall every day.

🍁 MOUSEHOLE

Mousehole, situated on the western side of the lovely sweep of Mount's Bay, is nowadays a much photographed village, beloved by hundreds of tourists. The name is derived from two Old English words, maew meaning gull and holh, a depression or basin. It is a description still valid today, the gulls having moved from the offshore island of St Clements, where they lived and nested happily for many years, to the village, where they have become a nuisance.

Later called Porth Enys, Mousehole was an important fishing village with its own maritime courts. Exposed to the heavy seas, a pier was built, the first to be constructed in the county of Cornwall, with a Harbour Board of 15 commissioners, which it has to this day.

Mousehole may be small, nestling in a semi-circle round the harbour, but it is full of history. Tom Bawcock's Eve is still celebrated at the Ship Inn on Christmas Eve's Eve, with a huge Stargazy pie, to remember Tom Bawcock, a fisherman who braved dreadful winter storms to catch 'sebn sorts of fish' as the song goes, for the starving people of Mousehole. Guise dancing at the New Year has died out now, but in the olden days folks would dress up in disguise and burst into the cottages to make the occupants try and guess who they were. It always finished with a glass of ginger wine and away they'd dance to the next cottage. No one locked their cottage doors in those days! May Day is still celebrated. The small May Queen and her attendants chosen from the primary school, process through the village, followed by the boys blowing the May Horn. It is often cold and windy, but they look so pretty and tiny with their bouquets of spring flowers.

Typical of a village so close to the sea, every summer there are Harbour Sports with swimming, greasy poles and general great fun for children and visitors in particular. The Rowing Club's regatta draws racing boats from all over the county and the 'smeech' from frying hot dogs hangs over the harbour as local and visiting crews fill up between races. All summer the visitors throng the narrow streets like Duck Street, where legend has it that ducks were swept down the flooded streams from Paul village above Mousehole, swimming down the stream to the harbour! Then there is the story of John Stone – he went to the local stone quarry where he worked to say he wouldn't be working that day as he was poorly! Even now folks say, when they state the obvious, 'as John Stone would say'.

Mousehole is renowned for its bright Christmas lights – Christmas trees, puddings, robins, and serpents and dolphins in the harbour. Carols sound from the twinkling church all made with lights. Only once have the lights been turned off; when the Penlee lifeboat *Solomon Browne* was lost with all hands, going to

The Keigwin Arms, Mousehole

the aid of a stricken coaster in atrocious weather. It was a tragedy that filled and overwhelmed the hearts of the entire village; but time passes and there is now a high-speed lifeboat still putting to sea unflinchingly, whatever the weather.

The fishermen who pace up and down the harbour front, reminiscing, discussing the weather and generally putting the world to rights, have all gone. The women standing and sunning themselves in the cottage doorways, gossiping with their neighbours have gone too and many cottages are now let to summer visitors. The fishing boats that were once so many that the children could jump from boat to boat right across the harbour have gone, but the harbour is still used by 'toshers', small single-handed fishing boats and yachts. The young lads still dive and swim there, showing off in front of the giggly girls. There's plenty of life in the village, plenty 'going on'.

🍁 MULLION

Mullion today is a thriving village with 20 shops including the post office and chemist. There is a health centre, Abbeyfield House, the Royal British Legion Hall, junior and senior schools, and a fire station with firemen trained to cope with medical emergencies. The WI has its own hall and serves coffee on Fridays for locals and visitors. There are several hotels, restaurants, guest houses and football and cricket clubs. There are three coves, Poldhu, Polurrian and Mullion Harbour.

The Old Inn in the centre of the village in part dates from the 17th century. An entry in Francis Kilvert's diary states: 'Visited the Old Inn on 22nd July 1870. Kept by Mary Mundy, a genuine Cornish Celt, impulsive, warm-hearted, excitable, demonstrative, imaginative and eloquent'. The visitors' book of this period records the names of members of the aristocracy including Randolph Churchill the elder, and Mrs Craik, the well-known authoress. Later, Marconi stayed there when the first wireless message was transmitted from Poldhu to Newfoundland. It is still an inn, and a social centre for villagers and visitors alike, who raise large sums of money for good causes, especially Guide Dogs for the Blind.

The sturdy granite church dating from the 15th century was built to withstand the violent storms that beset us from time to time. Features include a striking stone carving of St Mellanus, one-time Bishop of Rennes, over the entrance door. This solid oak door has a 'dog door' to allow the shepherds' dogs to slip out during the long services. There are also both Methodist and Roman Catholic churches in the village.

Trenance Farm is now a guest house and self-contained accommodation for visitors made from outbuildings. It was built in 1858 in front of the original farmhouse, which was recorded in the Domesday Book of 1086 as Trenant. This older house was the home of the Jose family. The family comprised the brothers William and Jeremiah, their wives, children and household servants – about 20 in all. On the evening of 5th December 1827, a dispute arose between young Francis, aged 26 and his uncle Jeremiah who was known to be hot-tempered. This quickly deteriorated into violence, and then murder. As Francis came close to his uncle, using abusive words, Jeremiah lost control, and taking a nail from his pocket lunged at Francis, striking him in the temple. The blow was mortal. Jeremiah was found guilty of wilful murder at Bodmin in March 1828, and sentenced to transportation. There are no court transcripts of what happened, but a contemporary account states that the Judge reopened the court, and commuted the sentence to two years' imprisonment.

Jeremiah returned to Mullion to farm once again, but not at Trenance. He died in 1845, and lies buried in a separate grave from that of the family. How the village must have been shocked at this happening, and the story must have been told for many a long year.

🍁 MYLOR

Redgate, Vat and Vane, Park and Browse and Lurk, these are some of the field names in Mylor, once a small farming and fishing community, now a yachtsman's paradise.

The village takes its name from the Celtic bishop-missionary who sailed from Brittany into the shelter of the Fal estuary in around AD 411, and landed in this well-wooded marshy inlet. Authorities tell us that the church would have begun as a shrine, where St Mylor taught pagans and the newly-converted round a standing stone or menhir, which in due course would have been christianised with a Celtic cross. That same 17½ foot cross still stands (seven feet being underground) by the south porch of the parish church. The Saint would first have built himself a wattle cell, which with other primitive buildings, would have formed Lawithick, 'the monastery among the trees'. A farmhouse opposite the church still bears the name Lawithick. It was once an inn called the Clinton Arms, closed down by a 19th century vicar, the Rev Hoblyn, because more people were worshipping Bacchus than God. Later it opened as a tea room, specialising in Cornish cream teas. A second church was built further up the creek at Mylor Bridge in 1892, for the use of servants.

Village life revolves around several halls, the largest being Tremayne Hall, where one may sing *Jerusalem* with the WI, have tea with the Darby and Joan Club and do-si-do with the Mylor Folkdance Group. It is odd that a place which now gives the village so much entertainment was once the poor house. Then there is the Ord Statter Pavilion on the creekside George VI playing field. It was opened as the first village youth centre in Cornwall by Lord Hunt of Everest in 1966, but is now well used by sportsmen, the Floral Art Society, the Gardening Club and the playgroup, who paint and sing and, on sunny days, spill out to play on the grass. The smallest venue is the Parish Hall, home to painting and other classes, parish meetings and very popular Saturday Coffee Mornings.

Water and electricity came comparatively late to the village. Today several pumps can still be seen, perhaps the best kept one being the Gilbert pump installed in 1852. It stands resplendent in the old farm colours of blue and red between the Lemon Arms and a terrace of tall houses built of bricks which had been ballast. Captain Garland had been refused permission to extend his house and said 'Right, you will rue the day' and built the houses of the ballast as a form of curse.

Until recently blacksmiths have plied their trade near the bridge in the village. William Oak was blacksmith at the end of the 17th century. Later the Reese family took over the forge, first David and then William. Amongst other things they produced dredges used by local oyster fishermen on the Fal. Past trades have also included a brickworks in Comfort Road, the salting of pilchards which came from Falmouth via Saltbox Road, and a coal yard on the quay; a Mr Andrews remembered coal at one shilling and sixpence a cwt and a wheelbarrow was lent free to wheel it away. There was also quarrying for granite a little way down the creek. There were various shops and pubs, ten at one time, and there were many thatched cottages in the village so there was a thatcher. There was a small tin mine on Mylor Downs at Wheal Lemon.

At its peak Perran Wharf Foundry, on the Truro Road, employed around 400 men, many of whom must have come from Mylor. Today there are still fishermen, shopkeepers and builders in the village, but many people go out of the village to work and use their own or public transport, unlike the days when a Mr Gilbert used to keep a cab in a shed under the oak tree on what is now the playing field. Another public spirited lady in New Row used to cook chips for the village on a Primus stove. She also did hairdressing.

Writers associated with the village include Katherine Mansfield who stayed in a cottage along Church Road for a while in 1916. A.L. Rowse wrote a poem *How Many Miles to Mylor*, and Howard Spring, who died in 1965, is buried in the churchyard. His novel *All the Day Long* is based on Mylor church and vicarage.

Past festivals have included that of 'Nutting Day' when journeymen tailors of Penryn proceeded to Mylor to elect a sham mayor. He would have to be one of the wittiest men of the village and there would be drinking bouts, processions and speeches mocking the parliamentary candidates of the day. For the present there is the May Fair held on the playing field which was presented to the children of Mylor in 1952 and was formed from reclaimed and drained land, and the regatta which takes place at the harbour.

❧ NANCLEDRA

Lying on the then main track to Penzance, then a coinage town, the village grew as tin mining boomed in the area in the early 18th century. With tin stamps and 22 mines in the parish of Towednack, and smelting houses at Chyandour, Blowing House, Ludgvan and St Erth, Cledry became the social and spiritual centre for the farming and mining communities. The population dropped and changed with the collapse of industry but, as now, the area continued to attract gifted people.

On the site of an ancient oratory, away from the road, a strong sense of quiet peace pervades Towednack church. It was a struggle for the people of the parish to find the time and monies to build the church, and later the chapels. During the rebellion of 1549, for which the then mayor of St Ives was hanged, the squat tower was still being built. Despite the spiritual decline which followed, the latent fervour of our forefathers somehow survived to welcome Wesley. The congregation is slowly growing again. Three of the bells are medieval. Though competitive ringing has gone, when the ringers from Ludgvan join Nancledra it is possible to hear the full peal of eight.

One of the most looked for days was the Easter Monday Treat. Towednack

Brass Band led the children round the district, with banners flying. Treat teas always consisted of the same repast: a one pound saffron cake and, a treat in itself, *sugar* in the tea. Afterwards, it was into the field for high spirited fun and games. In 1912 a newspaper reported 'a procession of 120 children from the United Chapel Sunday schools around Nancledra'.

Towednack Brass Band was formed in the late 18th century. In great demand, the band gave priority to Towednack Feast Monday and Annual Horse Race, and to Sunday school treats. As young miners left to work in Australia and elsewhere, often three or four at a time, it became difficult to keep the band together; disbandment came in 1950 when Mr Pope died. Band rehearsals for Cornish Christmas carols started in October, ready for the band's tour of the village and surrounding houses and farms on Christmas Eve and Christmas Day. Happily this tradition has been revived by Mr Ralph, family and friends.

Of the many notable artists, craftsmen and writers who have chosen to live in the village, Mr and Mrs R. Morton Nance lived and raised a family here. Mr Nance's series of plays based on the old Cornish droll-tellers' stories, starting with *Duffy* were produced in the school room with the children as the cast. Mrs Nance designed and made the costumes. The performances led to the start of the Old Cornwall Movement in St Ives, and later to Mr Nance being made the Chief Bard.

✤ Nanstallon

Nanstallon is on the banks of the picturesque river Camel, situated two miles south-west of Bodmin and one and a quarter miles off the A30. The river meanders along the edge of the village, flowing through hilly farmland and wooded slopes.

Immediately above the river is the site of the old Bodmin/Wadebridge railway line. Now the popular Camel Trail for walkers, cyclists and horseriders alike, in its heyday this line saw as many as 30 passenger trains daily, carrying schoolchildren to Bodmin and housewives to do their shopping.

Up in the village is the popular village shop and post office, a friendly meeting place for locals and visitors alike. There are several family-owned farms around the village, some dairy herds, others beef and sheep, plus a little arable land. It gives a pleasant pastoral scene, the fields divided by attractive flower-studded Cornish hedges.

The village butcher purchased on the hoof from local farms, the animals being taken to the abattoir at Wadebridge. Not only did he have a shop in the village but a big country round to outlying villages. But again change, the shop closed about 1970 when topside was four shillings and sixpence a pound!

Beneath the turf of Tregear (Cornish for the place of the camp) lies the early history of Nanstallon. The village has the distinction of having the only known Roman fort in the county, dating back to AD 55 and finally abandoned about AD 80. It was first discovered in 1800 and was last excavated in 1968 by a team from Exeter University. The garrison consisted of about 500 cavalry and infantry and may have been built to protect the ford over the river (now the bridge) below the modern day village, and the mines in the area.

Of scientific interest is Mulberry Pit which lies in a south-westerly direction on the edge of the village. This open cast mine was already a feature of the landscape when Thomas Martyn published his map of Cornwall in 1748. However earliest records of the mine only go back to 1859. They show that the average content of tin per ton was six to seven lbs. It is believed that copper is also in Mulberry, though none has ever been mined.

Before the mine closed in 1916 the employees walked a number of miles daily to work there, having to arrive half an hour before starting time and remaining half an hour after clocking off to clear up.

In the centre of the village stands the school opened in 1878. On the register today are over 80 pupils. During the Second World War some 50 evacuees arrived dirty, tired and very bewildered at the school. But so welcome were these children made, that 60 years on many still return to the village to look up old friends.

St Stephen's celebrated its centenary in the mid 1980s with a Flower Festival, at which time the church had been refurbished. The Methodist church celebrated its centenary in 1989 with special events in each quarter of the year. The Methodist schoolroom is the venue of various organisations including the WI, Get Together Club, Sunday school, playgroup and gardening club. The latter holds an annual Garden Show each July in the village school. The other public building in the village is the institute. In the past there has been a cobbler's, a blacksmith's shop and a cornmill, but all have now either completely disappeared or the buildings been converted.

❧ NEWLYN

Newlyn is a picturesque fishing port about a mile west from Penzance in the south-west corner of Cornwall. It is tucked away in the western corner of Mount's Bay, with the famous and beautiful St Michael's Mount in the background. The cottages and houses cluster round the large harbour which has for centuries been the lifeblood of the village. There are records of what is known as the Old Quay being repaired in 1435. Nowadays Newlyn boasts three more fishing quays creating the spacious harbour.

The South Pier was completed in 1846 and is the site of the Greenwich Tidal Observatory established early 1900, chosen because of its proximity to the Atlantic swells. All tides in Great Britain are measured from the Ordnance Datum Point – brass plaque on its floor – and reported to the Proudman Oceanographic Laboratories in Birkenhead. The North Pier, a quarter of a mile long, was opened in 1894. The Mary Williams Pier, Newlyn's most recent pier, was built in the middle of the harbour, and was opened by Her Majesty the Queen in 1980.

Catches of all varieties of fish net £24 million per annum, with a large percentage being shipped to the Continent. Where once only small craft, long liners, pilchard drivers and trawlers ventured many miles into the ocean, now the harbour teems with beam trawlers as well, capable of staying at sea for ten days or more, and where once jousters and donkey-carts carried fish landed from the boats onto the sand, the village now roars with the sound of huge refrigerated lorries leaving the new fish market, which was opened by HRH The Princess of Wales in 1988, making their way to the Plymouth ferries. As well as local craft, Newlyn is used by boats from other UK ports, the Channel Islands, Brittany and by the seaboard of western Europe during bad weather, all bearing their distinctive registrations. Anchored at all times in the harbour is Penlee's *RLB Mabel Alice*, a 52 ft Arun Class lifeboat.

Near the market is the Newlyn Iceworks built in 1903. The water from its reservoir, situated just outside the village, is served by a nearby borehole. The Iceworks produce 50 tonnes of crushed and sliced ice daily for the fishing fleet.

The two ancient villages of Newlyn Town and Street-an-Nowan are now connected as one by The Strand, aptly named, for here stretched the sea shore before many present buildings and piers were built. Along the Strand runs the Coombe river with its five bridges within a distance of 200 yards. Beside the seaward bridge is the fine structure of the 'Mission' or 'Institute'. This Ship Institute, taking its name from the gleaming model ship on its clock tower, is one of the establishments of the National Mission to Deep Sea Fisherman which has for over 70 years given invaluable service to fishermen and sailors of all nations as well as comfort and help to the local community.

Outside the Mission stands the war memorial, and other important buildings include St Peter's church (1886), Trinity Methodist chapel (1834), the Centenary Methodist chapel (1927), two primary schools, six public houses, several potteries and a fine art gallery.

At the southern end of the village is a large granite quarry which still supplies road stone, loaded and taken away by 'stone boats' for use on motorways and by industry in this country and abroad.

Because of its quaint cottages, net lofts and cobbled streets, Newlyn has its own peculiar charm. Its quality of light attracted many artists in the 19th century. One such artist was the well known Stanhope Forbes who started his Newlyn School of Artists. These all contribute to the exhibitions all through the year at the Passmore Edwards Gallery and play an important part in the culture of the local community.

Mary Kelynack was a Newlyn fishwife who decided, at the age of 74 years, to walk to London to see the Great Exhibition of 1851. She is reputed to have carried with her a pound of tea as a present for Queen Victoria! It is known that the Queen wished to meet her and she was later entertained at the Mansion House to tea, where the Lord Mayor gave her a golden sovereign as a present. She then returned home, walking all the way.

❧ NORTH HILL

North Hill – north of what? There are many theories but no one really knows the origin of the name. It is one of the largest parishes of Cornwall; the picturesque Lynher valley runs through. On the south side of the river are the boulder-capped Hawks Tor and Kilmar where, tradition tells us, the ancient Druids worshipped.

There are traces of people inhabiting North Hill parish from the Bronze Age, 1500-1000 BC. A bronze urn was turned up by the plough in a field of Trebartha Farm in 1975. Evidence of continuing habitation is found in hut circles in what is believed to be a hill fort at Allabury and the early medieval fortified manor house overlooking the Lynher river in Upton Woods.

Four farms are mentioned in the Domesday Book: Trebartha, Tolcarne, Treveniel and Trevague. Battens Farm House is held in Knight Sergeantry from the Duke of Cornwall – feudal dues of one lb of cumin are still presented to the Duke of Cornwall on his first visit to the county.

The church of St Torney is a fine granite building dating around 1289. The impressive tower has 100 steps to its roof with six bells. The village consists of stone cottages, a Victorian terrace and three farm houses (Battens being the home of the Vyncent family). One unique building has two living rooms over apartments with separate little doors where in ancient times the house pig was kept.

Some farm barns have been converted into desirable dwellings and the old chapel has been turned into a very attractive home. There is a shop and post office, a public house and garage. The village hall – North Hill Victory Hall – was built just after the Second World War and is now a thriving meeting place for all the village activities.

North Hill had a public house until the late 19th century – the Ring of Bells, later changed to the Rodd Arms. This was closed by order of the Rodd family because of a drunken orgy. A man on his homeward journey was thrown from his horse and trap and killed. The Church of England school was closed about 1961 and sold. It was then bought by Mr R.B.M. Budge who obtained permission to modernise and convert to a new public house and so after some 70 years a new pub, the Racehorse, opened in 1965.

Trebartha estate remained in the same family from the Conquest until 1940, having passed through the female line twice; to the Spoures in 1498 and Rodds in 1729. The estate was sold to the Latham family in 1940 – the beginning of a new era. Trebartha Hall was taken over by the army and became a RAMC hospital. Many of the men came straight from Dunkirk, wounded and exhausted. The Hall was demolished during 1948.

Wood pigeon shoots in February and rook shoots at the end of May organised by the gamekeeper for tenants were long standing events. Following this pigeon pudding and rook pies were on the menu of many homes (the rooks were skinned and only the breasts used).

Much timber was cut here for the war effort with the help of 'Lumber Jills' (some girls came from London) cutting trees and working the saw mills. There are still fine trees around Trebartha. Sadly the largest Sitka Spruce (Christmas tree) in Cornwall succumbed to the January 1989 gales, as did a large beech at Kingbear which was approximately 300 years old – one of a row of trees thought to mark a land boundary prior to the Land Enclosure Act.

Based at Stonaford was a small toy factory making unique wooden toys – jointed animals, dolls houses and furniture. These were sold all over the UK throughout the 1930s.

Just off the road on Ridge Hill stands a granite cross, erected by the Rodds of Trebartha Hall where a lady fell from her horse when hunting and was killed. Along this road is the Bastreet Water Works, built just before the Second World War to supply piped water to St Germans and the seaport of Looe.

❧ NORTH TAMERTON

North of the Tamar lies the village of North Tamerton, with its 15th century church standing tall above the river. The high tower houses six well-cast bells though today ringers are hard to find.

John Wesley once came to preach in the church but, finding the door locked, took his following to the barn of the nearby Well Farm and preached to them there. The present chapel is a little further up the road, and is approximately 120 years old. This replaced the old chapel which is now a house. Still further on from the chapel is Trebarrow, now a farm but once an ancient burial ground. Rev Hawker once lived at the farm whilst curate of North Tamerton; he was supposed to have introduced the Harvest Festival service.

The Tamar saw fighting in the days of the Civil War. The owner of the Vacey estate who fought for the King had his lands sequestered by Cromwell, but had them restored on the return of the King. At the other end of the village lies Ogbeare Hall, now a residential home for the elderly built by the Love family in the days before the first Elizabeth. On the boundary of the parish the manor of Hornacott stands; it is still a family house and was mentioned in the Domesday Book.

The Bude-Launceston Canal ran through the village; an aqueduct crossed the road and nearby cottages were built for the workmen. Canal Farm served as the stores. Beyond the stores was an inclined plane with a house where the keeper lived. Little now remains of the canal.

After the First World War a village hall was built by the Squire and people as a memorial to lost sons and husbands. This is still in use today for meetings, clubs and entertainments and is run by a local committee.

Eastcott Farm is now a holiday complex with Swiss-type chalets built amongst the trees. Many people come to enjoy holidays here, also at Well Farm in the village. A few of the local people also offer accommodation. The Tamar offers good fishing to visitors and to Bude Fishing Club.

❧ PADSTOW

Padstow's name is derived from Petrocstowe, after St Petroc who arrived in the 6th century to make his monastic home there. Historically important throughout the centuries for fishing, trading and boat building, it is now a great attraction for the discerning visitor and tourist alike.

A fine Elizabethan manor house, Prideaux Place, where descendants of the original owner still live, has a deer park and is a great feature of the area. The

15th century church, surrounded by ancient yew trees, is on a site of Christian worship for some 14 centuries.

The oldest building in the town by the harbour is Abbey House. It has been a guildhall and a portreeve's office in the past and, it is believed, it was along a tunnel from Prideaux Place to this house that Charles II escaped en route to France after the Battle of Naseby. South of the harbour, Court House is said to be where Sir Walter Raleigh, as Lord Lieutenant, held his maritime courts.

Padstow is not without its legends. One is of a mermaid inadvertently shot for a seal, who wreaked revenge by causing a large area of sand (the Doom Bar) to rise at the mouth of the estuary. This was to be the downfall of some 300 ships which foundered there. A happier legend concerns the little mounted horses on the roof of a local bank, who it is said gallop through the streets when children are asleep.

It is the celebrated 'Obby 'Oss Day' on the 1st of May for which Padstow is best known, when exiles come from the four corners of the world to rejoice with families and friends. Considered to be one of the oldest European dances and pagan in origin, it is a day of festivity and gaiety. Through streets bedecked with flags and greenery, crowds follow the 'osses singing and dancing to the accompaniment of accordions and drums. A happy, joyous welcome to summer. With fishing and tourism, Padstow is now a busy little place with friendly pubs and good restaurants, and employment is very much geared to these industries.

Padstow is special for having its own carols, and Christmas for the inhabitants really begins on the first Sunday evening in December after worship, then the carollers unaccompanied voices echo around the streets and quays, which are decorated with Christmas lights.

At High Season there is an annual sea service by the inner quay, with all denominations taking part. The lifeboat, fishing boats and holiday craft fill the harbour. On a lovely summer's evening, this can be a very moving ceremony. The lifeboat and its crew has enormous importance to the area, ever ready to perform its valiant service of help and rescue. The original boat of 1827, named *The Mariner's Friend*, was rowed by four oars, and was said to be the first in the Duchy.

The Camel Trail, which runs along the old railway line beside the river from Wadebridge, is now extremely popular for walkers, and cyclists in particular – an area of great beauty for family parties to ride in safety.

Padstow keeps its character as a fishing and working port and it is a pleasant sight to see some of the older fishermen still strolling around their beloved harbour, laughing and joking with friends and passers-by.

❧ PELYNT

Anyone travelling up from Cornwall and taking the road to Looe or Polperro will automatically pass through the village of Pelynt; for it lies just three miles inland from each holiday resort. The name Pelynt is a corruption of the Celtic Plu-nent which means 'the Parish of St Nonna'. The church was dedicated to St Nonna, the mother of St David of Wales, who was the patron saint of the chapel (now destroyed) and the holy well at Ninnies near Hobb's Park on the West Looe river which divides Pelynt parish from Duloe. There is no tradition that the well cured anybody of anything, but offerings in the shape of bent pins in return for a wish or the expectation of recovery remain a tradition.

The earliest reference to education in Pelynt is contained in a report made in 1745: 'John Francis Buller of Morval, about ten years ago gave £100 to Pelynt parish ye interest to be applied for a charity school. The number of children not limited, but twelve at least will be taught.' This may have started the old part of the school building. The new part was built about 1900 with local labour – some older farmers remember their fathers 'drawing' the stone from a quarry at Trelawne Cross now named Granite Henge. Pelynt now boasts a brand new school, but the original building has been renovated and is now a thriving social club.

The nearby manor of Tregarrick was the seat of the Winslades, hereditary squires of the White Spur. John Winslade took part in the Cornish Rebellion and was executed in 1549.

The Trelawney family is undoubtedly the most famous in Pelynt's history – from the manor of Trelawne, now a large holiday complex. Bishop Jonathan Trelawney, Baronet 1650-1721, was quite a character. During Monmouth's rebellion he organised the military defence of his wavering county and was rewarded with a bishopric at 35. He remained mute on the Romanising practices of King James, until he was bidden to read the Declaration of Indulgence throughout his diocese. Then, venturing his life for Protestantism, he went to his trial after being imprisoned in the Tower of London with six other bishops, and was with them triumphantly acquitted. The Pelynt Male Voice Choir proudly wear Trelawney's mitre and staff on a badge on their blazers today. Naturally they look on Parson Hawker's famous song *Trelawney* as their own special song.

The village has certainly changed a lot – both by way of buildings and jobs. There used to be carpenters-cum-wheelwrights-cum-coffin makers, masons, cordwainers and cobblers, baker, butcher and watchmender. These days a new bunch of traders and services exist for the same purpose – to cheerfully cater for all the needs of villagers and parishioners alike.

🍁 PENROSE

References to the village of Penrose appear in records as far back as the 13th century. The name probably indicates its location at the end of a hill spur where the lane from St Ervan divides. To the south the lane dips steeply to Lower Town where a stream crosses beside Trethewel mill. The branch to the north is known as Becky's Lane – Becky's identity is a mystery, but her lane winds down to another stream and Lewidden mill. A ghostly figure is said to appear near the mill from time to time. If this spectre is Becky then it must surely be friendly.

Both mills were in use until about 1850, grinding corn produced on the many small farms in the area. Sugar beet was grown during the First World War and later, in the 1930s, broccoli became a speciality, the variety bred from home produced seed. Trethewel mill was part of the ancient manor of that name. The manor house, dating back to the 14th century, is situated further up the lane where there was once also a windmill.

While the inhabitants of Penrose were attending the harvest festival service at St Eval church in September 1922 a tremendous rainstorm flooded the lane by Trethewel mill. The returning worshippers had to be rescued with great difficulty by horse and cart. In consequence a new bridge was demanded. It was recorded that the construction took a long time – 'like all public works'. Rebuilding of the new bridge was undertaken by Jim Hawke and his mates Jim Bunney and Jont Caddy. A doggerel poem about the saga comments on 'the industry displayed by all three to finish the bridge in 2000 odd year'. Perhaps the three spent their crib time (ie break-times) playing the popular game 'Shaking Hats'. Participants placed pennies in a hat and, after shaking it, turned it over – all 'heads' coins were claimed by the owner of the hat.

Until the 1930s there was an inn in Lower Town. For many years the game of 'kale', a kind of bowls, was regularly played in the yard outside. At that time there were blacksmiths, shoemakers, a tailor and two shops in the village. The tiny Methodist chapel, built in 1861, has been taken over by the Historic Chapels Trust. Billy Bray came to preach there. He stayed overnight in a nearby cottage. So revered was the event that the bed in which the great preacher slept was turned into a table for all to use.

❧ PENSILVA

Pensilva's panoramic views stretch from St Austell, along the coast to Plymouth and Dartmoor. They are breathtaking. Charles I enjoyed them when he reviewed his troops on the slopes of Caradon in 1643. Another ruler lived here in the Iron Age fort (800-200 BC) at Tokenbury. This is surrounded by oak trees (the name means oak tree fort) and has its original entrance flanked by two formidable granites.

Pensilva was born in 1840, three years after rich deposits of copper and tin were discovered on the Caradon – a name which became synonymous with great wealth. There were a few farms on the edge of the moorland where the village was built. The principal ones were Bodmonland Manor (renamed Jubilee Farm in 1895) and Penharget. The village's first name was Bodmonland, and it was built on Penharget Down and Silva Down. Miners brought their families to live in the two-bedroomed terraced houses which mushroomed as more mines were opened in the area. Eventually the name was changed to Pensilva combining the names of the two Downs.

The first chapel was built by the miners in their spare time at Charston Cross, a neighbouring hamlet. They began in 1842 and by the time it was completed it was too small and too far from the new village. The staunch Methodists, who laboured for eight hours a day in the mines and were paid an average of fifteen shillings per week, built and paid for three chapels in the village of Pensilva. One remains. A small church was built at the beginning of the 20th century as a result of a bequest by Rev Reginald Hobhouse, one of the most famous vicars of St Ive.

The miners emigrated to the USA, Canada, Australia and South Africa when the mines closed, and now almost all the children leave the village to seek work. Fortunately some remain and work on the industrial estate which has been built on the edge of the village. This has proved such a success that it is being extended. Others commute to the neighbouring towns or Plymouth.

The village has every modern facility except gas. Street lights twinkle and it is a landmark for many miles. It is possible to be involved in an activity or organisation every evening, and classes and meetings are held in the women's and men's institutes each day.

Almost all the houses have lovely gardens and one of the prettiest has two friendly ghosts. An elderly couple in Victorian dress appear beside the fire smiling and appearing to talk to each other. They reflect the happy, warm atmosphere of the house, and must have enjoyed the village carnivals and flower show which are annual events now. Every year almost all the inhabitants join in or enjoy these. The Women's Institute promotes the Flower Show tradition and organises one every summer.

🍁 PENWITHICK

Penwithick is situated three miles north of St Austell and is one of the villages in the Treverbyn parish. Years ago it was called Penwithick Stents and consisted of one road, the east side was known as Cannamanning and the west side as Penwithick. Stents was derived from the fact that many years ago it was washed for tin, the waste stones were thrown back and the tin was washed down by the stream that still flows down through the village and winds its way through to Par. The rejected stones were spoken of as stent. This name was dropped in 1906 and the village became Penwithick.

It is reported that many years ago it was a haunt for smugglers. There was a large cave capable of holding 25 people and from this there branched several tunnels. It is said that whiskey, rum etc, on which duty was payable, was brought to Par by boat and conveyed to Penwithick by horseback.

On Easter Monday 1906 the stone-laying ceremony for a Methodist chapel was held. For all the worshippers that attended, this building was not big enough and in 1914 a new chapel was built and the old building became the Sunday schoolroom. Besides chapel activities it is used as a hall for the playschool four mornings a week, and any charitable event.

In the 1930s when there were a great many unemployed, the idea of building a social hall started and, given a piece of land, these men cheerfully promised to do all the necessary labour. A gentleman who had a controlling interest in the clayworks guaranteed the money. When the stonelaying took place it was visited by HRH the Prince of Wales, the late Duke of Windsor, who expressed his admiration at the success of the project. In 1981 an extension was built and is now used for discos, bingo and private organised parties.

There were no regular supplies of letters before the First World War as the postman was not allowed to go off the main road and so letters were delivered to the nearest house. It could be three or four days before the letters got to the right owner. One postman was deaf and stamps could only be obtained from him; if it was raining he would not sell any and if he was riding his bicycle he would pretend not to hear if they shouted to him. The owner of the village store applied for a licence to sell stamps to oblige the villagers, and she had permission to hold a stock to the value of five shillings. After some time she canvassed the village asking for support to get permission for a sub post office. This was granted and is still operating from the same building today.

The men of the village worked mostly in the clayworks which were situated near the village, Greta Treverbyn, Baal Ninestones and Lantern (now closed). Today a great number of men and women have been employed at John Keay House, headquarters of ECCI. There were also many lorry drivers who worked for two lorry depots in the village, mostly carrying sea sand as fertiliser for the farmers, rough sand and building blocks. Now the lorries for these drivers are at the heavy transport depot, Par.

There were many farms and smallholdings scattered about the area but most of the fields in the village have been used for building council estates and private dwelling houses. One farmer has turned some of his fields into a residential caravan site with a siting for 50 mobile homes and caravans.

🍁 PERRANPORTH

Perranporth is in the parish of Perranzabuloe (St Piran in the sands) and is situated between sand dunes and the majestic cliffs on the Atlantic coast. At low tide the beach below still bears some evidence of the many wrecks which have happened here. It has developed over the centuries from a small mining village and pilchard fishing area into a favourite holiday resort, the three miles of golden sands being one of its main attractions.

Legend has it that, buried beneath the sand dunes, is the city of Langarrow. Its people, rich from mining copper and tin, became too high and mighty to work and so they imported England's worst criminals to do the job for them. Gradually, these workers infiltrated into the city, which became a den of iniquity, corrupt and degraded. One night, a wind came swirling down, driving the sand before it. For three days and nights it blew and the wonderful city was buried.

The name Perranporth comes from St Piran, patron saint of tinners, who sailed to Cornwall from Ireland on a millstone and landed on the beach in the 6th century. He founded a monastic settlement nearby, where the little church or oratory was built. This is said to be one of the oldest places of Christian worship in Britain, with parts of all four walls standing when it was excavated.

In this oratory were deposited the relics of St Piran. These included his head, his staff and his bell, which were carried around the district on festival occasions. Only a Celtic cross remains near the spot where the now reburied oratory stood. The cross is almost nine foot high and, unusually, has three pierced holes, rather than four. It is a thousand years old and was already a landmark in documents of AD 960.

The present parish church was dedicated in July 1805 and is set well away from the dunes in the centre of the parish.

In earlier days the village was small, with a few dozen stone and cob cottages and five shops – three grocers, a butcher and a fruit and icecream shop. Trade in the winter was not brisk, especially for the latter, and the proprietor was heard to remark that she 'made her rent on August Bank Holiday and her rates on Carnival day' – the only busy days the village ever saw. Today is rather different, with many more shops and hotels bringing in the holiday trade, helped at one stage by the railway, which came in 1904 and was one of the victims of the Beeching axe in 1962. The village owes much of its shape and development to a body of inhabitants now known as the Perranzabuloe Garden Charities, whose founders had the foresight to preserve the centre as a long open space, running from the bowling green and boating lake through the gardens to the seafront promenade and car park. The income generated is used for the upkeep and improvement of these and other parts of the village. Some of the old cottages still remain among the new buildings, with the old houses which belonged to the mine captains standing like sentinels on the cliff top overlooking the village, monuments to the past.

Beyond the Perrancombe valley, leading towards Trevellas, you will find Harmony Cott, the birthplace of John Opie RA, the famous Cornish painter, who was born in 1761. Another much later resident of Perranporth was novelist Winston Graham, who wrote the Poldark novels, later made into a television serial. The village of Sawle in his books is partly based on old Perranporth as a small mining and fishing village. Nampara itself is the name of an area near the centre of Perranporth. Winston Graham became a patron of the Perranporth Folk Museum.

In the early 1930s actor Peter Bull brought a summer repertory company, which gave Perranporth quite a publicity boost. Among its members were Robert Morley, Nicholas Phipps, Richard Ainley and many others who later became well known and their amateur successors, the Perranporth Players, still flourish.

🍁 PERRANUTHNOE

Perranuthnoe was first documented in the Domesday survey of 1086. A constantly recurring name in the area is Trevelyan, since the title of lord of the manor passed to John Trevelyan through his marriage to Elizabeth (his cousin), daughter of Thomas Whalesborough (the previous owner). The family coat of arms hanging outside the Trevelyan Arms in Goldsithney perpetuates the legend that the sole survivor of Lyonesse was a Trevelyan.

Mines and mineshafts are rife in the area – all with their own names. It was hoped that copper would make the area's fortune, so much so that Gundry's issued their own bank notes. These of course have not survived. When in 1861 Wheal Charlotte's boiler blew up many men were killed, and the local people say that their voices can be hard to this day.

Perranuthnoe clings to the hillside overlooking the sandy beach and Mount's Bay. There was a silver mine there 100 years ago, but now it is a quiet haven with just a pub, the Victoria Inn, and a square-towered church where the clock strikes the quarter hours, while men work in the broccoli fields which surround the village. This part of Cornwall is the produce growing area. The greater part of the population live in Goldsithney which lies beyond the crossroads. Here is the village hall, the centre of all activities. Also St James's hall still stands in South Road, on the route of pilgrims who went to Spain to the shrine of St James at Santiago, Compostella, in the Middle Ages.

To the east of Perranuthnoe, in the parish of St Hilary, lies the jagged promontory of Cudden Point, and beside it Prussia Cove. Here lived John Carter, known to the locals as 'The King of Prussia', an infamous smuggler. Some of the old cottages still stand where underground passages led down to the sea, thus hiding the silks, lace and brandy stealthily brought in from France and Brittany on dark moonless nights. Today this is a peaceful cove for fishermen, and a haven for walkers on the South Coast footpath.

Sadly the local shop has now closed – which means that the residents have to venture further afield for both the necessities of life and the gossip which was the life line of many!

🍁 PERRANWELL

It would be easy to think, as you drive through Perranwell, in the parish of Perran-ar-worthal, that this is just another dormitory village for the city of Truro. You would be wrong. In spite of its residential appearance, Perranwell has a history stretching back into the ancient past, researched and recorded by the late Mr Eric Ryall.

A tumulus or Stone Age burial mound lies on a hill within the parish and later, as Christianity came to the Celtic western lands, so St Piran left his mark. A quiet pool, festooned in greenery, St Piran's Well, can be discovered only yards away from the busy A39 and a stone's throw from the sturdy, grey parish church of St Piran.

Industry has always been closely connected with Perranwell. The Perran Foundry was established by the creek in 1791, where it is said the Industrial Revolution truly began. George Croker Fox, followed by his two sons, George and Robert, built up a towering enterprise here, but like other industrial sites in the area, this is now derelict. It will, however, rise like a phoenix from the ashes, rejuvenated as a residential and interpretive centre, if all goes well. One of Perranwell's most famous sons, William Jory Henwood, a scientist of national repute, started his work here. He died in 1875. The surrounding mines, notably on United Downs, gave work to many and brought distress when they closed. Finally, the railway came through in 1863. 'Perran was an awful place at that time', with drinking and fighting amongst the navvies. Who would now believe it?

Life now is very different. Green fields have been developed for comfortable and pleasant dwellings. Where once a busy rural and farming community lived have come commuters, business people, white-collar workers and the retired. Cars and buses hurry through, but it is pleasant that tractors still rattle by with potatoes and broccoli; that the village shop and post office still look down on the bridge over the Trewedna stream; that children still straggle up to the school on the hill; that Mrs Hattem still has time for a word with Mrs Ivall; that the postmen still cycle their rounds; that Hugh Kneebone still waves cheerily to the people at the Hoppa bus stop.

To celebrate the new Millennium various groups worked on projects to improve and enhance the village. These include a natural stone bus shelter to be erected opposite the Royal Oak, another shelter at the railway station, and a history of the village based on local walks. Furthermore, the planting of over 13,000 daffodil bulbs and primroses in hedges, on verges, waste ground, around the playing field and the war memorial will brighten the local scene each coming spring with a golden glow.

🍁 PETHERWIN GATE

Petherwin Gate is situated in the parish of North Petherwin in the area bordering Devon. The village is situated at one end of the parish in the vicinity of the parish church, which is dedicated to St Padern, or St Paternus. The present building was erected on a true Celtic site where previously there had stood a wooden church. Dating from Norman times with Norman piers and chancel, it is probably the oldest church in these parts. The magnificent medieval pulpit at St Mary Magdalene's church, Launceston, was at one time part of North Petherwin church and is believed to have survived the dissolution by being coated with thick black 'paint'. A fine view is obtained from the belfry, looking far across the Tamar into Devonshire, of which North Petherwin once formed part until it was incorporated into Cornwall in 1966. During 1998 and 1999 the Holy Well, which had been 'lost' for many years, was refurbished by parishioners. It was rededicated in 1999 and the water is now used for baptisms in the church.

Centuries ago, Petherwyn was a land of marsh and moor, inhabited by

Bronze Age man who built his barrows, or tumuli, at Bodgate and Buttern. The Domesday Book records Petherwyn under its section on 'Devenescire'. Forming part of the large manor of Werrington, it was royal land held by the Countess Gytha who made a grant of it to the Abbot of Tavistock. There being no proof of the grant at the time of Domesday, the Commissioners rightly treated the land as belonging to the King. However, the Abbot regained Petherwyn in 1096 and it remained church property until the Dissolution.

Not all the parish of North Petherwin was owned by the Dukes of Bedford as can be seen by the architecture. There are numerous low-ceilinged farmhouses and cottages which escaped 'modernisation' by not belonging to that family. However, the parish owes a great debt of gratitude to Francis, seventh Duke of Bedford. He drained all his land in North Petherwin and built new farmhouses and cottages in a distinctive style well ahead of the time. These now provide fine modern residences. Local labour, stone and slate were used and the bricks and drainpipes were made, and lime kilns worked, on the border of the parish near Egloskerry.

The parish consists of numerous small hamlets. However, Petherwin Gate has been somewhat transformed by residential development which has brought people from all over the country to live in this rural community. Some residents commute to Launceston or further afield for work, whilst others have their own crafts or small businesses within the parish, occasionally operating from rural workshops. Sole reliance on a livelihood from agriculture has become almost impossible, leading to many people seeking to diversify to gain additional income.

From its earliest days, the Methodist church found great support in this area and the chapels at Maxworthy and Copthorne are still in use. The church school, dated 1844, is a listed building and is used as the Parish Hall. The well-built primary school at Brazzacott celebrated its centenary in 1976 and is still going strong!

Tourists regularly visit this, until recently, unexplored area, staying in the variety of holiday accommodation now available. Local attractions include the Tamar Otter Park, an award winning nature trail and a farm implements museum. In 1999 the Barton Millennium Wood, an eight acre Parish Community Woodland, was planted with indigenous trees and is for use by everyone.

Skittles, darts and clay pigeon shooting are enjoyed within North Petherwin. A working village with old, middle-aged, young and children who enjoy each other's company and the surroundings, the villagers and parishioners of Petherwin Gate look to the future with a caring eye to make sure too much is not lost unnecessarily to what is called 'progress'.

☀ PILLATON

Pillaton is an attractive village overlooking the Lynher valley on the south-east border of Cornwall.

Mentioned in the Domesday Book, its name is believed to have been derived from 'pile of stones', probably because of the seams of shale which run beneath the surface of the soil round about.

The church of St Odulph, consecrated by the Bishop of Exeter in 259, makes a pleasing impression on visitors entering the village from the east. Those stopping to look inside will notice how tranquil and well kept this beautiful church is. A recent exciting discovery has been of a medieval niche which probably housed a statue of St Odulph. Medieval ceiling plates have also been uncovered – two on the porch and two inside the church.

It is believed that the nearby inn was a resting place for monks building the church and early in the 1960s the then proprietors changed its name from the Royal Oak to the Weary Friar. It is now a well known hotel and restaurant and provides a traditional setting for the Christmas Eve meet of the East Cornwall Hunt.

Pillaton formed part of the Newton Ferrers estate until 1924 when the whole village was sold, farms and cottages being mostly bought by the sitting tenants. Clapper Bridge is a well known local beauty spot at the lower end of the village and near the weir there is an adit to a manganese mine where a young man lived in hiding for the duration of the First World War to avoid conscription.

Until 1949, Pillaton was a small hamlet of some 20 houses with agriculture and horticulture as its main industry. To support this there was a wheelwright's and carpenter's shop and a smithy where agricultural implements such as cultivators, ploughs and hayrakes were made and repaired. Two farms were situated at each end of the village. A grocer's shop and post office were then separate establishments, but sadly these have now closed and been altered into private accommodation.

Another interesting example of then and now is that at Kernock Farm the cultivation of white heather and pittosporum was begun commercially and a number of villagers were employed in picking, packing and despatching to all parts of the country, including Scotland. Today part of the same area, Kernock Park, has been developed as a wholesale nursery for plants and hanging baskets. This industry is expanding and now employs about 60 workers, some of whom are local people.

In 1959, a road bridge across the river Tamar from Plymouth to Saltash was built and thus brought an explosion of house building to Pillaton. It is now within easy commuting distance for business and professional people and those connected with Devonport dockyard. Today there are some 115 houses and a population of 500 people among whom has grown up a real community spirit, resulting amongst other things in the winning of the Tidy Village competition and three times winning the CFWI award for the best kept small village. There is a successful team of lady hand bell ringers and the peal of six church bells is regularly rung by an enthusiastic band of tower bell ringers. The church also has a talented choir. The very active membership of Pillaton WI enjoys a varied programme of meetings. The annual gymkhana provides valued financial support towards the upkeep of the village hall, which is to have an extension to allow better facilities for all ages and organisations in the village.

❀ POINT & PENPOL

These two villages, situated on the north shore of Restronguet and Penpol creeks, which form part of the Fal estuary, today present a very peaceful scene. It was not always so, for when tin and copper were being actively mined they were a hive of industry. Both products came down from the mining hinterland, the tin to be smelted at one of the many smelters which lined the shore of Penpol creek and the copper exported to South Wales to be smelted there. Coal and pit props for the mines came in by boat and were then transported back up the valleys. In the 18th century this was done by pack animal and later by mineral railway.

There are signs of this earlier industrial activity all round the area. A fine old stone quay, initially built by a Mr Daniell and named after him – Daniell's Point – now known as Point Quay, has come into the ownership of the parish of Feock, the purchase aided by a generous public donation, as a public amenity area. There are other old stone quays along Penpol Creek. At the same time that Point Quay was purchased a small overgrown orchard was also acquired and as this was cleared by volunteers an interesting lime kiln came to light.

The track of the old mineral railway (the Redruth & Chacewater Railway), long defunct, ran from Point along the creek side to Devoran, a mile away. This section of track only used horse-drawn waggons, Beyond Devoran steam locomotion was used. This track is known as the Old Tram Road, it makes a good level walk and there are delightful views over the creek.

Also at Penpol there was a tidal bone mill; very little is left to see, but there are stepping stones over the creek, visible at low water.

Point is unusual for a Cornish village in that it has a village green.There is a working pump on the green and it has typical early 19th century cottages and houses around it. Here was an inn called the Bell, reputedly haunted, now two dwelling houses, a mission hall and a shop, all private cottages nowadays. There

Lime Kiln, Point

are several documented stories of the smuggling of spirits involving the innkeepers.

Tin mining also took place 75 feet under the bed of the creek and at low water the remains of the wooden stakes surrounding the air shaft in mid-creek are clearly visible.

Also by Point Quay there is a brick built semi-detached house, said to be made from the bricks of the huge chimney of one of the smelting works. The chimney appears in two local paintings, one dated mid 19th century and one from the 1880s. The picture showing Penpol smelting works may be viewed at Truro museum.

There are no longer any shops in the villages, nor a pub but the local tradition of boat building is continued and also half a mile away towards Devoran, rowing gigs are being hand-built to a traditional design.

The nautical connection carries on with many people using the water for a variety of sports, two hours either side of high tide providing sufficient water in the creek for most boating activities. The Point and Penpol Regatta, held during the summer, is a function of many years standing and was even held during the years of the Second World War. On the Monday following the regatta, the gig rowing races are held. The crews and clubs come from many parts of Cornwall, the competition is fierce and the cheering from the spectators on the quay is intensely partisan!

❧ POLGOOTH

The meaning of Polgooth is 'Goose Pool'. However, the mining of tin and copper is undoubtedly the major factor in the history of the village. Polgooth is particularly distinguished for its extensive and rich tin works.

The Great Polgooth mine employed more than 1,000 people by 1800; this included underground miners, blowing house men, bal maidens and children. The mine was one out of eight mines in the area to be still at work at the dawn of the 19th century. Above Polgooth on the golf course today, the stump of its engine house stands as a reminder.

The South Polgooth mine on the hill west of the village, near Five Turnings, was a smaller mine – 136 persons employed. The old dressing floors of Polgooth are now the golf course; at South Polgooth you can see a large area, presumably arsenical, on which nothing grows.

The engine house at East Rand has been renovated by Brendan Sweet into a dwelling. A lot of these engine houses have perished over the years but at East Rand much hard work has been completed to the roof and lintels where the stone walling was unsafe. Many of the houses in Polgooth were built with stone reused from engine houses which were pulled down.

Through volcanic eruptions thousands of years ago, a belt of elvan stone was pushed up between tin bearing lodes. This comes to the surface at Bal-East quarry in the lane near the Polgooth inn. Yellow burrow, by the road junction near the inn, is a mound of waste from this quarry and is so called from the colour of this stone.

The Polgooth stone, as it was called, was used by the Leyland Barratt Company for the houses in Moorland Road, St Austell and for most of the mansions in the town and also the cottage hospital.

Polgooth is very fortunate to have a magazine, *The Polgooth Times*, which is published some three or four times a year. The village institute is also a very important element in village life. A new hall at the rear of the main institute has been completed and is very much in demand by village groups, clubs, playgroup and other organisations.

🍁 POLKERRIS

The hamlet of Polkerris is sited on the north-eastern shore of St Austell bay between Par and Fowey, and was mentioned by the great traveller Leland as a haven of refuge in 1549.

Polkerris and most of the surrounding land belongs to the Rashleigh family of Menabilly, which lies towards Fowey. Menabilly was made famous by Daphne du Maurier as Manderley in her romantic novel *Rebecca* (for the film, Caerhays Castle was used to portray Manderley).

After the Second World War, Daphne du Maurier and her husband, Sir Fredrick Browning, moved from Menabilly to Kilmarth, a large house overlooking Par above Polkerris, where Lady Browning lived until her death in 1989.

How different the hamlet of Polkerris is now from the village in the 19th century, when it had a flourishing pilchard fishery, 63 allotment gardens and various furze (gorse) plots for fuel, a chapel, school, shop, post office, public house, plus the coastguard station and lifeboat station.

Nowadays, gone are many of the dwellings, the chapel has been converted into a summer holiday let, the old life-boat house into a beach shop and 'take-away'. The Rashleigh inn was previously the coastguard station and home, and the present car park for the pub was the site of the General Elliot public house, which was washed away by a fierce storm, as was a thatched cottage nearby. The last post office, in one of the cottage's kitchen, after running on a part-time basis for two years was finally closed in June 1990, through lack of use.

The fishing industry declined towards the end of the 1800s; at one time around 200 people were involved in the curing and packing of the pilchards. The remains of the old Elizabethan 'palace' or pilchard curing cellar, one of the largest ever to have been built along the coast, still stands above the beach and is used by the Scouts to keep their canoes and other equipment safe.

Nearby, to the landward end of the quay, built by Philip Rashleigh in 1790-91, is a lime kiln, where limestone was burnt to produce lime for the local farmers to 'sweeten' their soil.

Before the lifeboat station was opened in 1859, the Polkerris coastguards would launch their 14 ft galley and many a daring rescue took place. During the years from 1859 until 1922 when the lifeboat was moved to Fowey, the succession of lifeboats from the *Catherine Rashleigh* in 1859 to the *James William* and *Catherine Courtney* in 1904, performed 15 rescues and saved 52 lives and a ship's cat. Gold and silver medals were also won for bravery and seamanship by lifeboat crews. For many years after the fishing industry declined, the launching of the Polkerris lifeboat was the only source of excitement for the village and they would all turn out to help or watch the boat rumble down the slip and enter the water with the crew at the ready.

POLPERRO

Polperro has had many names in its long history. In 1300 it was known as Porthpirie, by the 1500s it was Poulpier, today the name Polperro is thought to mean 'the mouth of the river Pol', from the small stream which runs through the village. The population is about 1,300.

Polperro nestles in the valley with hills on three sides. A lovely little harbour is to be found at the end of the village, which has been a working harbour since the 1300s and probably before that. In early days pilchards were the main catch. Today any number of fish are brought to the fish quay, and fishing is still one of the main industries in the village, the other being tourism.

Tourists come from all over the world to walk through the narrow winding streets – straight lines do not exist in Polperro. Visitors to Polperro cannot bring their cars down into the village, but they can park and ride on a 'horse bus' which is pulled by a large shire horse, into the village.

There is much to see on a visit – the model village, the Heritage Museum, and also the Shell House which is decorated with shells, all done by a local man who decorated the house as a hobby and created a tourist attraction. There is a Saxon bridge and also a Roman bridge, beside which there is a house on props.

Many of the buildings date from the 16th and 17th centuries. Some of the fishermen's cottages still have the original clome ovens and not long ago a pilchard press was discovered behind a boarded up wall in one of the cottages. In the old buildings the thickness of the walls – some of them almost three feet thick – help to keep the residents cosy as they keep the houses warm in winter and cool in summer, but some of the cellars near the river and quay are damp due to the residue of salt which penetrated the walls when the pilchards were salted and stored there.

There is a preservation order which operates in Polperro to ensure that the original character and appearance of the buildings are not changed too much – one has to obtain permission to even change the colour of the paint on the houses.

Polperro's famous son, Jonathon Couch had a house here, named 'Couch's Great House'. He was a local doctor and an eminent naturalist. The village also had its share of smuggling, influenced greatly by Zephaniah Job, who organised lawyers for smugglers who were caught and sent money for those in prison. He was also adviser, banker and accountant to many.

The House on Props, Polperro

One of the traditions linked with Polperro is that of the Cornish Guernsey or Knit Frock. The local women used to gather together to knit their original designs. They often knitted the initials of the owner either underneath the armpit or on the bottom line of the Guernsey.

A strong sense of community spirit exists here and there is no better place in which to live in times of trouble as everyone rallies around to help each other. In 1976 the village was severely flooded but with everyone's help things soon returned to normal. In the bad winter storms of 1989/90 the pier and harbour walls were badly damaged and many local organisations sprang into action to raise funds in various ways to help towards their repair.

❈ POLRUAN

Polruan is a quaint old seafaring village on the east bank of the Fowey river at the harbour mouth in the parish of Lanteglos-by-Fowey. Off the beaten track, it can be reached from Fowey by passenger ferry or by car ferry via Bodinnick. It can also be reached by road from Liskeard to the east.

At the top of Polruan is an ancient granite cross marking the site of the old village well. Fore Street runs down the hill (1 in 6 gradient) bordered by old stone cottages. From this road East Street and West Street branch out along the shore line, West Street to the old blockhouse or castle which was connected by chain to one on the Fowey side as a harbour defence in the 15th century. East Street boasts two working shipyards, one of which still builds traditional wooden fishing boats.

There is a Methodist chapel and St Saviour's church, near to which are the ruins of an ancient chapel which has been a landmark through the centuries. The parish church, where Daphne du Maurier was married, is situated out in the country about one and a half miles from the village.

The village is unusual in still having an active Town Trust which meets in their reading room near the quay. The Town Trust dates back certainly before 1688 when existing records began and administers the Town Land and car parks.

From earliest times Polruan has been inseparable from seafaring, particularly so as access from the landward side was hampered by bad roads and difficult terrain until this century. The sea was the little town's highway and all necessities not locally produced, or surplus goods for sale, were carried by ship. Links with the continent, always strong, were further strengthened by the Norman Conquest; and there was constant traffic between Polruan, the Channel Islands, and the French ports.

With the wars of the 14th century, activity in the port greatly increased as local shipping was used to carry men, horses and arms to France for the royal campaigns. Less legally, Polruan men engaged in privateering and piracy, experience which schooled them well when they joined other Cornish ships to face the Armada and, more recently, the smuggling boom of the 18th and 19th centuries. As horizons widened they fared further abroad; and old ships' logs of Polruan master mariners tell of voyages to the Americas, the Far East, South America and Australia. They joined the fishing fleets which went to the Newfoundland Banks for the cod trade and nearer home fished off shore. The pilchard trade was of great importance, and there were pilchard 'palaces' or large cellars and, later, a pilchard canning factory. All these activities were reinforced by ancillary services; pilots, coastguards, ferrymen, lightermen, keepers of harbour lights, jettymen and, not least, boatbuilders, who all played their part.

One of the old surviving customs is Polruan Carnival Day held on August Bank Holiday when there is a sailing regatta during the day and a colourful and humorous fancy dress parade and Flora Dance in the evening. Villagers and visitors throng the streets on this special day and join in the fun.

🍁 PORT ISAAC

The name Port Isaac is derived from Port Izzyck, one of many spellings, and is thought to mean 'corn port'.

Slate-roofed cottages huddle together for protection against the Atlantic gales along the narrow lanes and alleyways winding down the steep side of the valley to the harbour. Two notable features are Temple Bar, recorded as the narrowest thoroughfare in the world and known locally as 'Squeezee-belly Alley' and the 'Birdcage' so named because of its unusual shape. It was built by a Mr Valentine Powell Richards and was used at one time as a cobbler's shop. It is now owned by the National Trust.

There were nearly 50 boats fishing out of Port Isaac in the mid-19th century and now there are only about a dozen but, during the summer season, there are always long queues of visitors at the old fish cellars wanting crabs and fish packed in ice in polystyrene boxes to take home with them. There was some boat-building carried out in the village in the 19th century but not any more and a major industry now is, of course, tourism. The old village itself is unspoilt except that like so many attractive villages, many of the old cottages are occupied only during 'the season'. However, the new part above the old village is thriving and there is a good community spirit.

Some years ago the old school, overlooking the harbour, was closed and a new school was built amongst the new houses. Now the old school building is an hotel and restaurant.

The Port Isaac branch of the RNLI is very active and well supported at various functions and a new inshore rescue boat was recently commissioned. The first lifeboat stationed in Port Isaac in 1869 was the *Richard and Sarah*.

St Peter's, the parish church, was built in 1889. Before that parishioners had to walk two hilly miles to St Endellion. Roscarrock Hill Methodist church celebrated its centenary in 1969. This chapel replaced one built in 1837 which had become too small but the first chapel was built in 1750 after John Wesley had visited the village.

Either side of Port Isaac are two smaller ports, Port Gaverne to the north-east and Port Quin to the west. Port Gaverne, apart from fishing, was the port from which the slate from Delabole was shipped before the railway was built and Port Gaverne was a busy trading port at that time but is no longer so, the busiest trade being at the old 17th century Port Gaverne Hotel. Up through the Port Gaverne valley to Pendoggett there is said to be gold bearing rock. Port Quin was also a small fishing village with fish cellars and cottages around the harbour but it is now deserted and the National Trust have renovated the cottages for holiday visitors. It is said that the village died when all the men were lost at sea many years ago and their families moved away.

Until the Beeching cuts of 1966, there was a main line train service through North Cornwall and Port Isaac Road station was only a few miles away. Now the nearest station is Bodmin Parkway, a distance of about 20 miles. Port Isaac is, however, well served by the local coach firm. Although travel is rather limited for those without cars or who, for one reason or another, do not drive, Port Isaac is fortunate in having a doctors' group practice in the village and enough well-stocked and friendly shops to provide for everyday needs.

🍁 PORTH

The small coast-line village of Porth lies two miles to the north of Newquay and used to be called St Columb Porth, being the port for the then busy market town of St Columb Minor, long before the existence of Newquay. Vessels brought in the staple requirements of the community, including coal from South Wales, salt and lime, and later, when Newquay became established as a china clay port, used to continue round to Newquay to pick up the clay. The salt was for use in the fish cellars situated on the quay, the remains of which can be seen in the sea wall near today's post office.

At that time the only way out of Porth to the north was by fording the river to Watergate Road. On this side of the beach is Porth Island, now linked to the mainland by a bridge constructed by Richard Tangye, the then owner of the large house on the Newquay side of the bay called Glendorgal, who also owned the island, so that public access could be made. The island is one of the finest examples of a cliff castle, and excavations have disclosed it was used as a settlement from the 3rd century BC to the 6th century AD.

On the mainland facing the island used to stand the Banqueting Hall Cavern – a huge cave enlarged by mining rock which was lifted up through a hole in the roof by a rope pulley called a whip and derrick; the area above the cavern subsequently being called Whipsiderry. Concerts were held in this cavern during the 1920s and 1930s, for which a harmonium was hauled across the beach and over the rocks. These concerts could be held on about six occasions per year at exceptionally low tides, and about 1,000 people could be accommodated at a time. Recently this cavern was proclaimed unsafe by the local council and was blown up, although traces of it can still be seen from under the bridge.

Glendorgal is a very striking house in a superb position on the cliffs overlooking Porth Bay and Island with its own access to the beach and the small cove called Cupboard Cove. Built in 1850 by Francis Rodd as a summer home, it was owned by the Tangye family for many years and is now a well-known hotel. From the grounds of Glendorgal above Lusty Glaze Beach used to run a canal designed and built by John Edyvean of St Austell to carry sea sand to local inland farms and coal to St Columb Minor and neighbouring villages, with china clay and stone being brought to the coast from the St Austell area. This canal was in use until the early 19th century, and can still be traced in the fields above Porth valley, now a favourite dog-walking area. Porth valley was an important slate quarry in the 18th and 19th centuries with tin being mined from the valley gravels. The Morganna Mine adits can still be seen near the steps to Whipsiderry Beach, while in the cove at the bottom of Watergate Road was a busy shipyard where fishing smacks and three schooners were built during the 1800s.

Today Porth is a suburb of Newquay with a road bridge built in 1902 which takes the traffic which used to ford the river. The river is tidal and is very silted up, making it difficult to imagine a shipyard once working there.

Under the sandy beach lie the remains of a submerged forest, discovered when excavations were made for a sewage pumping station. Preserved leaves, twigs and even insects were all found and can now been seen at Glendorgal Hotel. Today the British Trust for Conservation are trying to recreate the wooded valley of Porth by planting a mixed woodland belt along the Newquay side of the valley. So far over 600 trees have been planted and most are surviving the salt-laden gales, which sweep in from the Atlantic. Hopefully, this generation will also leave a piece of history for Porth.

🍁 PORTLOE

Portloe is a typical little Cornish fishing village, sheltering in an inlet in the rocky coast. It is surrounded by hills, and the road runs steeply up at either end of the village. The cove is exposed to the east, and although a small sea wall, completed in 1959, breaks some of the force of the sea, boats must always be hauled up the beach on to the slipway (by means of a winch), out of reach of the tide. But inshore fishing is a dying industry, and Portloe is becoming more and more a holiday village, dependent for its prosperity on the visitors.

Entering the village you will see a row of ten terraced, two-storey houses, which were once neatly whitewashed coastguard cottages. Since the end of the Second World War they have been bought up and altered to individual taste, and have lost their uniform appearance. Trevanion, the large L-shaped house, standing in a garden below the terrace, used to be occupied by the coastguard officer. Below this again is the boathouse (now a private home), with its slip-way for launching the coastguard cutter.

The footpath leading down to the boathouse from the road continues up the hillside opposite to the Methodist chapel. The narrow road winds on down the hill, past groups of cottages, above and below it. The typical Portloe cottage is a two-storey building of colour-washed rubble (stones of irregular shape and size), with sash windows and grey, slate roofs.

The mission church of Portloe is an inconspicuous small building – usually being propped up by the backs of some of the men of the village! It is a chapel of ease attached to Veryan church. Originally, the building was the lifeboat house; the lifeboat was difficult to launch, as it used to hit the corner of the cottage next to the post office. Later, another house was built for the lifeboat on the south side of the beach.

The road widens out into a tiny square in front of the church, where you turn down sharply to the slipway and the beach. The post office/tearooms and licensed restaurant stand on this junction.

On the north side of the beach is the Lugger Hotel, formerly an inn, with a reputation as a haunt of smugglers. Later it became a private house and only reverted to the licensed trade after the Second World War. The present building is part converted fish cellars.

Past the church, the road starts climbing again with cottages on either side until you arrive at the Ship Inn. The inn was built in 1904 on the site of a two-room, cob-walled predecessor, which was known in the village as 'the Drinking Kitchen'.

The village ends at Sunny Corner, a cluster of cottages enchantingly set in a little dip among trees, with a stream running alongside, of which the gardening enthusiasts who live there have taken full advantage.

🍁 PORTWRINKLE

This was once a small but flourishing village with its early 17th century pilchard cellars, situated halfway between Plymouth and Looe, but like Topsy it has recently 'just growed'. Where the surrounding steep fields were once tilled with potatoes and swedes and the fishing nets were spread to dry, now stands a small development of houses with their colourful gardens – a tribute to the imagination and tenacity of the present villagers. Seating here and further west along the front of the village affords panoramic views of Rame Head and the Looe peninsula as well as out to the Eddystone lighthouse.

The ancient walls of the fishing cellars remain. A small inner area is used for garaging and the making of the original withy crab pots. The western part of the village also includes early 19th century coastguard cottages and a boathouse used by the first customs men who tried to outwit the local smugglers who flourished in the 17th and 18th centuries and well into the 19th too! In recent years the harbour and beaches have seen repeated attempts to strengthen the coastal defences against the south-west winds which reach storm force during the winter months.

The focus of attention on the eastern edge of Portwrinkle is the Whitsand Bay Hotel, once a large private house built in the Victorian Gothic style on the outskirts of Torpoint, until being rebuilt stone by stone in the early part of the 20th century on its present site.

During the first half of the last century there were many interesting characters inhabiting the village who lived in their fishermen's cottages to a ripe old age, including one elderly lady who it is alleged could well have introduced nude bathing to Cornwall. The older generations entranced us with tales of their childhood and of the harshness of making a living from the sea and surrounding fields. Now only two of the original families remain; the new inhabitants are mainly retired folk or commuters to Plymouth or the Royal Naval establishments. They have happily settled into the spirit of village life, co-operating in creating, for example, a sitting area where the original coastguard hut was situated.

Although one third of the housing is holiday accommodation and there is no chapel, shop, post office, public house or street lighting, nevertheless there is no lack of community spirit. There are also close links with the two other villages in the parish, Crafthole and Sheviock.

Since it is exposed to the prevailing south-west winds, very few trees grow in the village. The number of species of both resident and migratory birds has declined in recent years; some like the song thrush becoming a rare sight. Similarly the richness of life in the rock pools is disappearing, reflecting the scarcity of the fishing in general. There is still a wide if changing variety of wild flowers and plants to be found and the less common salt-loving varieties thrive in rocky crevices.

Alive with colour and people in the summer, Portwrinkle becomes its own unique self in the winter; a place of the sound of the sea and wind and of its own inner stillness.

🍁 POUGHILL

The village of Poughill (pronounced Poffle) is situated one mile inland north of Bude, North Cornwall. It has a unique place in local history and as long ago as 1086 it featured in the Domesday Book, but was then known as Pochehelle.

It was a typical rural village with its water-mill which is believed to have been a manorial mill for Trevalgus manor lying at the foot of Trevalgus Hill in thick woodland. It was powered by the stream which runs south towards Stratton called the Stratt. The mill still stands located on the footpath towards Bush. Poughill mill was described in 1972 as having a slate floor with ten millstones of various shapes and sizes embedded in it. Part of the building was formed of timbers of wrecked ships from along the coastline.

At the heart of the village is St Olaf's church, named after the Danish St Olave. Built in the 14th century, with some parts being older, it is square towered. It seems to have a motherly position as the cottages nestle close to it as if for comfort. An interesting feature of the church is the wall frescos, which were rediscovered in 1894. Its other points of interest include a memorial to Sir Goldsworthy Gurney in a tablet above the main entrance.

Sir Goldsworthy Gurney, born near Padstow in 1793, was an inventor, and lived in a house named Reeds in the village. He built a manorial size house on sand dunes in 1850 at Bude because he wanted to prove a house could be built on sand and he achieved this by building on a concrete bed for the foundation. He also invented the 'Gurney Stove' for the form of heating to keep this large house warm for family living. It was a private house until 1942 when it was bought by Bude and Stratton Urban District Council, and is to this day the town council offices. He was also the father of incandescent lighting and invented the

Bude light which was used in lighthouses for a century, and was a flashing beam signal. He superintended the lighting and heating of the Houses of Parliament.

The famous battle of Stamford Hill was fought in the parish on 16th May 1643, when 2,500 of Charles I's men fought the Roundheads. There is a copy of a letter of thanks from Charles I from his address at Sudeley Castle, on the church wall at Poughill.

The people of Poughill were called 'Cuckoos'. Legend has it that the villagers would attempt to wall-in the first cuckoo of spring. From this came the annual 'Cuckoo Revels' held in the summer. The event was started in the late 1920s to finance the building of the village hall, which is dated 1932.

There are some very old houses in Poughill. Burshill Manor is proven medieval and is listed as an open hall house; another old house is Church House dated 1525.

🍁 PRAZE-AN-BEEBLE

Praze-an-Beeble literally translated from Cornish means 'praze' – meadow and 'beeble' – culvert, 'meadow with a culvert in it'. There is a stream running through the village which is called the Beeble and for the most part it is visible along the edges of the fields but a part is culverted past the pub through the Square (under the main road) which one assumes is the original meadow with the culvert in it, hence the name.

The village, apart from being at the centre of the farming community, used to be a hive of industry and although there has been a decline in such industry with the increase in residential development, commercial life is now on the increase. The village today sustains a general store, newsagent's, post office (which has been run by the same family for many years), garage, petrol station, pasty (baker's) shop, agricultural merchant, time-share exchange, ornamental iron worker, hairdresser's, sandwich shop, video shop and fish and chip shop. The video shop helped Praze to set up its own Internet web site (www.praze.org.uk).

Crowan is the site of the parish church which serves the village and was the original site of the village school. There used to be two Methodist chapels in the village, one at the top of Fore Street and the other in the middle. The top chapel closed some 30 years ago and the central Methodist chapel closed in 1999. Praze Male Voice Choir was formed in 1924 by a group of enthusiastic local lads to raise money for oil for the street lighting in the village. Praze is fortunate in having a village institute which provides a meeting place and is home for the playgroup and mother and toddler group; Praze Women's Institute also meets there. Sports activities in Praze include cricket and football teams. Praze Fair Show week takes place every July and includes a carnival, flora dance, horticultural show and gymkhana.

Bordering the village is the Clowance estate and mansion house which was owned by the St Aubyn family until about 1919 when death duties forced its sale. They now live at Pencarrow, Bodmin. The estate covered some 6,000 acres with dozens of tenant farmers who gave their loyalty and work to the family and land. In the 1830s the Molesworth-St Aubyns launched what must rank as the very first Job Creation Scheme. Mining was in one of its periodic slumps and hundreds of miners were out of work, their families hungry, so many of them were hired to build a very grand – but totally unnecessary – wall, five miles long, encircling the Clowance estate, some of which still stands. In 1786 the Molesworth-St Aubyns arranged for Messrs Head and Johns, apothecaries of Camborne, to treat the sick of Crowan parish at Sir John Aubyn's expense. The estate is now a timeshare development and well maintained. The village pub is called the St Aubyns Arms.

The village has more than doubled in size in the past 20 years and although a number of residents work locally or on surrounding farms the majority commute to work in outlying towns. A number of service personnel from RNAS Culdrose live in the village.

🍁 PROBUS

Probus, or Lamprobus, was the seat of a Celtic monastery ('Canons of St Probus' were mentioned in the Domesday Book). It was afterwards re-established as a collegiate church but in 1242 Bishop Briwere decided to abolish the college and devote its revenues to the Treasury. Because the church, tradition says, was founded by a king (King Athelstan AD 925-940) its choir is allowed to wear red cassocks. It has the right of sanctuary, one of only five Cornish churches with that privilege. The church tower, carved of St Stephen's granite is, at 125 ft 10 inches, the highest in Cornwall.

The first steam threshing machine was built in Probus in 1811 by Richard Trevithick for Sir Christopher Hawkins and is now in the Science Museum in London.

Trewithen, the local manor house, was built over the period 1723-1775 on the site of an older house. It is not only a fine country house of that period but has world famous gardens. The Hawkins family were at Trewithen for many years and the village pub, the Hawkins Arms, has certainly been named after them.

The estate descended to a nephew of the Hawkins family, Mr George H.

Johnstone, and the squires of Probus, both Hawkins and Johnstone, have been great benefactors to the village. The Cornwall Education Committee Demonstration Garden is on former Trewithen land.

Near Truck Hill, on Trelowthas land, there was once a tucking mill and Probus has also had at various times, to name but a few, rope-making and basket-making industries, a soap factory, malthouses and a workhouse.

The eminent Probus school was demolished to make way for housing. Lewman Road in the village (leading off the appropriately named College Close), was named after a beloved headmaster. One of Probus school's greatest treasures was a signed photograph of Scott of the Antarctic. It was given to the school in thanks for the money they sent to help with the expedition. One of the sledges on the expedition was called Probus School.

Nowadays the very large population (about 2,000) works mostly outside the village, in either St Austell or Truro. A few are employed by the meat packers which occupy the abattoir site, near to which was the now demolished toll gate where John Wesley halted, but did not stop to preach.

There are still two flourishing village shops, the local garage and post office, and the village also benefits from three restaurants, a fish and chip shop, a pub and a social club. Although it would seem, because of this, that Probus people spend their lives eating and drinking, there are many groups in the village which have growing memberships. The old Methodist chapel is now a second-hand furniture shop.

🍁 QUINTRELL DOWNS

Four roads converging onto a roundabout, an unmanned level crossing, busy roads, a busy shop, a petrol depot, an enormous shop selling jewellery, a busy garage, a printer's, a steak house, a country club and lots and lots of new houses. This is the Quintrell Downs of today – quite different from the Quintrell Downs of over 20 years ago.

The name Quintrell comes from the French meaning fop or dandy and dates back 600 years. The Downs is the area to the south of what is the Two Clomes Country Club – this area was called the common. The village is surrounded by three farms – Trethiggey, Trewollack and Bejowan and all of these can be traced back at least 200 years.

As far back as can be remembered the Downs of the common area was the 'village' and there were twelve cob houses in the area of the Magda Park camping site. Five of these were up Wherry's Lane – the back lane going off the bridle path which runs through the Downs.

The inn was called the Union and was very different from the current building, as it was a cottage-sized house with a large 'brew house' adjacent. People from the clay works area and Redruth used to rest at the pub. A Mr Trudgian and his daughter Nellie used to run the pub and they also provided a service for food. The next building was the chapel (this is now the printer's). Treviglas Farm and buildings were opposite. For many years the cows were brought along the road to the buildings for milking.

There used to be a brickworks in the field adjoining the recreation ground. This was built around 1910 by a Mr Thomas who made a substantial number of bricks at this time but six months later he died.

The village had a growth period in the 1930s, houses appearing above the railway line on the way to Newquay and also from the chapel eastwards. In the late 1940s buildings were restricted for want of materials, growth started but was very slow.

The advent of the sewerage system brought about a rapid increase in the number of houses in the late 1960s, which was accelerated by the granting of planning permission for Treviglas Farm in the 1970s and other areas. Today there is still considerable building in the Treviglas area, the number of houses in the village now totalling more than 400.

Years ago people in the village knew exactly where everyone lived, only in recent years have houses with numbers on them come about. Such is the growth of Quintrell Downs that it has been likened to a suburb of Newquay, but thankfully that day is a long way off.

🍁 ROCHE

The village of Roche, situated in mid-Cornwall, derives its name from a remarkable mass of rock, known far and wide as 'Roche Rock'. The parish of Roche stands well above sea level and is surrounded by moorland wastes; on the south by the Hensbarrow downs, where on a clear day it is possible to see both the north and south coasts, on the west and the north by the Goss and Tregoss Moors.

As Cornish villages go, Roche is now considered to be a large village. In the last decade many houses have been built, and estates sprung up. Roche is blessed with good shops – an excellent butcher's, supermarket, wool shop, two greengrocers, a post office, fish and chip shop, Chinese takeaway, a baker's, two hairdressers, launderette, and a newsagent's too.

In days gone by there were three fairs in a year; May, July and October. These were mainly where cattle and horses were bought and sold. They were held in the mornings – then later in the day would be the 'pleasure fair', with the wonderful fair organ playing. This used to be held in the field at the rear of the school. The fore street would be lined with (standings) stalls, where one could buy home-made sweets, toffee apples and cheap jewellery! The school is at the top of the hill and a field opposite is the 'school field' where the school sports take place and all the outdoor activities. Alongside the school field is the recreation ground, which was given to the village by a Mr Bennett.

At one time there were seven places for worship, now there are just three – the parish church and two Methodist chapels. Feast Week was always held in June. After the two chapels had their Sunday school anniversaries would come Feast Sunday; this was followed in the week, starting with first Tremodrett, then Trefaise, then Roche chapels, by a faith tea. Then came a procession around the village with banners and a band heading the teachers and scholars of the Sunday schools. Church Feast was the highlight of the week when after the tea there was dancing on the Rectory lawn.

The main occupation for the inhabitants of the village is based on the clay. The waste tips from the clay are now being landscaped, thus beautifying the area. Farming too plays a large part in employment, and a new industrial estate at Victoria Roche has provided jobs.

Roche Rock is a very famous landmark. Ladders will get you up to the top of the Rock where, as legend has it, a 'hermit lived'. Again legend says his daughter took him food and water from a well found amongst small rocks. Tregeagle too was supposed to have sought refuge in the hermit's cell. He was given the task of emptying the Dozmary Pool with a leaking limpet shell, was chased by the Devil and found refuge at the top of the Rock.

🍁 ROSE

Rose is a small village in the parish of Perranzabuloe, between Goonhavern and Perranporth. The name is thought by many older scholars to come from the Cornish word 'ros', meaning heath or moorland, because much of the land was just that.

It used to be said, though, that true Rosillians believed that many years ago their ancestors had lived in the sand dunes. One night, during a violent storm, the village was overwhelmed with sand and almost all of the inhabitants died. The survivors moved a mile or so inland and built a new village which they called Rose, because, they said, it rose from the sand. In all their celebrations they used a red rose as their symbol.

More recently the idea has been put forward that the name comes from a

Celtic word meaning circle or wheel, because of the ancient earthwork known as Perran Round. This has been a focal point of religious and social life in the village for over 2,000 years. It has been described as Britain's oldest theatre and has been the location for fetes, markets, tea treats, wrestling matches, political meetings and the Cornish Gorsedd, which has been held there several times since its revival in 1928.

During the Middle Ages miracle plays, written in the Cornish language and telling the story of the Bible and the Cornish saints, were performed there. It is thought that in the Middle Ages the 'Devil's Frying Pan' was used as Hell and because of this a tradition has arisen that if you run round the Frying Pan seven times and put your ear to the ground in the middle of it, you can hear the Devil frying.

During the Dark Ages, the heyday of the Celtic Christian church, a road passed through the Round and on to St Piran's oratory in the sand dunes, which had become a place of pilgrimage. The first pilgrims were mainly local, but later pilgrims came from all the Celtic countries. Now known as 'The Lost Church', because for many years it was covered by sand and rediscovered first in 1790, it is thought to have been built by St Piran and his followers in about AD 500. A concrete cover was built over it in 1907 because of the encroaching sand once again, and in 1981 it was buried in order to preserve it for future generations.

A story is told of the Methodist minister from Truro on one of his pastoral visits to Rose, who noticed that the curtains were drawn in every house he passed. Thinking there had been a death in the village, he asked on his first visit who this could be so that he could meet the family and pray with them. He was told, 'Tedn't nothing like that, maister, just a boat load o'candles washed up on the beach last week and now 'tis cheaper to burn candles than daylight.' To a hard-up mining community this cargo was like striking gold.

Conditions were particularly hard in the 1860s. Many miners went to work with just a slice of dry barley bread. One man was so concerned by what he saw that he ploughed up one small field that he had, and filled it with parsley. This was done to 'slock' (attract) the rabbits from nearby Penhale and Gear Sands so that the miners and their families could trap them for food. This is still known as Parsley Field.

For many years Rose was a self sufficient community with mining as the main industry. Over the years villagers mined copper, tin, zinc, lead, iron and small quantities of silver. During the heyday of mining the village had four shops, two pubs, a bakery and a shoemaker, and a population of about 1,400.

Today the village has become a dormitory for people working in Perranporth and Truro, and a haven for the retired. It has no shop, no pub, and all the traces of its once flourishing industries are buried under the tents and caravans of the thousands of tourists who visit it each year.

🍁 RUMFORD

A stream bisects the village of Rumford, the original ford across the waterway giving the village its name – Rum, meaning wide. Perhaps ancient man who erected the Long Stone at Music Water where the stream rises, only a mile away, used the rum-ford.

The stream with its wide ford, no doubt stimulated the original settlement and work for the inhabitants. On its short hastening course to the sea at Porthcothan, the stream once provided power for at least three corn mills, one of which was upstream of the ford. The mills were working until about 1850. The present stone bridge was built around 1860.

Other industries also owe their origin to the important crossing. A carrier firm has progressed with industrial technology from ox waggons and carts to modern lorries. And the present agricultural engineers started as blacksmiths and wheelwrights. The early wheelwright's lathe was turned by a succession of small boys and the carrier's housed the first steam driven threshing machine in the locality. The machine, known as the 'Black Maria', had previously been dragged from farm to farm by horses. At one time a saw-pit was situated near the middle of the village. In the early 1900s the village supported two shoemakers, two carpenters and two blacksmiths. These services were used by the many small farms in the area.

Sugar beet was grown on a large scale in the First World War. In the 1950s a particular strain of grass seed called Cornish Eaver was sown. The growing of broccoli developed as a speciality, using home produced seed in the 1930s and continues today.

The most the village has ever boasted is three shops – and no inn. The present Methodist church united two nonconformist chapels. One of the shops in the 1930s was a chemist's owned by Mr Astley Chattock. This well remembered gentleman was responsible for dispensing pills and potions and even drawing teeth. He peddled his wares around neighbouring parishes on a tricycle and is reputed to have concluded every conversation with the words, 'Oh! my giddy aunt!'

Today the hub of the village revolves round the sub post office and stores. A post-bus journeys daily across the bridge and up Primrose Hill to the market town of Wadebridge. Away from major roads and holiday routes, Rumford continues to enjoy a rural charm where the Music Water stream hurries down to the sea.

❧ St Anthony in Meneage

There is a tradition that the church was built as an offering of some shipwrecked Normans who came shore safely at this spot. The church, derelict in the 19th century, was restored in 1890 and is now well supported and maintained. There is an ancient well in a corner of the churchyard.

The Dennis, the headland between the Helford river and Gillan creek, was a Royalist fortress in the time of the Civil War. The last battle of the war is said to have been fought in the area.

Once a farm, the buildings around the church have been tastefully converted to holiday homes and there is a thriving sailing, boat hire and chandlery business on the shore. The creek, now silted up, was once used by barges carrying grain, coal, fertilizer, etc up to the mill at Carne.

The Bosahan estate boasts sub-tropical gardens and is occasionally open to the public. The present house was built in the 1950s on the site of an old mansion.

Trewothack on the south side of the creek, once housed a monastery for both monks and nuns in Celtic times. Boden Veor was mentioned in the Domesday Book. In 1743 Mr Anthony Hosken of Lanne (Lannarth) gave an annuity of £4 charged on the estate of Boden Veor for the purpose of teaching the children of the poor to read and write. This money is still paid and through an arrangement with a local shop, some children get a discount on shoes. Roskruge Barton is an Elizabethan house with an imposing entrance. The beacon nearby is the highest point on the Lizard peninsula and on a clear day you can see Rame Head (East Cornwall). An Armada fire would have been lit there and in more recent times to celebrate mid-summer and historic events. At Lannarth Farm there is an ancient thatched cart house.

Most of the modern development is at Gillan and Flushing the south side of the creek. Tregildry, the one hotel in the area, has panoramic views across Falmouth bay.

❧ ST BREWARD

St Breward, named after St Branwalader, lies at the edge of Bodmin Moor, a long, straggling village, descending from the windswept church at the top of the hill to Wenford tucked away in the valley. Until comparatively recent times it was composed of small groups of houses spaced out at intervals over a length of nearly two miles. The oldest part started round the church, built nearly ten centuries ago, and includes the pub which claims to be 'the highest in Cornwall'. The middle section expanded greatly in the latter part of the 19th century, in the heyday of the granite quarries which employed hundreds of men. During the last 20 years, in a great flurry of building, the gaps have been filled and houses and bungalows hug the road all the way down, shooting off into side roads and cul de sacs.

The chief employment for the village in times past was provided by the three quarries, the clay industry and by farming. Clay has been mined on the moors since the beginning of the century and the Dryers at Wenford were opened just a bit later. In the early days this was grim work, for the clay was dried by means of under-floor heating of such intensity that the men, despite their heavy wooden clogs, would find their socks burned and their feet blistered. One of the quarries, the clay pit and dries still exist, but, with the aid of machinery, a few can now do the work of many.

People can remember a time when you could buy just about everything needed in the village itself. There was a shoemaker and a hat shop; a sweet shop, run by a blind man, who could put his hand on any of his stock without hesitation (unless his wife moved things!); a fish and chip shop; a blacksmith's; and several general stores. Today St Breward can still boast a post office and a general store.

Cars didn't appear until the 1930s and horse-drawn vehicles were the means of transport, or Shanks' pony. The roads were unmetalled, and in various places throughout the village men would sit, with sacking over the shoulders and round their waists, surrounded by immense piles of stones which they patiently broke up with a hammer into small pieces for use by the road-menders.

Two figures have disappeared from village life: the local 'bobby', a comforting presence and the scourge of small boys bent on mischief; and the district nurse, the best remembered of whom is Nurse Crahart, who died at a ripe old age in the early 1960s. Several generations were brought into the world by Nurse Crahart. In her early days she travelled to her patients by horse and trap. Later she acquired a car, but at first was none too sure of the procedure for stopping it. Coming down hill from Churchtown, she failed to apply the brakes and called out instead. 'Whoa there! Whoa!' to the car which rolled heedlessly on into a wall. This busy lady also found the time to knit the socks for the football team, which still plays in the local league. The team now have a smart new social club house on the edge of their ground, which has proved very popular and is packed to the doors on Saturday nights.

Many newcomers have settled here over the past 25 years, some to retire and some to work. There are those in the village who travel to jobs in the surrounding towns, and there are those who work from home or who have started businesses locally, showing a wide range of skills. A recent craft exhibition demonstrated just how much talent and creativeness there is in the village, which, though greatly changed, still thrives as a community.

🍁 ST BURYAN

St Buryan is situated five miles from Land's End and is steeped in history, dating back to 2000 BC. Bronze Age people lived here in 1700-1600 BC. They erected two stone circles – the Merry Maidens and Boscawen-un circle. The first-ever Cornish Gorsedd was held at the Boscawen-un circle and there are more Cornish crosses in St Buryan than any other parish.

The patron saint, St Buriana, was an Irish virgin saint and she made an oratory at St Buryan where King Athelstan and his army rested after a battle against the Danes in AD 931. The next morning the king made his communion in the oratory and vowed if he conquered the last remaining Danish stronghold on the Isles of Scilly he would build a church on the site of the oratory. The expedition was successful, a church was built and because of its Royal Charter the church choir wear red cassocks.

The present church was built in the late 15th or early 16th century, but the tower, which is 92 ft high, is of 14th century work and houses what are believed to be the four heaviest bells in the world. The treble bell weighs nine cwts (1681), the second eleven cwts (1676), the third 14 cwts (1738) and the tenor bell 21 cwts (1901). These have all recently been rehung and were pealed for the first time for 90 years in February 1991. There is also a beautiful rood screen in the church which depicts an unusual hunting scene.

St Buryan Feast is held on the Sunday nearest the 13th May and is still celebrated vigorously each year with special services in the parish church and Methodist chapel. A cricket match, clay pigeon shoot, bazaar and concerts as well as special entertainment on Feast Monday for the children is arranged annually.

John Wesley visited and preached at St Buryan on three occasions and the first chapel was built in 1783. A new and larger chapel, built on a different site in 1832, remained in use until it was badly damaged by storms in 1979 and replaced by a modern one opened in 1981.

The present village hall was used as a deanery school in 1801, the earliest recorded school in the village, and has always been the centre of village activity.

The drill hall was built for training army volunteers but from the mid-1940s it was the village blacksmith's shop until 1989, when it was converted into four dwellings (Pengelly Court).

The present blacksmith was commissioned to make five pairs of wrought iron gates for the entrance to a military cemetery in America. The gates cost about £26,000 to make and each pair measured 15 ft high by 18 ft wide.

In 1914 a typhoid epidemic broke out in the village and this was traced to water from a local well. Fifty people were affected and six died.

Boskenna is the largest local manor and was the home of the Paynter family. It was also the first house in the county to have electricity.

William Noye, who was Member of Parliament for the St Ives constituency in 1625, was born at Pendrea in 1577 and later became Attorney-General to Charles I. Legend tells that Charles II hid at Burnewhall before fleeing to France at the end of the Civil War and Queen Catherine of Braganza, Portugal also visited Burnewhall on her way to marry the King in 1662.

A school was built in the village in 1910 and is still used today. Other buildings include a post office, village store, hairdressing salon and a public house, but before 1900 St Buryan had two public houses, a bowling alley, two blacksmith's and a pound for stray cattle. Each year horse and greyhound races were held, the horseracing being started by the ringing of a ship's bell. A ploughing match was held each Easter Monday. This thriving village is still expanding and has recently had 26 houses built by the council for first-time buyers as well as several for senior citizens.

❦ St Columb Minor

St Columb Minor was a place of importance in the days when Newquay, which it embraced, was just a small fishing village. Now St Columb Minor is a part of Newquay.

The village name, appearing over the years as Lower St Columb, Nether St Columb and St Columb the Little, stems from the legend of St Columba, the daughter of an Irish king who sailed to Cornwall to escape marriage with a pagan prince. She landed at Porth Island and was chased through the forest, now Porth Beach. The prince captured her and cut off her head. Where her blood fell, a spring appeared and formed the river which flows to Porth.

In the Domesday Book, we find Rieltone and Trelloi, the two manors in this parish. Rieltone was the largest manor in Pydar Hundred and until the Reformation was owned by the monks of Bodmin Priory. Prior Vivian enlarged and beautified the house in the early 16th century. After the Restoration it was granted to the Godolphins and Sidney Godolphin became Viscount Rialton. Much of the house was destroyed by fire in the 18th century. It is now owned by the Duchy of Cornwall and privately occupied. The garden is beautiful with a holy well in the old courtyard.

The other manor, Trelloi, is now a farm, and in its orchard is the famous holy well of St Pedyr. Down in the centre of the village are the church, the inn and very old cottages. Honeysuckle Cottage, a listed building was a farmhouse in the early 17th century and ships' timbers were used in its construction. Although three quarters of a mile from the sea at Porth, there are several former smugglers' cottages and it is known one smuggler was shot by a soldier in 1741. In about 1842, Rev Chudleigh found his horse steaming and a keg of brandy in his stable – hire for the horse!

Before Celtic missionaries came to build a wooden church, it is believed an ancient barrow, site of pagan rites, existed here. In 1100 a Norman church was built but the present church dates from around 1430. It has the second highest tower in Cornwall, a landmark for generations of fishermen. The font is in memory of James Carne, 'the Parish Clerk for 64 years who with his father and grandfather filled that office successively for 163 years'. He died in 1909 aged 103. This may be the same James Carne who used to lead the choir up the aisle with his flute. Later were added a clarinet, bass viol and cornopean. The lads practised in the parlour of the Farmers' Arms for an hour before the service and were known as Nebuchadnezzar's Band.

Opposite the church is the Farmers' Arms where in October 1913 a boy threw a sparkler which set alight the thatched roof. Newquay Fire Brigade were soon on the scene and connected to a hydrant. When St Columb Major firemen arrived, after rushing six miles with their horse-drawn pump, they were told not to use the mains water so they resorted to pumping from an old quarry. Newquay firemen, unwilling to share their fire, turned their hoses on them and their rivals retaliated with muddy water which ruined Newquay's uniforms. Poor Samuel Argall, the innkeeper for 42 years, watched his inn burn down while firemen played hoses on each other. During the rebuilding, a slate tombstone was found upside down in the kitchen floor.

Burton's Stile dates from 1857. Burton was a pedlar who, after falling here with crocks on his head, gave up alcohol and later built the stile as a warning against strong drink.

The recreation ground, where the village football teams play, was given to the inhabitants by Judge Bingham of Kentucky, USA, American Ambassador. He was a friend of Rev Paul, the vicar, and wanted to do something for the parish. Another benefactor was Dr 'Willie' Stephens, a great friend to the village both as a doctor who made no charge to its working people and as a noted antiquary who researched its history. His memorial inscription reads, 'The beloved Physician'.

In 1894 the urban part of St Columb Minor was created a civil parish and renamed Newquay. Of the 1,000 or so villagers at that time, many were farmers and traders, but there were also blacksmiths, a horse-breaker, wheelwright, maltster, shipowner and shoemakers. Later, employment was provided by the five quarries which were here, one of which supplied the stone for St Michael's church, Newquay. Many people started taking in tourists, but in more recent years, visitors have tended to stay nearer Newquay centre. Residents now work mostly in hotels and shops in Newquay, in the service industries, at RAF St Mawgan or travel to other towns. The present population is about 2,500.

There is still a community spirit and a village life but few now remain of the once close inter-marrying village folk nicknamed 'Bradleys'.

🍁 Sᴛ Dᴀʏ

The name St Day derives from a Breton saint who was a bishop in the year AD 655, and was known as the Happy Saint.

The area was once known as the richest square mile in the world. This was because of the tin mines, where most of the local men worked, as well as young girls who were known as bal maidens. But, with the drop in the price of tin after the 1920s, many of the mines closed. This depression left its mark. In 1968, the mines were started again, but were successful for only a few years. Wheal Jane and South Crofty were the only ones to keep producing, but they were finally closed on 25th February 1991.

Also, in those early days, there were 17 public houses in the St Day area serving the thirsty miners. Nine of these pubs were in St Day village itself. Now there are only two.

St Day Brickworks, making fine bricks and tiles, was founded in 1860, and closed in 1912. A sports ground now covers this site. St Day also had a workhouse. This was on the site of what is now Burnwithian Terrace.

The St Day clock was erected in 1821, when a market was held each Saturday with live animals, as well as local produce, being sold. At one time the base of the clock was used as the local gaol for one-night prisoners.

Once, there were at least seven places of worship in the village, and John

Wesley visited the district no less than 17 times between 1743 and 1789. Alas, now there is only the Methodist church at North Corner, and Holy Trinity at Church Street, but both are well attended.

A well-known village landmark is Vogue Shute, which once supplied the whole area with drinking water at the nominal price of one penny per pitcher from the local barrel vendor.

The Feast of St Day is still the most important day of the year in the life of the village. Feast Day is held three weeks after Whitsun each year and dates from the laying of the foundation stone of the old church (approximately 1826). Unfortunately, the celebration almost died, but was brought back to life on the 18th June 1928 with the opening of the playing field. An old St Day boy, W.J. Mills, gave a lump sum of money to be invested and the interest used for a tea for the old folk, and a bun and a shilling for the children on Feast Day. Also, a Christmas gift for the poor and elderly. Mr Mills bought Simmons Street for the elderly of the village. On the 3rd July 1933, Simmons Street was officially opened and renamed Mills Street.

Nowadays, most livings, apart from shopkeepers, carpenters, farmers, etc are earned at nearby industrial estates and towns, but St Day is still an excellent place in which to live. There are many local organisations to join, and always someone ready to raise money for the various charities in the area which are in need.

🍁 ST DENNIS

The roots of St Dennis go deep into the past. It is understood that St Denys' church is the only church in south-west England built on the site of a fortified Iron Age settlement. 'Dinas' is Cornish for fort. It stands on a conical hill above the village and part of the fortification remains. Around this hill, Carne Hill, are massive 'hedges' built of huge stones, presumably from remains and clearance of the hut dwellings of the Iron Age community, making a patchwork of small fields.

The parish church, over 600 ft above sea level, is tree fringed and has a Norman tower and arch. Outside by the south door stands a Cornish cross. The interior and roof were completely destroyed by fire in May 1985. It has been restored carefully in a pleasing style, the woodwork and beams in Columbian pine. The stained glass windows were restored from previous photographs.

Around the village is the industrial heartland of the china clay industry, the economic life of this area with its dereliction and fascination of open cast mining – pits, tips and pools. Environmentalists watch this landscape which

The Village Pump, St Dennis

dominates the skyline in places, while the clay companies are seeding and planting, attempting to keep the air clean and the tips stable. The village is termed an 'island' settlement for planning purposes – no industrial development inside and no encroachment from outside.

The Goss Moor nature reserve is the largest wetland site in Cornwall. It has been affected by tin-streaming and mining leaving numerous pools and streams forming tributaries of the river Fal – with dry and wet heathland, grasslands, swamps and dense willow thickets. This area is a Site of Special Scientific Interest – one of the most important wildlife habitats in Cornwall. On farmland adjacent to the moor some hedges date from pre-Saxon times and are managed and retained, tall and dense, to provide rich sources of food and cover for wildlife while maintaining landscape features and shelter for cattle and sheep to graze. There are two places alongside the farmland and moors recorded in the Domesday Book; Marsalen – Carsella, Dimililoc – Domellick.

The village homes and buildings are diverse in character, style and period. Undoubtedly the oldest are those showing they once had open chimneys, hearth fires, and the Cornish clome ovens. Several are seen along Hendra Road, Fore Street and Trelavour Square built of granite some 200 years ago. These were farmhouses or cottages of smallholders with a few acres of land as a sideline to tin or clay mining, so common in Cornwall. There are examples of homes with lovely dressed granite fronts, single and terraced, dating back into the 19th century. A manor house named Hall is tucked away beside the low Commercial Hotel at Trelavour Square, and there, too, is the 'gallows field'.

Providence chapel, now a carpet store, is dated 1836. The Arundel Trust in 1859 built a village school; now the church school. The council school came later in 1905. In the playground is a small garden of trees put there by the then headmaster unofficially as a memorial to those of the school who went to war in 1939. The blacksmith's shop has closed but a metal disc outside lies flat where untold cartwheels were clad. Long gone the organ maker but his fine organs remain, one at Hendra Road chapel. Gone also the saddler, watch maker and cinema, but not the post office, pharmacy, bakery, newsagency and village shops or parish council.

For the Millennium, St Dennis Parish Council erected a Celtic Cross on 'Freda's Triangle' and a sundial on Trelavour Prazey. And the future? A population way over 2,000 – about 850 homes – and predictions of the clay industry going the way of Cornish tin-mining! Only time can tell.

🍁 St Dominick

St Dominick is said to derive its name from a young Irish nun, St Dominica, who with her brother St Indract and seven companions came up the river Tamar in about AD 689 to Halton Quay and founded a religious settlement at the site now known as Chapel Farm and where a holy well still exists. A tiny consecrated chapel stands at the water's edge at the quay and this is used for outdoor services on Sunday evenings in the summer months. The parish church, which is dedicated to St Dominica, dates from 1259 and the more modern parts are built on the original 13th century building. It has been the centre of village activities for many years, and a patronal feast is still held every year at the beginning of May. Until recently there were two thriving Methodist churches, one of which, Trinity church, was sadly closed after being badly damaged in the gales of 1990, but Ebenezer church is still very active.

One of the oldest houses is Halton Barton, down near Halton Quay. Sir Francis Drake is reputed to have fought a duel there. It was owned at one time by Sir Anthony Rous, who was High Sheriff of Cornwall and lord of the manor of Halton, and the tomb of Sir Anthony and his son, Ambrose, is in St Dominick church.

The village of St Dominick with the neighbouring hamlet of Bohetherick is today very different from the rather isolated self-contained village which existed at the turn of the 20th century. In those days few people left the village as everything that was needed was on the spot. The main occupations were farming, growing fruit, vegetables and flowers, and, apart from running the small shops which provided for everyone's needs, most of the inhabitants were involved in these. The Tamar valley strawberries and cherries were always far earlier than those from other parts of the country and considered to be superior in flavour. Everyone joined in the main harvesting, the children being given time off school to participate, and the produce was sent to Devonport market down the river from Halton quay. Few cherries are now grown as labour is not available, although there are still plenty of strawberry growers – often selling their fruit on a 'pick-your-own' basis.

In the 1920s Fred Rogers (a member of one of the old village families) started manufacturing flower and fruit boxes for transporting produce to Covent Garden market. Growers began to raise new varieties, often depicted in many of the paintings by Mary Martin, a well-known local artist, who paints from life almost exclusively within this parish. She is also preserving the older varieties of apples, such as American Mother, and cherries (including the Burcombe cherry). Primroses were once prized by the women and children of the village who picked hundreds of bunches for market, especially for Primrose Day, 19th April, and Mothering Sunday.

The northern end of the village, known as Churchtown, near the parish church has changed most, with many new houses being built, but the one part of the village which is almost unchanged is the hamlet of Bohetherick. The properties were part of the Cotehele estate belonging to the Earls of Mount Edgcumbe and were provided for the workers on the estate. The beautiful medieval fortified manor stands high on the banks of the Tamar with its own historic quay and ancient watermill. It is now the property of the National Trust, having been handed over by the sixth Earl in lieu of death duties. Villagers remember the Earl from wartime days with his big bushy beard, which he had vowed not to shave off until the war was won. Cotehele is still a good source of employment in the village and the influx of visitors from all over the world adds to the prosperity here.

There is now only one public house in the village – the Who'd Have Thought It. This was originally the Butchers Arms, but was known locally as the 'Sheffield' (pronounced 'Sheffel' by the locals) because when St Dominick Fair was held in front of it, men used to come and sell Sheffield cutlery. The bar was used as a courtroom on one occasion for a murder trial. It is possible to get a good view of Plymouth and the Tamar bridge from the pub, and many villagers remember watching the raids on Plymouth during the Second World War.

The village is lucky to have a thriving post office and general store, owned by Nesta Martin (another of the old families) – the place to go to find out what's happening.

❧ ST ERME WITH TRISPEN

St Erme with Trispen is a village situated four miles north of Truro alongside the A39. It is the centre of a large agricultural parish set between the parishes of St Clement, St Allen, Ladock and Probus. It is watered by the St Allen river on its western boundary and by the Trevella stream flowing north to south across the centre. In 1960 the population was under 400, today the number has practically trebled. This marked increase is due mainly to a large estate built in the 1970s, which effectively joins the two separate hamlets of St Erme and Trispen.

St Erme and Trispen were once two separate entities, St Erme having the church, the school and the village hall and Trispen claiming the pub, the post office and the chapel. The old rectory has been converted into a home for autistic sufferers. Trispen Inn and the post office and village stores are the sole survivors of a number of traditional village businesses which thrived a century ago. Then there were two blacksmith's shops and a cycle repair shop as well as a carpenter's and wheelwright's and a cobbler's. There was also a local butcher, who slaughtered his own meat, and two little grocery shops – all situated in simple cottages mainly built of cob, with Cornish kitchen ranges and open chimneys.

In those days the men worked for the local squires who lived on the neighbouring farms, each with its small mansion. Today Trevella and Tregassow house the local 'gentry'. Trehane is the base for the village's biggest farming enterprise which is run by a single family. Today's residents no longer depend on the farms. They mostly work in Truro, and Trispen has become a dormitory village.

There are, of course, the usual village activities. A lively football team has been formed. There is also a long established Horticultural Society which holds its annual show in August. The church and the chapel continue to provide Christian witness and to organise jumble sales and harvest suppers. The church fete is one of the year's great days. The village also has a cricket club.

Let us not forget though those characters of yesteryear who have made St Erme known. One such was a Francis Carthew, who is reported to have died one night and mysteriously revived the following morning. This strange event took place in 1699. Another person of note was Cornelius Cardew who was rector of St Erme and headmaster of Truro's old grammar school in the early 19th century.

St Erme and Trispen has nothing spectacular or particularly beautiful to commend it, but it is a good community in which to live, offering its inhabitants pure country air, organisations to suit all ages and tastes and with a goodly share of friendly people with a welcoming spirit.

🍁 ST ERTH

The name is derived from St Ercus, to whom the church is dedicated. He was probably an Irish missionary who introduced Christianity to the area in the 6th century and died in AD 514. The original name of the village was Lanuthnoe.

There are several manor houses in and around St Erth village which are mainly run as farms and bed and breakfast accommodation. Trewinnard Manor is the home of Sir John Nott and his family. The manor house itself has a Queen Anne shell porch. There is also a coach from the estate which is now in Truro County Museum.

The parish church is late 14th and 15th century with a 20th century beautifully carved Lady chapel. The Methodist church is over 160 years old.

St Erth bridge, which spans the river Hayle, was for many years part of the main thoroughfare from Penzance to London. It was built in 1340 and widened in 1860.

The Star inn, a very popular meeting place for locals and visitors alike, was built in 1686. Parts of Mena House, adjoining the Star, are probably older still, this house was previously the New Inn which was a coaching house.

Local people of note include Davies Gilbert – born Davies Giddy, the son of the curate in 1767. When he married he took the surname of his wife. He was MP for Helston and Bodmin and became President of the Royal Society and also of the Royal Geological Society of Cornwall. He encouraged many new ideas and inventions and did much to help such men as Thomas Beddoes, Richard Trevithick and Humphry Davy (who he discovered in 1797). William Husband, 1823-1887, invented many things including boiler safety plugs, hydraulic and mining machinery. He also worked on the Severn tunnel and lies at rest in St Erth churchyard.

In May 1908 a young girl, Emily Tredrea, was murdered by her boyfriend William Hampton. Such a tragedy in a small village aroused much local interest and more than 1,000 people attended Emily's funeral. Her murderer was the last person to be hanged at Bodmin gaol.

The Feast of St Ercus is held on the Sunday nearest to 2nd November. In bygone days 'Feast' was celebrated for the whole week following this. Streets were decorated and filled with market stalls selling many things including sweets (or niceys), fairings, water pistols, whips and tops, etc. Concerts were arranged and there were visiting fairs. More recently celebrations have only taken place during the weekend and on Feast Monday.

Early in the 20th century great excitement was aroused by the visits of Sir Alan Cobham's Flying Circus. Everyone gazed in wonder at the low flying aircraft, wire supported wings, wing riding and other daredevil feats.

Occupations of the inhabitants of St Erth are varied. Latterly they were mainly farm and mine workers, but today there are no miners as all mines are closed because of the low price of tin. However people seem to like the remoteness of the village and travel many miles to their places of employment. The blacksmith has retired and the building is now a woodcraft workshop. There is now only the one post office and general store.

🍁 ST ERVAN

The little church in John Betjeman's poem, *Summoned by Bells* lies at the end of a shady lane, nestling on the side of a hill and proudly portrays both the bell and the poem in the belfry. St Ervan church was dedicated around 1210, the origin may however go back to an earlier Celtic saint. At the time of Betjeman's visit the tower, deemed unsafe, had been demolished. In 1955 the tower was rebuilt and three of the refurbished bells rehung. One other bell suffered some damage and now rests within the church.

Tucked away off the lane, the parish hall was built by voluntary labour in 1982. Like the rectory the village school is now in private use, the small belltower providing a clue to its previous life.

The leafy lane beyond the church plunges steeply down to end abruptly at a ford beside Millingworth mill. Powered by a leat from the hurrying stream, the mill ground wheat until around 1850. Beside the lane a spring bubbles up into an ancient well and overflows to feed the abundance of verdant ferns. At the time when the mill was supplying flour for local use, St Ervan had an annual fair on 10th October. An alehouse, known as the 'kiddlywink', served refreshment to the participants. The kiddlywink was however closed before St Ervan's cricket club played in a nearby field. In 1924 it is remembered that John Barton, the rector's son, was such a fast bowler that rival teams refused to accept any challenge.

The quiet of St Ervan Churchtown was interrupted in the Second World War when a Royal Naval Air Station operated on the edge of the parish. At present the airfield is used by the Cornwall Parachute Centre and free-fall parachutists perform more peaceful feats.

Those who follow Sir John Betjeman's journey today find St Ervan Churchtown much as it is described in his autobiographical poem. They may even see, as he did on that memorable day, 'large red admirals with outspread wings – basking on buddleia'. For the buddleia bush still blooms beside the little iron gate leading to the church.

🍁 St Gennys

The parish of St Gennys lies on a noble stretch of Cornwall's rockbound coast with cliffs rising to over 200 metres, the highest in Cornwall. It falls wholly within an area designated as of Outstanding Natural Beauty and much of its coastline is also classed as an area of Special Scientific Interest.

There are two sandy beaches, Crackington Haven with safe bathing and Strangles (a corruption of Strangehill – Strange being a 14th century family name). There is a public house close to the beach and a few holiday establishments. It lies at the end of a deep valley which divides the parish geographically into two and so consequently supports two thriving Methodist communities dating from the days of John Wesley, who was a frequent visitor here when George Thomson was the vicar.

Being of an independent nature the parishioners were always known as Wreckers and Wrestlers; the Gennys family were notorious wreckers as early as the 14th century, William and Robert being outlawed for their exploits but later pardoned. It used to be said that if you removed the wreckwood from St Gennys the houses would all fall down.

The church, restored in 1871, is of Celtic foundation and still has original Normal stonework in its structure. Sadly the oak bench ends were removed with only one or two being incorporated in the pulpit. The parish enthusiastically supports a silver band founded in 1908 which over the years has won many awards.

The parish has a number of hamlets but for topographical reasons has no central village, although the addition of a housing estate in 1970 has tended to centre activities on the south side of the parish. It supports only one post office and stores, namely at Crackington Haven, the St Gennys post office accentuating the problems in being situated outside the parish boundary.

St Germans

You will find the village of St Germans in the south-east corner of Cornwall, lying at the head of the tidal estuary from the Hamoaze and on the banks of the river Tiddy. Called Lanaled in Celtic times, by the 7th century it was known as St Germanus, possibly derived from Germanus, Bishop of Auxerre. The substantial Saxon church became the Cathedral of Cornwall and a priory was built. By the time of the Domesday survey the see had passed to Exeter. The church lands were divided and from Elizabethan times each priory had an MP until the Reform Act 1832.

In 1565 a Devon merchant, John Eliot, bought the priory of St Germans which became known as Port Eliot. In the 18th century diversion of the river in front of the house created an attractive wooded parkland. Although never available to the public in general, Port Eliot's gates have always been opened generously for village fetes, festivals and carnivals.

The church, in its present form, was built soon after 1066, the great west door being one of the finest Norman doorways in England. Sadly neglected after the Dissolution of the Monasteries, restoration work was completed in 1888 and 1893. The beautiful stained glass east window was designed by Burne Jones and William Morris & Co. A fine Methodist chapel was built in 1825. By 1968 the main building, being unsound, was demolished and present activities take place in the original Sunday school building.

Originally a busy fishing port, the heyday of St Germans' commercial activities on the river was in the 19th century. Lime kilns were already in existence but a new quay had to be built, the present one. Despite the advent of the railway the river remained important and barges plied their trade until 1950. Passengers and other goods went to London by train as the turnpike roads were costly. The railway viaduct enhanced the character of the quay. Originally wooden, it was replaced with local stone in 1908.

Built in 1583, the attractive almshouses were modernised in 1967 for six widows instead of the original twelve. The past generosity towards the poor is well-known, expressed today in great fund-raising efforts for charity. The Elliot Hall, a memorial to the Earl's eldest son, in 1911 replaced the old town hall. It provides an essential venue, as does the Masonic lodge next door, for the varied village activities.

Founded in 1647, the new purpose-built school opened in 1992 stands in a magnificent site and provides excellent facilities for village children and neighbouring areas.

Villagers are well catered for by a shop/post office, mobile vans, a charity shop, rural workshops, and the long established Eliot Arms.

A walk through St Germans reveals its hidden past – Fox Cottage of Quaker fame, the site of Nut-tree Square, the ancient churchyard, the smithy, the slaughterhouse and the river Slatterbourne which provided water for the medieval potters, the monks' fish ponds and their mills. A hermit's cave lies in Craggs Wood, reputedly Celtic.

St Germans is a mixture of old and young from all walks of life, professional, manual, naval, estate and dockyard. The influx of outside people has injected new life and a spirit of unity into the community.

🍁 St Hilary

St Hilary is the adopted name of a French pagan turned Christian in the 5th century AD. He was well educated and produced many religious books. The parish was very much under the influence of the chapel dedicated to St Michael on the Mount, and in the 12th century monks were brought to build the church. The first service was conducted by the prior from the Mount, and it was also confirmed by the Bishop of Exeter to the abbey on the Mount.

The longest serving vicar was Rev Thomas Pascoe, 1758-1814, who was the first to live in the vicarage. He also farmed the glebe land, and made a great contribution to what was known as St Hilary Churchtown. He planted many trees, including what is now known as The Avenue leading from the road to the church, alongside the public footpath and a parking area for horsedrawn carriages. In 1929 there was a great storm which wrecked The Avenue, and from which it has never recovered.

St Hilary Churchtown is now a small complex of houses, a farm, and of course the church. Previously there was a small school, a general shop and a wheelwright's and carpenter's shop, but most important – a public house, the Jolly Tinners, which served the miners on their way to and from Friendship and Penberthy mines. It used to have a board outside, now in the archives at the Mount, by John Tyzack. Painted on it were the words – Come all true Cornish boys walk in – here's brandy, beer, rum and gin to copper, fish and tin'. In the 1920s Rev B. Walke turned the pub into a children's home for deprived Londoners, and also some displaced persons were housed at the vicarage.

In 1927 the first outside broadcast from Cornwall came from the church when a Nativity play was performed, with local people as players.

The vicarage became a Land Army hostel prior to becoming a private hotel, and a new rectory was built in the grounds. The glebe land is let to a local farmer, and the farm is now a lovely house.

❧ ST ISSEY & LITTLE PETHERICK

It is not surprising that the adjoining parishes of St Issey and Little Petherick were founded by saints – the Saints Way from Padstow to Fowey passes through both. St Petroc, that much travelled saint to whom so many churches are dedicated throughout the West Country – and indeed in Brittany – lived at Little Petherick (or Nansfounteyn, the Fountain in the Valley) after leaving Padstow. St Issey was founded by St Yse (or St Ida), one of 24 children of the Welsh King Broccan, though whether the saint was male or female is still a matter of debate. He or she, too, must have 'got about a bit', being the co-founder with St Meva of Mevagissey and the founder of Plouisy in Brittany.

The industries of the parishes in the main have been those associated with Cornwall for centuries – farming, fishing and mining. Farming led to milling, and both parishes had several mills, including a tidal grist mill at Sea Mills in St Issey parish, which was in use for many years during the 18th and 19th centuries – harnessing the tides is not new! The remains of the old sea wall which trapped the tides can still be seen. One of the owners, a Mr Tregaskis, being a member of the Total Abstinence Society, attempted to persuade the people of Padstow to abolish the 'Obby 'Oss celebrations with the associated excesses by offering them an ox for roasting for seven years in lieu. He and his wife were driven out of town, and the 'Obby 'Oss remained. Two blacksmiths had workshops at St Issey, and the use of the sand and seaweed for fertilizers led to the establishment of several 'sanding roads' (which gave access to the foreshore) in both parishes.

Because of the proximity to the sea (many of the inhabitants being fishermen) much of the diet of the people was fish, which was for the most part plentiful and cheap. Fennel was therefore widely grown to eat with the fish, and many a dairy farmer in recent years has found his milk to be tainted with the pungent smell of the herb which his cows had found to be palatable.

Mining and quarrying have both been industries in the parishes, the former, mainly for copper, having been discontinued, while the latter is still of importance – the decorative stone being much in demand.

The Molesworth family of Pencarrow were for many years patrons of Little Petherick church, two of them being rectors, while Mr Athelston Riley, who became patron in 1898, was a great benefactor, providing the church with many vestments and ornaments and the village with a village hall. He is also remembered as being the author of the hymn *Ye watchers and ye Holy ones*, which is sung at every Coronation of the Sovereign.

St Issey church was called 'Eglos Cruk', The Church on the Mound, and 1990 saw the celebration of a church having been on the site for 800 years. Both parishes were thriving communities each with a school and chapel. Little Petherick school closed in 1910, the chapel in 1967.

The villages have one parish council; they encompass almost 20 hamlets, but still have a population of just over 600. Widespread but very much a community, family names found on old records are still 'on register', and several whole family groups live within the parish bounds. A number of 'incomers' of all age groups number among the residents, and have become part of the community, their help and skill being appreciated.

Now mainly a family farming area, diversifying into providing caravan camping and holiday sites in a few instances, tourism has become a secondary business; attracted by the beaches, walks and coastline of the Camel estuary. People who do not work locally follow a variety of professions in the surrounding towns. The mills have become homes and a guest house; the Mellingey mill is used as a willow workshop, and the stream for a trout farm, before running into the creek at Little Petherick. A woodcraftsman works from St Issey, and one farm is a shire horse complex. A modern village shop, post office, diary, antiques shop, two garages, guest houses and two inns are part of the village scene.

❧ St Ive

St Ive is a parish of scattered hamlets and farms between Liskeard and Callington. There are five manors listed in the Domesday Book – Bicton, Appledore, Haye, Woolston and Trebeigh. Trebeigh was owned by the Abbey of Tavistock until the Norman Conquest. In 1150 the King gave the manor and the patronage of the parish churches of St Ive and Temple, on Bodmin Moor, to the Knights Templar. In 1314 they were transferred to the Knights Hospitallers. Traces of their ownership can still be seen in the house and farm buildings at Trebeigh. A damaged Cornish cross from their time has been erected in the churchyard. The church has a fine royal coat of arms from 1660 and a sundial dated 1695. There are six bells which are regularly rung. Old church registers from 1683 are deposited at Truro record office.

A well known rector of St Ive was Reginald Hobhouse, who was the first Archdeacon of Bodmin. He built the Victorian rectory in 1852 with the architect William White. His youngest daughter, Emily, left St Ive when he died and went on to achieve international fame as an early human rights campaigner in the Boer War. In South Africa she is revered as a saintly heroine. She continued her work in Europe. A plaque marking her birthplace is attached to the rectory, now called The Chantry and a private house.

There is a fine medieval bridge called 'Newbridge' over the River Lynher. Note the granite hooks above the four arches on the upstream side. Here the monks suspended nets to catch their fish as these swam under the bridge.

Nearby is the most ancient feature of the parish, Cadsonbury, an Iron Age hill fort over 2,000 years old. It was constructed on the top of a prominent steep hill with a single large rampart and a ditch. There are panoramic views of the surrounding countryside.

The main road was constructed as a toll road in the 18th century and marked with a matching set of granite milestones. Extra horses were needed to pull the coach up the steep hills. Granite stones carved 'Put On' were erected at the bottom of the hill at Newbridge and Coombegate, and a 'Take Off' stone was put at the top where the extra horses hired for sixpence were unhitched. Two stones are in situ on the old, straighter toll road.

There is an active Methodist church built in 1860. The Butchers Arms is an old pub which used to hold a monthly market chiefly for cattle and pigs until the mid 20th century. Some locals still remember helping to drive animals to the market. Since the Second World War the village has seen the closure of the school, the cattle market, the three shops, a blacksmith's, a post office and a petrol filling station.

❦ ST JOHN-IN-CORNWALL

St John is approximately three miles west of Torpoint. The village is situated at the head of the estuary called St John's Lake opposite Devonport and the parish extends southwards to the English Channel and adjoins Millbrook and Antony. It takes in part of the coast and a narrow boundary road connects it with the King's Highway from Cremyll. The present road connecting it with Antony was once the old drive to Woolsden House, a large building on a hill overlooking the village, and the name comes from the family that lived there for many years after the Norman conquest. In the 16th century it passed to the Boger family, who occupied it until quite recently. It is now divided into three flats. An ancient oak tree used to stand halfway down the back drive under which villagers would place food for the house at the time of the plague and which provided a boundary past which they were forbidden to go. The RAF was billeted there during the Second World War and they cut down the tree.

A great deal of the past history of St John has been lost because church records were stored for safety during the war in nearby Mount Edgcumbe House, which unfortunately received a direct hit in the bombing and all documents were destroyed.

The main building of interest is the church, built in about 1150 but much altered over the centuries. It was originally dedicated to St John the Evangelist but around 1490 the dedication was changed to St John the Baptist and it is thought from this the village got its name. It has a massive squat Norman tower with small Norman windows.

The area is mainly agricultural but was once a place of considerable trade and it is thought that it gave its name to St John in Newfoundland, taken there by sailors from the village. Before roads were constructed market boats plied between St John and Devonport with produce from the surrounding farms. At low water in St John's Lake, bodies of prisoners from the convict ships used to be buried in the sand and rumour has it that sometimes they can still be seen walking along the shore at night.

Today it is a quiet hamlet with no shop and only one inn, which dates from the 13th century but has been much altered over the years. The mud flats of St John's Lake are a haven for wild birds. In October 1985 osprey were reported over the lake, the first time they had been seen in this part of Cornwall. The area, being one of outstanding natural beauty, also attracts many walkers.

St Just in Penwith

St Just in Penwith, from its town to its lovely moorland, its magnificent granite cliffs and beautiful valleys, offers scenic delights in this special and unspoilt corner of Cornwall. Much of the coastline is now in the care of the National Trust.

It is a town grown from a village, with a mayor and town council. It goes back to prehistoric times, with Chûn Castle, Lanyon Quoit and Bollowal Barrow among local landmarks. Its past centred on mining; mostly tin with some gold, silver and other minerals – mining, alas, has ceased, though many buildings remain.

The town centre is marked by a beautiful church which was founded in AD 596, with the present building dating from 1336. The church was saved from a serious fire in 1974, which started in the belltower among the surplices and soon spread to the main body of the church. Unexpected afternoon visitors alerted the authorities and averted a greater disaster.

Across the Square lies the Plan-an-Guare, which means 'plain of sport'. Its circular area is 125 feet in diameter, and it has held 2,000 people. Medieval mystery plays were performed here, and other activities included athletics and wrestling. It was once surrounded by six rows of stone seats, but only a few stones remain, with holes recalling their use for rock-drilling competitions in the 1920s. Charles and John Wesley both preached here. It has been used for plays as recently as 1968, and has been the setting for assemblies of the Gorsedd.

Midsummer Parade is held at the end of June, and a bonfire lit on Chapel Carn Brea to celebrate the summer solstice. There are water sports at Cape Cornwall, where the bravest swim to the Brisons, and the less hardy enjoy boat trips or watch the raft race. There is a music festival in June, culminating in Lafrowda Day with stalls and processions, and St Just is also the home of a nationally-known steel band – Hammered Steel.

There are many local artists, with several galleries displaying local paintings and crafts. For three weeks in August there is an Art and Craft Fair at the school, exhibiting and selling local work, and raising record amounts for charity. Cape Players and St Just Operatic Society each produce a show annually.

St Just prides itself on self-sufficiency, and has shops catering for most needs. It also has two banks, an estate agent, a launderette, and two garages. Five public houses and hotels provide accommodation and food, along with several cafes, a fish and chip shop, and take-always. St Just has a library, a fire station, a health centre, a dentist and a vet. There are primary and secondary schools, and an invigorating golf course at Cape Cornwall. The parish church is also used by the Roman Catholic congregation, and there is a Wesleyan chapel and a Free church. The main local employer now is the bakery, which supplies Cornish pasties and saffron cakes nationally and internationally.

🍁 St Just in Roseland

The fame of St Just in Roseland lies in its church and churchyard nestling beside the creek. In a natural bowl, sub tropical plants grow beside native trees and flora. Legend has it that Joseph of Arimathea was a tin merchant and that when he came on business to the Fal, he brought the boy Jesus with him and landed at St Just, where Jesus talked to the religious leaders.

The village itself is away from the church on top of the peninsula ridge, once nestling around the crossroads where the main road to St Mawes and Truro links with the King Harry Ferry road. At the beginning of the 20th century a fire started by a chimney spark alighting on thatched roofs, destroyed the cottages on one side of the road. In the 1950s, a council estate of some 25 homes brought the centre of the village back towards the chapel on the King Harry road. In the early 1980s the bowling green, a permanent pasture field used for village sporting activities, was sold and an estate of 16 bungalows was erected, housing mainly retired couples. Another small housing estate was completed in the

1990s and there is now a car park in the centre of the village. Apart from the main concentration of houses around the crossroads at the top of the hill, there are some twelve houses and cottages at the bottom of the hill on the way to the creek and the bar.

The school closed in the 1930s, then was reopened during the war for St Just children and the evacuees. Now money is being poured into the building, which is the home of the Roseland Outdoor Education Centre. Children and young people use the building for almost nine months of the year, using the creek and the river for water-based activities. Their fleet of boats and canoes float among the hundreds of boats now using the creek as a safe recreational haven. Pascoe's boatyard was originally opened for boatbuilding, but now its activities are more geared toward repairs and fitting out. This apart from farming is the only industry.

St Just in Roseland is unique among the Roseland villages in that it is now dry – there is no public house. Two were recorded in the 19th century, one of which is known to have been burnt down more than 100 years ago. St Just Feast is celebrated in October, with a special service in the parish church followed by a lunchtime feast in the institute. Representatives from all the parish organisations parade banners and emblems.

A cup of coffee or a cream tea can be enjoyed on leaving the church at Anna's. The local hotel has been converted into residential units and many farm buildings are now holiday homes.

🍁 St Kew

St Kew is probably the most extensive rural parish in Cornwall; Chapel Amble, Pendogett, Trequite and Trelill – all good Cornish names – are part of it. These outlying hamlets have changed little over the years though their Methodist chapels are now, sadly, redundant or converted. Trequite still has an old Celtic granite cross and Chapel Amble traces of the medieval chapel of St Aldhelm, pulled down at the Reformation, in the stones from which the oldest cottages were built. There is a house called 'Dover' and an orchard called 'Calais', names deriving perhaps from the time when barges carrying coal and sea sand, some actually from the Continent, came up the river Amble at high tide before it was tamed at the Camel estuary by the sluice built below Trewarnon Bridge. The Maltster's Arms gave and still gives refreshments to inhabitants and visitors.

Trelill sits on top of a disused railway tunnel and besides an Elizabethan manor house has 16 houses, many of them now holiday lets. Men used to work on the farms, the railway and in a stone quarry.

Trequite has a tiny triangular green where the Celtic cross, found in an old barn, has been placed. It used to have two notable characters, a retired headmaster of St Kew church school who lived to be 96 and a stone breaker's wife called Fanny who would take her husband's mid-day meal to him with a bottle of beer. One day along comes the vicar and, not wishing him to know what was in the bottle, she said, 'Sir, we have not got any money to buy milk so my Johnny is drinking 'tea water'.' Immediately the vicar took a coin out of his pocket and gave it to her. He probably knew quite well what was in the bottle!

St Kew Highway, just off the road between Camelford and Wadebridge, is expanding. There are two housing estates and some new bungalows and it still has a sub post office, the Red Lion, a garage and small supermarket, fish and chips and a small surgery. The people have got together in the last few years and rebuilt a community hall and acquired a community bus.

But the real heart of this parish is a mile and a quarter away – St Kew Churchtown. There the 15th century church dedicated to St James, the 200 year old inn and the old vicarage, an elegant Georgian house, stand unchanged in a sheltered hollow among trees alongside the stream which becomes the river Amble. There beside the church is the parish hall, previously the old stone village school which is now rehoused in a modern building nearby. Cornish wrestling once took place in front of the pub and a member of the Cornish team, an old man now, lives on a nearby farm.

The St Kew Inn, renowned for its excellent steaks, is still giving Comfort and Content. The garden of the ex-vicarage still sees the annual event, the St James' Fete, which unites the whole parish of St Kew, or 'Kewa' as perhaps it should be called, for it was a female Celtic saint after whom this place was named.

🍁 St Keyne

St Keyne, in the past variously spelled Kayne, Kaine and Kean, lies on the B3254 between Liskeard and Looe and is thought to have taken its name from one of the 24 holy children of King Braghan, founder of Brecon in Wales, about the year AD 500. In the 16th century it was one estate, Lametton, the present farmhouse being 'the big house' mentioned in the Domesday Book owned by the Coplestones, a landowning family. When in 1561 the owner, John was found guilty of murdering his son and godson, he had to sell 13 estates, one of which was Lametton, in order to buy a royal pardon. It was then owned by the Harrises of Mt Radford in Devon, one of whom was MP for Liskeard in 1661 who married a daughter of John

Rashleigh of Menabilly. Ownership passed to that family until 1911 when the whole estate was auctioned off in separate lots at Webbs Hotel, Liskeard.

It is famous for its well with its strange legend, captured in the poem *St Kayne's Well* by R. Carew, 1603:

'The quality, that man and wife
Whose chance, or choice, attaines
First of this sacred stream to drinke
Thereby the mastery gains.'

and today 'well water' is used for baptisms at the parish church which is part Norman, but mostly 15th century and drastically restored between 1868 and 1877. The church will have witnessed many weddings when couples followed the rectory path through the kissing gates to the road leading to the well to adhere to the legend. Whether the legend holds true or not the same happens today but by a different route. The well was rebuilt by the Old Cornwall Society in 1936. Nearby is the Well House Hotel, formerly Dhoolie, understood to have been built on profits from an Indian tea plantation.

With the influence of John Wesley the public house gradually lost its importance and on its site Zion chapel opened in 1861. It closed in 1932 and now houses a bakery.

Research has shown the great distances covered for employment. Villagers travelled to Herodsfoot to work in the mines; also to Looe to work on the quay, as this was once a cargo port kept busy by the Liskeard to Looe canal which opened in 1828 and was abandoned some years after the railway was built in 1859; and Liskeard as it became the main East Cornwall cattle market. St Keyne was well known for Lametton Mill which at one time supported four teams of horses, two to collect the corn from the farms and two to deliver the flour to Looe and Liskeard. The mill was worked until 1966 and now houses a collection of 'Magnificent Musical Machines' catering for the holiday industry. Farming was carried on, there was a busy blacksmith's forge and a thriving foundry and agricultural business which prompted the village to support a football team called 'The Ironsides'. There was also a cricket team and a working men's institute later handed over to the Women's Institute and then to the village.

Looking at the village today it is hard to visualize it even a couple of decades ago but many of the old houses still stand and primroses continue to adorn the lanes in the spring. In the past these were picked by the bath full, bunched up and despatched to markets 'up country'. A modern estate was started in the early 1970s on land belonging to Churchtown when it changed hands. The majority of residents, 360 at a recent count, are retired, some commute to Liskeard or

Plymouth for employment, and farming continues. A large new village hall opened in 1998.

❦ ST LAWRENCE

Although St Lawrence is now little more than a hamlet, it must at one time have been a comparatively large village. In fact writers in the 13th century frequently wrote of it as the town of 'St Lawrence juxta Ponteboy' (the latter part of this name signifying 'by the ford, or bridge'). In addition to the then leper hospital and chapel, which was consecrated by Bishop Brentingham in 1382, there were also a number of dwellings, a prison and dungeon and a corn mill.

The village has altered greatly in appearance in the last 150 years. The chapel, which was standing and being used as a stable in 1814, has now completely disappeared, as has the ancient market house. Many of the old houses have been demolished, and several inscribed stones, spoken of by certain old writers, have disappeared.

In 1476, it is stated that John Cole was 'Prior of the Priory of St Lawrence Juxta Ponteboy'. The seal of St Lawrence appears to have been executed at the end of the 15th century. The seal shows St Lawrence under a canopy with a gridiron, the symbol of his martyrdom, in his left hand, and the figure of one of his followers kneeling at his feet.

King James I, immediately after his accession, granted certain privileges upon St Lawrence. He granted it a market to be held each Wednesday and an annual fair on St Luke's day in October; this was held in the fair field adjoining the hospital. A good deal of drunkennness characterised the occasion, with a temporary licence being granted to one of the houses, known as the Miners Arms. The drunkest man in the fair was chosen as 'Mayor of St Lawrence'. He was placed in a wheelbarrow and tipped into the small nearby river.

The last patients admitted to the leper hospital were William Francis (who was the governor from 1774-1778), and Anna and Temperance Webb. The last named of these died in 1800. However, the last leper in Cornwall was a negro who landed at Polruan in 1907, who finally died 13 years later in 1920.

🍁 St Levan

The parish of St Levan lies ten miles west of Penzance. Porthcurno, home of the Cable and Wireless Telecommunications College and site of the first cable laid across the Atlantic Ocean, is part of the parish. From Porthcurno we travel along the cliff top to the Minack Open Air Theatre, founded and built by Rowena Cade in 1932. We then arrive at St Levan parish church. When the first church was built is not known, but the present building stands on the site of the shrine of St Levan and is 12th/13th century work. St Levan – from the Celtic saint Selevan – is believed to have landed at Port Selevan, or as we now know it, Porthchapel, in the 6th or 7th century and his name was the Celtic form of Solomon.

The holy well of St Levan lies beside the path to Porthchapel beach down a flight of about 50 stone steps. Following the cliff-top path from the church, we continue to Porthgwarra. This was once known as Sweethearts Cove. Nancy, daughter of a farmer, fell in love with a sailor called William. The lovers were forbidden to meet. They did meet, however, before William joined his ship. Nancy watched for the ship's return for many months. She became quite mad and one night walked down to the cove and sat on a rock surrounded by the incoming tide. The tide turned but still she gazed out to sea. Suddenly a sailor appeared and put his arm around Nancy, who was never seen again. News arrived at this time saying William's ship had foundered with all hands.

All the houses in Porthgwarra were built on the proceeds of shell fishing. Wells where fresh fish were kept are still in use. A lucrative trade was making miniature crab pots for the tourist industry.

Until the 1980s the nearby coastguard station at Gwennap Head employed four regular coastguards. Now it is manned by auxiliaries. The road from Porthgwarra and Gwennap Head leads to the Wesleyan chapel which was built in 1868. The fields surrounding the chapel form part of Chegwidden Farm, which still uses water from a well of many years standing. Chegwidden Farm is the destination of – so the story goes – the spectre ship which sailed overland across the sands from Porthcurno Cove. The ship was said to have been black, square-rigged and single masted. No crew was ever seen. The ship was said to be connected with a mariner and his servant. The servant never spoke to anyone apart from his master. They kept a boat at Porthcurno and at daylight would start for sea, not returning until night. They also used to hunt, and the howls of their dogs could be heard for many miles. The man died and the servant enlisted the help of local people to take his master's coffin to the churchyard. The body was laid to rest, with the servant and dogs surrounding it. As soon as earth was thrown on the coffin, servant and dogs disappeared, along with the boat. To this day, no boat has been kept in Porthcurno Cove.

Bertrand Arthur William Russell, third Earl, resided in the parish from the early 1920s. He was a philosopher, mathematician and essayist celebrated for his work in the field of logic and theory of knowledge and remembered for his moral courage, belief in human reason and championship of liberal ideas. Although he left his home in the parish, his family still own the house and reside there.

❧ ST MAWGAN-IN-PYDAR

St Mawgan lies about two miles from the north coast of Cornwall in a secluded and beautiful wooded valley. For centuries it was known as Lanherne, after the manor of Lanherne, and also the Vale of Lanherne, which was recorded in the Domesday survey. The river Malanhyl flows through the village to the sea at Mawgan Porth.

Following the Reformation it became known as Mawgan-in-Pydar, the Pydar defining the boundaries for municipal and political purposes. Today the Pydar Division still exists in the judicial system. It was only during the second half of the century that the Saint has been added.

Probably the oldest building is part of Lanherne convent where a monastery is known to have existed in AD 603. It is now, and has been for many years, the home of the Carmelite enclosed order of nuns. The village also has two other places of worship, the 13th century parish church and the Methodist chapel.

St Mawgan's history is varied and fascinating and excavations in the middle of this century have revealed that an Iron Age village flourished at least two centuries before the birth of Christ. Personal possessions found, including jewellery, and household chattels gave insight into community life centuries ago. During the reconstruction of the airfield, slate kist gravestones were exposed and subsequently recovered.

In more recent times the influence of the Bridges Willyams family of Carnanton, is found through the village records. The estate cottages are incomparable to any others in the village and give a vision of life long ago. Similarly the architecture of the almshouses, built by Edward Bridges Willyams in 1905 in memory of his wife, is unique. A delightful feature set in the surrounding wall to these houses is an enclosed fountain with two drinking troughs of different heights for dogs and horses.

Until the mid 19th century, the Falcon inn was known as the Gardener's Arms but Mr Gilbert, an eminent local man, decided to change the name to the Falcon inn which is the crest of the Willyams family. The inscription in Cornish on the sign reads 'Many thanks to God'.

Before the Second World War the blacksmith's shop was one of the prominent places in the village. Being an agricultural area there were many horses to be shod and farming implements to be mended. With the coming of the tractor, and later more mechanised machinery, the blacksmith's became a garage which in its turn has sadly now gone.

Although St Mawgan is an agricultural district, mechanisation has resulted in few job opportunities for local people. Some find work on the local airfield, at St Austell clayworks, the construction industry, and some seasonal jobs in the tourist trade. For others, moving to a new area has been the only way to find employment.

Like most villages with a long history, St Mawgan enjoys its traditional village events. One of the more notable is the Feast Sports held on the Wednesday nearest to 25th July to celebrate the Feast day of St Nicholas and St James.

🍁 ST MELLION

On 17th October, 1259 the church of St Mellion (or St Mellyan or St Mellanius) was dedicated by Bishop Bronscombe of Exeter. The original patron saint was probably a Breton missionary monk, St Mollien, but he was superseded by St Melaine, Bishop of Rennes in the Middle Ages.

The church, primary school and pub are the principal buildings. There is no industry, except for the farms, although in the past there were many packing sheds for locally grown fruit and most women were involved in agricultural work on the farms.

Now the biggest employer is St Mellion Golf & Country Club, which boasts two 18 hole courses, one designed by the great American golfer Jack Nicklaus.

The Coryton family, now of Pentillie Castle, in a neighbouring parish, originally lived at Crocadon Farm in the village. The church contains a finely executed brass to 'Peter Coryton Esquyer (died 1551) and lie wife Jane which had XXIV children between Them'. These are all shown on the brass – seventeen boys and seven girls!!

Captain Jack Coryton allocated the land for the WI hall at a peppercorn rent of 1/- per year when the Institute was formed in 1932 with 42 members. By 1936 the members had raised £300 to build and equip the large wooden hut, in spite of the low incomes of agricultural workers in those days.

The present primary school was opened in 1891. As with so many village

St Mellion Primary School

schools, its future has been in the balance, but without it the village would lose an important focus. Before the primary school was opened, St Mellion had a small pay school. This building, which has also been a forge and a carpenter's shop, is now a Community Project, and villagers are providing money and, more importantly, a few of them are giving their labour to transform it into a parish hall, principally for parish meetings, but also for other gatherings.

The most important event is the annual Cherry Feast, held for church funds. This is a joint effort by Pillaton and St Mellion, held in the church and vicarage grounds at St Mellion. Since the Tamar banks were originally famed for their cherry orchards and strawberry beds, the fruit being taken to Plymouth by river boats it was a custom at Pentillie Castle to give a cherry pie feast to all the children in the neighbourhood. As the custom died out, the church adopted the idea and each year, early in July, the event takes place. The most popular item on sale in the tea tent is, of course, Cherry Pie, but other stalls, in marquees, offer many tempting goodies.

Entertainment is provided by a brass band, dancers, dog agility displays and other different groups from year to year. Displays are also set out in the church, including samples of the school children's work, old photographs and manuscripts. Sometimes craftwork; sometimes old tools – it varies each year.

The small village shop and the pub, the Coryton Arms, are welcome village amenities. The cottages on the main road, both above and below the pub were originally built for Pentillie estate workers, but have since been sold off.

There is no record of ancient ghosts, but in the late 1970s, three separate people saw a large troop of soldiers, led by one on horseback, and accompanied by hunting-type dogs, come up the hill at Church Park and disappear near the church gate. One spectator thought there were about fifty men – somewhat different from solitary ghosts!!

🍁 St Michael Penkivel

The small village of St Michael Penkivel is hidden in the trees, and is situated between the tributaries of the river Fal. It has not changed since the houses were first built.

The church is the centre of the village – built originally in 1261, and rebuilt on the site of the old church in 1862. A western tower contains the four bells, with the spire which can be seen for many miles around. The church possesses an exceptionally ancient register dating from the year 1516. A piped organ was installed in 1989, coming from a chapel now closed.

The houses are grouped around the village green, which still has the old village pump. Some houses still have their leaded windows. The blacksmith's forge is now a house.

The parochial school built in 1844 was later used as a reading room, Sunday school, and for social occasions. Further down the road is Malpas Ferry, which was a flat-bottomed boat which once carried cattle or pony and trap going to Truro market, but now is only a rowing boat passenger ferry.

At Merther Lane stands the school built in 1889 at the cost of £3,000 for 120 children of the parishes of St Michael Penkivel, Lamorran and Merther. This closed when the numbers decreased, and has now been converted into a new village hall.

The people of the village all work on Tregothnan estate, in the gardens, woods, sawmills or on the farm. There are no shops and the post office now only opens in the morning. The mobile library calls twice a month.

The village has many activities during the year, including a cricket match between the farmers and the estate workers. A recital is held in the church every September and a Harvest Supper in the autumn. A Christmas party is held for village children who all receive a present from Father Christmas.

The name St Michael Penkivel is derived from St Michaelis de Penkievel, who came to Cornwall in 1261. Penkivel means 'horse's head'.

🍁 St Michael's Mount

The island of St Michael's Mount is just off the coast of south-west Cornwall, opposite Marazion, and connected by a causeway at low tide. It is generally agreed that it is the same island where, nearly 2,000 years ago, the inhabitants sold tin to merchant traders who had travelled from the Mediterranean area.

The name is believed to stem from a legend which tells how St Michael appeared to fishermen in the year AD 495. St Michael's Mount is recorded in the Domesday Book as Tremaras-tol, which means the market town with the cell or hole; cell or hole was a religious house. The building which stands high above the village became a priory and that holy place was much visited by pilgrims.

Starting during the reign of Richard I, St Michael's Mount had a troublesome history for many years. The island was forcibly taken by Hugh de Pomeroy who turned it into a stronghold. After surrendering to the Archbishop of Canterbury it was as much a fortress as a sanctuary. Possession of the island was fiercely contested during the Civil War. It was bought by the St Aubyn family in 1659 and they have lived there ever since.

Rebuilding of the harbour began, also houses, pilchard stores, a sail loft, shops and three inns. Schools were established and two wells provided fresh water. There was also a laundry building and dairy.

By 1811 the island exported pilchards, tin and copper ore. Iron, timber, corn and salt were brought in. The pilchard season lasted from July to October so, not surprisingly, many men of the village were fishermen. Others were sailmakers, seamen and pilots, or in the service of the St Aubyn family. Some of the women worked in the island laundry.

Queen Victoria visited the island in September 1846, along with Prince Albert and their children. They had sailed there in their yacht and Queen Victoria's footprint is preserved at the top of the harbour steps.

Lots of families have lived and worked on the Mount over the years, but not all stayed. Six surnames were prominent, the families living there from generation to generation. The Mathews family was one, the other five being Jago, Dusting, Sennett, John and Trannack. Six men wore the colourful ceremonial livery of Mount boatmen. That meant they crewed the St Aubyn family barge. In 1887 John St Aubyn became the first Lord St Levan.

A single line railway was constructed in 1900, climbing from the harbour to the summit of 650 ft. The single wagon has carried all kinds of things, even His Lordship's coronation robes.

In 1954 St Michael's Mount was given to the National Trust. Since then the working lives of the villagers have been largely affected by tourism, as thousands of visitors are attracted to the historic 'fairy tale' castle and island. Today the village has twelve attractive houses and two flats, with mains water and electricity. Other buildings include the Steward's House, Lodge, Barge House, and two shops. The inns have gone, the sail loft is now a restaurant and the laundry building a cafe. There is also a first aid centre and fire-fighting capability.

The island has an inshore lifeboat crewed by men and women, hastily dropping whatever employment they were engaged in, when a maroon is fired.

St Michael's Mount is the smallest parish in Cornwall. The village has seen many changes over the years, always, in one way or another, having been affected by the impressive building which dominates the skyline above it.

🍁 ST NEOT

There has no doubt always been a thriving agricultural industry in the parish of St Neot. In the Middle Ages the emphasis was on sheep, and people prospered from the production, dyeing and sale of wool. This is when the community was able to afford to build the beautiful parish church. The present building dates from the 15th century. The principal glory of St Neot's church is its stained glass windows, all but five of which date from the 15th or early 16th century.

Visitors to the church may question the branch which appears to grow from the top of the tower. Here is proof that St Neot during the Civil War was Royalist. Every year on Oak Apple Day the churchwardens go to the roof of the tower to take down last year's oak branch and haul up a new one. It was the custom, within memory, for village children to wear an oak leaf on the morning of the 29th of May and a sprig of boyslove in the afternoon, those without suffered the penalty of being chased with stinging nettles!

The holy well stands close to the river, about 300 yards from the church, in a well house made of stone with a wooden door, which was rebuilt in 1862. The water was said to have healing properties and weakly children used to be brought here to drink, especially on the first three mornings in May.

There are three active Methodist chapels in the parish, St Neot, Tredinnick and St Luke's.

Agriculture has always been the most important local industry but tin production was evident going back into antiquity. First of all the alluvial tin was recovered by 'streaming' on the floor of the valley from Twowatersfoot to Deep Hatches. Enough tin was found to justify the presence of a blowing house by the village to smelt it (hence Blowing House Meadow) and this operated from the 16th-18th centuries, using charcoal produced from the woods in the parish (the sites of old charcoal burners' pits can still be seen). The same oak coppices produced bark which supported a tannery in the village for many years.

The production of alluvial tin gradually gave way to hard rock mining, and in the 18th and 19th centuries, Wheal Mary, Wheal Sisters, Wheal Robins and Wheal Tregeagle were in production, the latter mine being the first one in Cornwall to use electricity in 1890. There is an adit within three yards of the village institute which drained mines on Goonzion Downs. In fact it is said that the whole of the village is like a honeycomb underground.

Slate production was of great importance. Slate from the Carnglaze quarry was taken by packhorse trains to St Winnow Quay for dispatch by sea, as well as supplying a wide radius of St Neot. More recently, china clay production in the parish has provided valuable and stable employment.

There are two expanses of water within the parish, the new reservoir at Colliford and the natural pool at Dozmary. The reservoir was completed in 1984 and was constructed using a barrage technique only previously tried in the Netherlands. A wide bank of china clay waste was used to build the wall and then coated in a thick layer of tarmacadam.

Dozmary Pool features in Arthurian legend as the possible site of Excalibur, and in the Tregeagle legend. It is said that it is bottomless, because no matter how hot the summer Dozmary Pool never runs dry. There are stone landing stages jutting into the water which are relics of the ice industry once carried out there. Large blocks of ice were cut from the centre of the frozen pool in winter and dragged out by horse. They were pulled into ready prepared cuttings and covered over with turfs of soil to a depth of six feet. In the warmer weather slabs of ice were cut and carried to Liskeard Station and thence to Looe to be used in the packing of fish.

❧ ST NEWLYN EAST

The village is said to have taken its name from the Celtic St Newlina. One tradition says that she came over from Ireland in the 6th century, landed at Holywell Bay and walked to where he church now stands. Here, striking her staff in the ground she said, 'Let a church be built', and from her staff there sprang the famous fig tree which may still be seen growing out of one of the church walls.

The village school has a strong connection with the church, the first school-room being built by John Oxnam in 1811 where the south-west wall of the churchyard now stands. His endowment provided the annual sum of £5, with 40 shillings for maintenance. Later the Oxnam Room (still standing) was added to the school as the boys' separate schoolroom. In order to attend the original school, children had to be approved by the vicar, which of course excluded the nonconformists, and a great deal of wrangling went on before the rules for the new school were drawn up, with a 'conscience' clause to allow for the inclusion of nonconformists. In 1877 a school was built on land given by William Oxnam and the family are still represented in the village. The growing population of the village and the need for more facilities has resulted in the replacement of this Victorian school building by a modern primary school in Station Road. The old school building remains and has been partially converted to a private dwelling.

There is also a strong Methodist tradition in the village and the famous Billy Bray preached here on numerous occasions at the Bible Christian chapel.

In the 19th century the village was a thriving mining community, due to the East Wheal Rose Mine, which employed over 1,200 men. The old miners' cottages in Metha Road still have on their deeds the right to keep animals on Newlyn Downs. One of the saddest events in village history was the disaster at East Wheal Rose. On 9th July 1846, at 1 pm a tremendous thunderstorm centred itself on the mine area. The deluge of rain continued for an hour and a half and was compared by those who saw it to 'casks of water being emptied from above'. The torrential rain flooded the valley, pouring down the shafts and flooding the lower levels. Many fought their way to the surface, but 43 men were trapped. When the water was pumped out the following day, four men were brought up alive, leaving a death toll of 39. The headstone for two of those drowned, William Pearce and his son Francis (aged 15) stands outside the south porch of the church. The mine was closed in 1881. Following this disaster, the miners dug the 'Pit' in the village both as a memorial and gesture of thanksgiving. It is situated on the site of an old cockpit and is one of only three in the whole of Cornwall. Sadly, the roof of the 'Tea Treat' hut next to the Pit was destroyed by fire in 1999.

The tithe barn at Cargoll Manor, built in 1240, is one of the few remaining in Cornwall, with the original hammerbeams still in place.

The village is justly proud of its war hero, whose name is commemorated not only here but in other places in Cornwall. Horace Augustus Curtis was born on 7th March 1890, the fourth of five children of a gamekeeper. His VC was awarded for valour at the battle of Le Cateau in October 1918.

Seventy years ago, the village had a large general store selling groceries, pots and pans, clothing and footwear, a tailor, butcher and doctor, not to mention Sara, who went around the parish with an old-fashioned push-chair selling haberdashery, accompanied by her dog Rufty-Tufty. The village today is still a thriving community, supporting one general shop, a butcher and a sub-post office.

🍁 ST STEPHEN-IN-BRANNEL

Local people from three sides of the village intending to visit the Churchtown of Brannel parish will say that they are 'going up St Stephen's' but when viewed from a distance one can see that the village lies in a hollow and only the tower of the Norman church rises above that hollow. Situated as it is on the very edge of the pits and tips of the china clay industry that has brought prosperity to the whole area, the village has grown by the addition of the new housing estates and now has a population of over 2,000.

To the south of the village another kind of mining once thrived. It is said that Madame Curie herself visited the Terras mine that produced the pitchblende ore from which she isolated the power source, the missing atom, that has revolutionised medical science and, less happily, modern weapons of war.

Brannel parish, which comprises some 9,000 acres (the name Brannel is thought to mean corn ground) was, before William Cookworthy's discovery of kaolin, mainly an agricultural area and once extended to the coast at Caerhayes. Following Cookworthy's discovery, a number of famous names in the pottery and china world such as Wedgwood, Minton and Spode became associated with the district and they took options on the clay-producing land. Only the cost of the transport of coal dissuaded them from producing their quality merchandise locally.

The church which was consecrated in 1261 and dedicated to St Stephen, the first martyr, succeeded an earlier Celtic church which is thought to have stood in a nearby valley at Gwindra. The churchyard contains a Crying Stone from where the news of the week was cried every Sunday following the morning service. Flanking the church are two inns, one at the head of a square where the village pump once stood. Further along the road stands the old Victorian board school with its 'gables and turrets' but which has now been divided into industrial units.

An early thatched Methodist chapel once stood near the east gates of the church and the surviving cottages are known as Chapel Row. The present chapel was built in a corner of a field on the then edge of the village which has now advanced and taken it into its midst. An imposing building of local granite it was completed in 1870.

When the village was much smaller as many as 16 shops served the villagers but today just six businesses suffice plus the doctor's surgery.

Mention must be made of the Tanner family who resided in the old manor house at Court and who held positions of power for generations. The original manor house is said to have been destroyed during the Civil War. The Tanners were also notable in that they were very tall and when the vault of the former lords of the manor was opened very large coffins were found – some over seven foot long. By a strange coincidence the present occupants of the farm at Court are also very tall.

🍁 St Stephens-by-Launceston

Records of St Stephens are Saxon whilst those of Launceston are mainly Norman.

'When Lanson was a Fuzzy Down
St Stephens was a Market Town'

says the old rhyme, but there is more to this than first appears. The town now called Launceston was formerly Dunheved. Until the 13th century, the name of Launceston applied only to St Stephens. The seat of Anglo-Saxon government in the Earldom of Cornwall, it boasted a royal mint as well as being an ecclesiastical centre.

Within two miles of the Devon border two imposing bastions of grandeur dominate either side of the Kensey valley. From Launceston Castle at the top of the southern slope, the main road descends 278 ft to the river Kensey at Newport and ascends 278 ft to the magnificent church of St Stephens.

The church was clearly central to the evolving community for the village nestles around and below it. Formerly administered by the Duke of Northumberland's estates, many of the properties are over 250 years old. Northumberland House was once an inn, whilst typical Cornish stone cottages line Duke Street and North Street.

Despite its proximity to Launceston, the community maintained a very definite independence, reiterating an ancient and legendary rivalry. Records reveal that separate Coronation celebrations have been held since the crowning of George IV on 19th July 1821.

Dedicated in 1259 and built on the site of the monastic church, St Stephens is the oldest church in the neighbourhood. The nail-studded door of the church features an ancient wrought iron sanctuary ring or knocker. The 1540 Act of Parliament granted continuance of the privilege of sanctuary to only eight places in England, St Stephens being one. Fugitives seeking refuge in the church were legally protected unless accused of sacrilege or treason. Protection for life might be granted in return for an undertaking to leave the realm within 40 days. This Act continued until the early 17th century.

In 1883 a spacious vault was disclosed under the floor of the choir. In it nine members of the North family, former owners and residents of Dutson Farm, had been interred. Two of the coffins were nine foot each in length – were there giants at St Stephens. Over its site is now placed a slate slab having a huge cross thereon and the letters IHS. The date is still clear.

A sizeable bequest towards the cost of building the tower was made by a wealthy benefactress from the nearby parish of Week St Mary, Thomasine Bonaventure (c1420-1512). Legend adds that she required the pinnacles to be high enough to be seen from Swannacott Farm in Week St Mary, some twelve miles away.

❦ ST TEATH

St Teath likes to boast of its one famous son, for it was here in 1753 that Vice Admiral William Bligh was born, he of *Mutiny on the Bounty* fame. He is reputed to have been born in a house sited on the village square, though he and his parents moved to Plymouth when he was just a few months old. Nearby St Tudy village also lays claim to Admiral Bligh, and thereby one of those ancient feuds begins. There is however some documentary evidence to support St Teath's claim, and it is nice to think he was born adjacent to the lovely parish church of St Tetha. The present church is 14th century, though records show a church was on the site in the 6th to 7th centuries.

It is from the church that the village derives its name, for St Etha/St Tetha came from Wales, and settled a collegiate establishment here. Regrettably the present day spelling of St Teath causes confused pronunciations; how easy it would be to return to the old spelling of 'St Teth' and a whole village would then be happy.

Sited on a plateau among green hills, St Teath today is a thriving community. It was once a staging point on the road from Camelford to Wadebridge, the original inn being at the top of Knights Hill where the horses took a much needed rest.

As in many villages, the shops act as communication centres for housewives and visitors alike, much momentous news can be gleaned from conversations taking place as you gather your shopping. At the village school parents and friends are encouraged to 'drop in'. They will always find a child who wants to be read to, or preferably will read to them. Then there is the local pub, owned by the same family for more than 30 years. A good 'yarn' can always be found there, together with a guaranteed welcome from the landlord. In the square is the community centre which arose from a derelict barn; records show that this barn was once the village poor house.

St Teath Clocktower

Springtime here is beautiful; the churchyard is a carpet of multi-hued crocus, the hedgerows abound with flowers, the woods are a mass of bluebells and anemones, and the many springs add their tumbling voices to the birdsong. Come again at Christmas for different sounds, the children's Nativities, the WI Christmas celebration concert, carol singing in the square around the clock tower, singing again in the square to welcome in the New Year, Christmas decorations and parties. All have become well established traditions of the village, along with the cattle, sheep and arable farming which is found here, on farms handed down from father to son.

At the bottom of the hill leading from the village to Trelill is a small hamlet known as Whitewell, once famous for its healing waters. Only cattle graze there now, drink from the stream and look up to fields where once flourished a silver mine.

❧ St Tudy

Yes, yet another saint! St Tudy was a 6th century Breton abbot who sent out his monks to convert the heathen Cornish. The church which they founded is mentioned in the Domesday Book. Today that church is central to the village. It is a beautiful 15th century building. In its porch is a relic from the ancient past of the village, a Saxon coped tomb, over a thousand years old.

Radiating from the church are the most interesting buildings in the village. The school, once under threat of closure, is now thriving again; an old rectory; an 'old clink', used as a lock-up by the village policeman in the 19th century, now restored and a popular venue for regular coffee mornings throughout the year; and a smithy, in use until recently. For their Millennium project the people of St Tudy had the binding stone restored to its original place outside this smithy, the village pump renovated and the whole area recobbled. To complete the project, commemorative slates were mounted on the adjacent smithy wall. On the perimeter of the round Saxon churchyard stands the granite war memorial in the shape of a Celtic cross. Adjacent to this memorial is a large chestnut tree. This glorious tree was grown from seeds brought home from the battle-fields of Ypres and is a constant reminder to the people of the village of the rebirth of hope after the horrors of the First World War.

The nucleus of the village also contains the village pub, the Cornish Arms, and the post office which is also a general stores. In this central area are some of the oldest cottages which have been carefully restored. Around the outskirts of the village are the new developments, thankfully on a small scale; also a thriving Methodist church founded in 1889, and lastly a village hall, now an extremely smart building after extensive renovations.

St Tudy is surrounded by very ancient manor houses, the oldest of which are Polrode and Tinten. The latter is claimed to be the birthplace of Captain Bligh of *Bounty* fame. The 15th century Tremeer estate became the home of the Lower family whose most famous member was Richard Lower. He experimented in the house with blood transfusions, later performing the first blood transfusion on a man in the presence of Charles II. Other ancient manors include Penvose, the home of the Nicholls family, one of whom, Anthony Nicholls, served in Cromwell's Parliament, and Hengar Manor, the former home of the Onslows, now a holiday complex. Much of the farmland surrounding these houses is now part of the Duchy of Cornwall estate.

The population of St Tudy is still quite small, about 600. In days gone by the local farms, granite and slate quarries and clay works provided this population with its living. Today however, apart from a few who continue in these occupations, St Tudy is a village of the self-employed, the retired and those who travel several miles to find work in the neighbouring towns. It lies close to the rugged North Cornish coast and on the edge of Bodmin Moor, so enjoying the best of both worlds, sheltered from, but accessible to both.

🍁 St Wenn

St Wenn lies just a few miles off the A30 on the way to Padstow. St Wenn is old, and there is an Iron Age fort at Demelza, the fortified mound called Castle, almost hidden in the woods. The manors, now farms, changed hands through the centuries, either by marriage or political or church intrigue. Some are mentioned in the Domesday Book. Lancorla had a ducking stool for nags – ladies beware! Vestiges of early Christian religion remain; 'Crossy An' on the parish boundary, a granite cross with hands; a Norman font in the church, a sundial on its wall. Gradually the parish changed, new houses appeared, settling in, mostly, by the older slate and granite cottages and farmhouses.

No famous person lived in St Wenn, but many are remembered. In Tregonetha, once called the village of spinsters, three market days were held, and nearby is a cottage, still known as Mary Ann Best after the lady who lived there. Later another Mary Ann made it her home. She had nine cats in a pram and would call on other villagers for waste scraps to feed herself and them.

The present school, built in 1855, replaced a private school once ruled by one Ezekiel Noweth, known as 'Zekey'. The record book shows many absences, caused by helping out on the farms, whooping cough and the dreaded typhoid fever. All was not sad though, remembered is the smell of burnt paper on the pasties warming on the range. Nearly opposite the school was the smithy, where the children stopped to see the great shire horses shod.

After the First World War, a Mr Percy Hawken studied a book of anatomy. He set up as a 'bone setter' and people came from afar to be relieved of their pains. His grandson, also born in St Wenn, became interested and became a qualified osteopath; he still practises in a nearby town.

In Rosenannon another healer, Mrs Taylor, had what is called 'the gift' handed down through generations. Everything she charmed, she always said, was taken from the Bible. People came suffering from many diseases. Locals called it 'charming' but she called it faith healing.

St Wenn is also known as the home of Cornish wrestling. The Chapmans, fathers, sons and grandsons, were all champions in their weight.

The village ladies worked and collected the money to build their own WI hall, a wonderful day in 1961 when it was opened. There each year a garden show is held – there are some good gardeners and cooks in St Wenn. The chapel entertains with many concerts. Only one of the three chapels now remains open. All were built by voluntary subscription and labour.

🍁 SHEVIOCK

Sheviock is the smallest of the three villages within the parish of Sheviock, the others being Crafthole and Portwrinkle. This parish is one of several in the forgotten corner of south-east Cornwall.

Very little development has taken place over the years, just a small estate and a few houses including converted barns, making a total of around 40 homes. Among the interesting dwellings is a toll cottage where the tolls were collected, but this was frequently bypassed by the local farmers when moving their cattle.

Sadly the A374, which is one of the main roads from the county boundary, passes through the centre of the village, which cuts off neighbour from neighbour and, because the increase in traffic makes it dangerous, great care has to be taken when crossing the road.

There are no shops, but tradesmen call regularly, which still leaves the walk to Crafthole, about half a mile, to visit the post office and general stores. Many retired people live here now. The village is quiet during the day as the younger villagers commute to Plymouth because there is a lack of employment, and the children are taken by bus to school.

Amongst the listed buildings in Sheviock is the 13th century church consecrated in 1259 by Bishop Walter Branscombe of Exeter and dedicated to St Peter and St Paul; later changed to the Blessed Virgin Mary. It is one of only six churches in Cornwall to have a spire tower.

In the south transept (Dawney aisle) is a raised monumental recess containing the effigies of Edward and Emmeline Courtenay; Emmeline was Dawney before she was married. There is an effigy of a knight of the same period on the opposite side of the church. At the back of the church are the parish stocks, much used in olden times, and indeed most uncomfortable for the occupants. In the 15th century the north aisle was built and some of the carved bench ends are attributed to this period. Until recently water was collected from a nearby well (Lady Well) for use at baptisms.

Records show that a local landowner named Dawney undertook to build the church, and his wife the tithe barn. On checking the cost afterwards, it was discovered the barn cost three halfpence more than the church. The same Dawneys built a manor house in 1330 across the road from the church and this later became Barton Farm.

Many years ago there was a public house situated adjacent to the church where Church Row cottages are now, and legend has it that people were visiting the pub instead of attending the church services, so the rector decided to have it closed. He did this by the somewhat devious way of purchasing the hostelry and then closing it down.

In bygone days when smuggling was the major industry, the cliff paths affording excellent facilities, imported spirits were said to have been hidden in Sheviock Woods, and on occasions in the church tower. Once there existed a secret passage leading from a well towards the sea!

❧ SITHNEY

The parish and district of Sithney lies about three miles to the north-west of the ancient town of Helston on the road to Camborne.

Modern Sithney is a pleasant area in which to live or to visit. It is in a district mainly concerned with farming, providing milk, beef, potatoes and cauliflower, the latter being referred to as 'broccoli'.

Here there were at least eight tin mines in the 19th century and those must have added considerably to the local prosperity. Tuckingmills, where homespun cloth produced from local wool was dipped and dressed were found in many parts of Cornwall where the local water possessed the necessary cleansing qualities to remove the fat from the wool. Four such mills were to be found in Sithney where, on Sithney Green, cloth was spread to dry.

The Trevarno valley stretches between Sithney Green and Chynhale and it is here that one of the few manor houses still stands. The word Trevarno when translated means 'big house' and it is interesting to note that the house was once owned by a Mr Oliver, the father of Dr Oliver of Bath the originator of the famous Bath Oliver biscuits.

Methodism came early to this part of Cornwall, possibly around 1750 when a society was formed in Sithney, and it is known to have been visited on several occasions by John Wesley whose preaching stone, or pulpit, is to be found in the yard at Trevarno. In the late 19th century the house was bought by a Mr William Bickford-Smith, whose grandfather will be forever remembered in mining communities as he was the inventor of the explosive time-fuse, which undoubtedly saved the lives of many miners. Trevarno is now owned by a company producing quality soaps and marine clocks. The gardens are being restored and provide a pleasant venue for gardening clubs and other societies.

Further along this same valley in an area known as Mellangoose is the ruin of an old farmhouse 'Plane-an-Gwary', meaning the 'place of the plays', and it was here that many of the Cornish Miracle plays were acted. This area later became a venue for Cornish wrestlers who displayed their prowess on feast days and fair days and were an irresistible attraction to men from miles around. Wrestling was denounced in 1790 by Methodist preachers who predicted 'a terrible judgment' against those who wrestled. However, Cornish wrestling continues in Cornwall to this day and age.

The village church is to be found at the top of the hill at the southern side of the Camborne road: this area being known as Church-Sithney. The 60 ft Norman tower was for many centuries regarded as a landmark for Porthleven fishermen, and the church itself has much to offer in the way of historical interest. In the 11th century a fair was held here on St James' day, the proceeds of which were used as a stipend for the poor priest. Nearby is a small granite cottage, which in days gone by was the village pub. It was known as the Tree Inn and still retains its name today, thus causing great confusion to many visitors. An excellent tea shop serving scones and cream is, however, situated close by.

❧ SOUTH PETHERWIN

South Petherwin or Petherwyn (wyn meaning blessed) was nicknamed 'Pethern' by older residents. One and a half miles from Launceston to the east, it is bounded by the river Inny to the south-west and served by the new bypass to the north. Its boundaries also include Daws House, Petherwin Water and Kennards House. It is an agricultural area with a population today of about 1,000.

St Paternus, the heart of the village, is one of the oldest Norman churches in the country, with the old church school once situated alongside. The new school was built to the west of the village in the Kennards House road. There was a holy well in one of the fields at a local farm, Oldwit Farm, and water was collected from there and brought to the church each time a baptism took place.

There have been several Methodist chapels in the village over the years but the present one was built of local stone in 1872. The stone was quarried from the nearby slate quarry, one of the main occupations of the villagers at that time. There were also stone breakers who worked at the side of the road, these being the old men who could no longer work a full day. Stone breakers were paid two shillings per yard and received about twelve shillings a week.

Other occupations were carpenters, blacksmiths and a cobbler, but mostly farm workers, there being several large farms in the area. Trebursye Manor was the largest house, now a residential home, with another at Trecrogo.

With the arrival of mains water and sewerage the village grew in population with three estates being built over the years and many houses but the businesses declined and workers moved to other areas. The first estate to be built was Tiny Meadows, the second Trelinnoe Close and the third Trelinnoe Gardens.

The village pump is in the centre of the village and served the population until mains water was laid on. A yearly charge was made for the use of the pump and it was locked during very dry weather and the local residents had to queue once a day for one bucket.

The village pub was the Brandreth Arms, which is now Beacon Farm. The local tenants of the estates brought their annual rent to the pub and were provided with a luncheon. A new pub, the Winds of Change, was built in 1989. In the village there is now a thriving general stores and post office, a garage for repairs and two taxi ranks.

The population has increased over the years, the majority of the working community being employed in Launceston and the surrounding district. The remainder of the residents enjoy their retirement in the village.

🍁 STICKER

Sticker is a small village set in rolling countryside between St Austell and Truro, with a population of about 1,100. There are several derivations of the name Sticker, the earliest being Stikier, or Stekyer, believed to come from the Cornish 'stockyer' meaning tree stumps, which as the area was reputed to be forested, would make sense. There is some evidence around the area of ancient inhabitants believed to be circa 200 BC to AD 300.

The village was at one time almost entirely dependent on mining, the last working mine being closed down in the early 20th century. One engine house remains standing on the outskirts of the village, South Polgooth mine, and another at the nearby hamlet of Hewaswater. Most mines produced black tin with some copper.

An interesting point of note is the now converted Peramore Methodist chapel at Lower Sticker, built by miners in their spare time in 1836, the present up-dated building having been opened in 1859. When the chapel was originally built, there were over 100 dwellings nearby occupied by the miners and their families, almost all of which have disappeared totally with the decline of the mining industry, although the building built as Sticker board school in 1878 and used until July 1961 still stands, and is occupied by a local doctor. Another Methodist chapel was built in Chapel Hill in 1876, and the church of St Mark in 1877 – the land on which the church stands cost £17 at that time!

One of the oldest buildings is now known as the Hewas inn, originally named the Great Hewas inn after the mine at Hewaswater. This suffered a devastating fire in 1826 but was rebuilt. Until the 1940s there was a working forge in the village, but this was demolished in 1983. There used to be several shops and inns, but over the years these have either been demolished or changed to just living accommodation, so that today Sticker is served by a small supermarket and one inn. The village hall in Retanning Lane is an extension of the reading room, which was built in 1890.

Farming is carried on extensively around Sticker, with the central village being mainly a dormitory for villagers working in St Austell and Truro. It is difficult to believe now when enjoying the many lovely walks through the lanes that mining once thrived here. Since 1992, when the bypass was completed, Sticker has become peaceful once again.

🍁 STITHIANS

St Stythian's church offers 800 years of history. Two chapels served the Methodists – Hendra, the older, no longer used for worship, and the newer Penmennor. The village also possesses Georgian mansions, Tregonning mill, and two cottages with 1719 cut into their stonework.

Stithians Agricultural Show, held on Feast Monday, began in 1834. It is held in July and is still a great attraction. It is the largest one day show in the West

Tregonning Mill, Stithians

Country. the show now has a 60 acre permanent site near to the village; this is also used for other events throughout the year.

This musical village has much to offer. St Stythian's Silver Band can be heard twice a week all summer at Falmouth, and there is a ladies choir and the male voice choir, all of which have been in action from three to six decades. A far cry from the fife and drum band which played at Penmennor tea treat in 1885 and peace celebration in 1919.

At Carn is the Stithians Dam which made the large reservoir. Not only does it provide piped water but is a tourist attraction and a venue for aquatic sport and bird watching.

With over 50 organisations, religious, sporting, educational and charitable, it is surprising that villagers find time to work. In olden days there was little leisure time. Apart from the usual village occupations, quarrying in the 19th century was the main employer, followed by farming and mining. Many men worked 'out of cor', eg quarrying by day and working a smallholding after work. The largest block of granite ever removed from Polkanuggo quarry was estimated at 2,000 tons.

One hundred years ago there were eleven shopkeepers, seven innkeepers and eight millers. Today there is one shop, a sub post office, one public house, a hotel, a petrol station with DIY store and a chip shop. *The Stithians Times*, a monthly newspaper of events and news of the village, is compiled by a group of villagers and enjoys a wide circulation in the area.

A private housing estate has been built and various plots of land are available for housing development. Villagers commute to adjacent towns to work or servicemen travel to Culdrose air station.

🍁 Stoke Climsland

There has been a settlement at Stoke Climsland since records were first kept. The Domesday Book of 1086 records that 'The King (William the Conqueror) holds the manor of Climeston containing five hides of land'. Today Climson is still a single farmstead while Stoke Climsland and its attendant hamlets of Bealsmill, Luckett, Downgate, Tutwell, Venterdon, Higherland and Bray Shop form one of the largest parishes in Cornwall.

In 1265 the first known rector of Stoke Climsland church was appointed. Through the following years the church has been added to and changed and was once consecrated, on All Saints Day, hence the assumed dedication. From 1337 the manor, with its central position on the River Tamar and tin interest, was a valuable part of the original Duchy of Cornwall, created for the young

Black Prince. Further on in time the village was involved in the Civil War when a battle took place at Horsebridge – the bridge crossing the Tamar between Devon and Cornwall which is the parish boundary.

The royal connection continued to the present day. After the First World War the Duchy Home Farm and the village saw many royal visits, and the development of a flower farm to provide work locally. Now on many village mantlepieces stand photographs of Prince Charles visiting tenant farmers or with local people at the opening of the Duchy Agricultural College, formerly the Duchy Home Farm.

The village has always had a strong agricultural leaning; although the centre of a large parish the actual village is quite small – a church and rectory, post office, school and sports club and clusters of private dwellings of different periods. Originally most people lived in small farming settlements and around mills, forges or tinworks; then as mining grew in importance in the 18th and 19th centuries more villages sprang up around the deep mines and Kit Hill granite quarry. At the height of the mining boom there were seven important mines within the parish employing over a thousand men, women and children.

As mining declined and helped along by the East Cornwall Mineral Railway recently built for the transport of ore, farmers and market gardeners began to specialise in early produce, particularly flowers and strawberries as well as the black mazzard cherries and apples for which the Tamar Valley had become famous. From a tiny smithy in the village of Venterdon an important firm, Dingles, grew up as contractor and manufacturer of agricultural machinery and steam rollers, making many vehicles with iron wheels.

The noted bellfounders Penningtons are buried at the foot of the church tower; they lived and had a foundry in the village and in 1771 were responsible for the peal of bells in the church, still rung enthusiastically on highdays, holidays and church days.

In the 18th and 19th centuries the Call family built a magnificent mansion, Whiteford, situated in beautiful parkland with lakes, Palladian bridges and summerhouse (now Landmark Trust) which brought fashion and employment to the village. When Whiteford was demolished in 1912 the Home Farm was built from its stone.

The school holds a May fete with maypole dancing annually and the church fete enlivens the village green in June. The Flower and Vegetable Show boasting over 1,200 entries takes place on the village green on the first Saturday in August – all evidence of the thriving village community. Most recent changes have brought a new primary school building, and new housing to the village centre, while the Victorian school building of 1866 has become a resource centre for the community. To mark the Millennium a large granite from

Kit Hill was lifted and placed on the green, and 2,000 daffodils were planted beside the hillroad leading up to the village!

🍁 SUMMERCOURT

Summercourt owes its origin and development to its central position in the county. It is dominated by the crossroads where the route joining the north and south coasts, from Newquay to St Austell, meets the A30. The name of the village is believed to originate from the travelling Assize courts held in the summer months in the locality.

The main claim to fame of the village is the renowned and ancient Summercourt Fair, which dates back to before 1234 when it was known as the Long Fair or Long Chipping. It was originally located at nearby Penhale but moved to Summercourt in 1711 and has always been held on 25th September, the old feast of the Holy Cross. The fair continues to completely close the length of the A30 through the village for the day. This causes much confusion to motorists who are diverted through the surrounding countryside, but tradition is upheld. Animals ceased to be a predominant part of trading at the fair in the 1950s and now a funfair provides the attraction in the 'fair field'. Privately owned, this field has always been the venue for the annual event. Folklore tells us that the custodian of the 'White Glove', which is associated with the granting of the original fair charter, was entitled to collect a toll per head of cattle and sheep. Although it has not been seen in living memory, the owner of the field is deemed to 'have the glove' and can demand fees from participating stall holders and showmen.

Summercourt is in the parish of St Enoder, first real mention of which appears in the Domesday Book as Eglosneuder, the church lands of St Enoder. It then contained some 22 farms, several of which can still be traced today. It is still essentially a farming community, most of the farmers to the south of the village being tenants of the Duchy of Cornwall.

St Enoder's church, Norman in origin, is to the north of the village. Extensive repairs started in 1464 give the basis of the lovely building which stands today and the original Norman font is still used. The Methodist church, built centrally in 1912, continues to thrive but the Wesleyan chapel to the west has recently closed.

The National school founded in 1828 continues today as Summercourt county primary school though much altered. At the hub of the village the corner shop serves the local community and a small post office still operates.

Understandably, because of its position on the county's main highway,

Summercourt's hostelry, the London Inn, is an old coaching inn. In the 18th century all Cornishmen talked of being 'forced' to London because of the wearying journey. Consequently the London Inn supplied a welcome change of horses and refreshment for passengers, and has altered little externally from that time. Modern travellers however, require the services of the local garage rather than the old smithy on the crossroads.

Built in 1969 to commemorate those who served in the two world wars, the village hall stands at the centre of village life and is the venue for several clubs and groups including the WI. To mark the new millennium two handsome wrought iron gates have been placed at the entrance of the adjacent Thomas playing field.

Summercourt bypass, opened in 1991 has made sweeping changes to village life. On Saturdays in the summer it is now the bypass that is gridlocked while the road through the village has little traffic. Life has become much safer and more comfortable for this friendly and lively community.

❧ TAPHOUSE

Of the three Taphouses, East Taphouse is the largest, having had several bungalows built by private enterprise besides the ones built by the local district council for senior citizens. Formerly known as the Eastern Taphouse, the name is derived (as in the other two) from the village inns where the coach horses were stabled and travellers found food and lodgings. Alas, the inn at East Taphouse became a farm for several years, then another owner sold the land and developed the farm buildings into flats for holidaymakers.

The mill is no longer used for grinding and crunching corn for cattle feed, but has been turned into units of various occupations. The village smithy is no more but the carpenter's shop is still in existence (greatly modernised) and run by a member of the same family who have been the village carpenters for generations. Gone are the massive tree trunks which used to be on the ground in front of the carpenter's shop, waiting to be sawn into timber by a saw powered by a steam traction engine.

Some people attend the parish church at St Pinnock, others may go to the Methodist chapel at Connon. The older chapel at Bethel closed some years ago, and is now home of the St Pinnock Band. In former years on Good Friday, Sunday school and Band of Hope scholars marched from Bethel for service and tea, headed by the St Pinnock Band and carrying a splendid banner. The band has been in existence for about a century.

At Middle Taphouse the inn is still in existence but a private house, and is situated at Braddock parish. There have been only two bungalows built in recent years by private developments. There is one farm, the barn of which is being developed, and an engineering (models) business – the rest being privately owned.

The Western Taphouse (West Taphouse) is in Braddock parish and has only two new houses built years ago by the former Liskeard Rural District Council. The school (once the parish poor house) is still used and had incorporated about 20 years ago the smallholding known as West House and which was the original toll house. The inn was a farm until traffic on the road made it impossible to cross the road with cattle. Hence, the land was divided among neighbouring farmers and the farmhouse sold. One can see in the dining room window the spy hole, where the policeman could look in to ensure that law and order was kept.

Originally the whole area belonged to a local estate but some has been sold. Barns have been developed, the chapel once a thriving place of worship has been developed into a private house and caters for bed and breakfast, while the smallholding of Cross Close does a great trade by breeding rabbits for food.

Near the village are several barrows or tumuli. Some say that the mounds are the graves of people killed in the battle of Braddock Down (1643), others say that they are burial places of tribal kings of the Iron Age. One was opened up in 1940 and found to contain pottery. It is rumoured that on the night of the aforementioned battle, ie 18th January, ghostly horses may be heard crossing the nearby downs.

🍁 THREEMILESTONE

The village of Threemilestone lies, as the name suggests, three miles from the centre of Truro on the former main road to Redruth and West Cornwall. Today the village is bypassed by a dual carriageway, opened in 1974.

It is an area which has increased in size over the past 40 years, probably more than anywhere else in the Carrick District. In the 19th century the hamlet, as it was then, comprised a few houses and other buildings surrounded by farms to the north and east, and by smallholdings to the south and west, the latter most likely occupied by workers in the extensive mines in nearby Baldhu and Chacewater. Associated with the farming were one, and at some time two, blacksmiths and a number of butchers. One blacksmith's shop, together with a carpenter and a small mill were situated at Stickler's Corner, at that time the turn-off from the main road for St Agnes and Perranporth. A stickler is the name given to a referee in Cornish wrestling, once a very popular sport with miners. No doubt mainly dependent on the mining community, there was a beer retailer in addition to the Victoria Arms, a public house still trading today under the same name, although somewhat enlarged and changed in appearance.

In 1939 the hamlet comprised the public house, a garage formerly one of the blacksmith's shops, a corn mill and a small general store, the blacksmith's shop at Stickler's Corner and some 20 private dwellings. This corn mill, a large structure clad with galvanised iron and typical of the period, but in 1920, has now given way to a group of small workshops and rural industries.

Today, the village has approximately 900 dwellings and is a community of its own with most of the facilities that a modern village desires. A new junior school was built and opened in 1966 and this accommodates some 320 pupils. The previous school for some 76 children, built in 1898, was just outside of the village and known as Chyvelah School. It was demolished when the bypass was constructed in 1974.

Although many of the inhabitants travel to Truro to work, there is considerable local employment. The Threemilestone industrial estate on the western outskirts of the village employs many local people and is still growing. To the east there is the Gloweth industrial estate mainly used for warehousing. Only a mile away from the village are the Treliske and private Duchy hospitals providing a good deal of employment.

Threemilestone is a modern village with none of the old establishments and few local families found in the older villages. A large proportion of the population have come to live in the village from outside of Cornwall, and have a very wide range of backgrounds. Despite this, and the fact that it is to a considerable extent a dormitory village for Truro, many well established organisations have developed with a strong community spirit.

🍁 TINTAGEL

The parish of Tintagel is made up of a number of small hamlets and is famous for its connection with King Arthur and the castle ruins. Some doubt remains as to whether King Arthur and his knights dwelt in these parts but, undoubtedly, Tintagel was the home of Cornish kings and princes. In 1990 archaeologists uncovered, among other things, a stone cross base in the churchyard of the parish church which supports the theory that Tintagel was an important place.

St Materiana's church, standing alone on Glebe Cliff and thus guiding sailors of a bygone age, was built entirely as it appears today in its cruciform shape between 1080 and 1150.

Many of the families are recorded in the parish records of some 500 years ago. These same families, ie the Browns and Dangars, still farm in the area. The Fry family, although of later origin, still run the village buses, having graduated from horses to diesel power. In the past, the highlight of the year then was Rogation Sunday, when everyone dressed in their very best with children and choirs singing. The following Monday there was a special tea of jam, cream splits and saffron buns. Games and races were held in a meadow next to the chapel. Nearby, Mr and Mrs Marwood Commins in their white aprons set up their stall of glass jars filled with home-made rock, cinnamon, barley sugar and other sweets, sold at an old halfpenny a packet. In those days Florence Richards lived in the cottage at the castle cove. She charged two old pennies to go up to the castle island, she gave you the key to go up on your own and would ring a handbell for you to come down. She served cream teas and told visitors that the cream was kept cool in the lavatory.

Today, many more visitors come to the village drawn by the Arthurian legend. Certainly, King Arthur has aided the present tourist industry with many of the various businesses reflecting his memory. There is King Arthur's Cafe, King Arthur's Bookshop, and the King Arthur's Arms public house, to name but a few. The Arthurian legend continues in the Hall of Chivalry, a most interesting place built by Mr Glasscock of the Monk and Glass family of custard makers. The King Arthur's Castle Hotel standing alone on the cliff has provided the location for several films, including *Dracula*.

Although a somewhat remote rural village, it is very much alive having a doctors' surgery, dispensing chemist, post office, newsagent, grocers, greengrocer, drapery and shoe store, electrical shop, butchers, banks, a well stocked hardware store and many gift shops. The village boasts a football and cricket club and their own clubhouse. There is also a village hall, a toy museum and a fossil museum.

Many of the tourists visit the castle ruins and The Old Post Office and go on their way and fail to discover the many interesting and enchanting facts and places of the parish of Tintagel, such as the beach at Trebarwith Strand, the dilapidated but once magnificent Trebarwith Farmhouse and buildings, and the peaceful Treknow with its share of traditional cottages and chapels. Trewarmett has its ghosts – a lady crosses the road and a headless motor cyclist makes his way to Delabole. The Min Pin inn at Tregatta, formerly Trewthen farmhouse, has a memorial stone as a hearthstone to John Bunt, a former owner who died in 1813. The Min Pin inn is now more famous for its small brewery operated by a mother and daughter and believed to be the only all-female operated brewery in the country. Indeed to the visitor, it appears that it is a village of drinking and praying, having nine public houses and eight places of worship.

Trebrae Lodge Hotel was the home of the Bray family for many years, situated at Trenale with its tales of things that go bump in the night and a tunnel to the beach to aid the smuggling activities. Bossiney was very important, it was a borough with its own court house which is now the Tintagel Pottery. It also has the old gaol with the village well in the grounds, the old forge and the mayoral house, from which was sent the Member of Parliament, the last being Sir Francis Drake. The last Mayor of Bossiney was Thomas Symons, a relative of the present owner of Bossiney Farm. Bossiney has a sandy bay, a petrifying well in Horn Hill and claims that King Arthur's Round Table is buried in the mound opposite Bossiney House Hotel and is said to rise on midsummer's night.

Trevellet has a trout farm and an old water mill built in 1472; the old workings are to be seen inside the now cafe. A breathtaking walk along Rocky Valley will reveal some old Phoenician markings.

🍁 TORPOINT

Situated on the Rame peninsula in the south-east corner of the county on the banks of the river Tamar, Torpoint enjoys the best of all worlds. It affords easy access to the amenities of the city of Plymouth and Dartmoor while to the west there is a choice of several pleasant beaches and bays and the listed garden and house of Mount Edgcumbe.

Torpoint's most famous features are, unquestionably, the Torpoint ferries. In 1991 the ferry service will have plied their way across the Tamar for 200 years. Originally steam-driven they now have diesel engines and in recent years were 'stretched' to accommodate more vehicles but still run on chains laid under the river and are basically to the same design as that devised by J.M. Rendel, the original 'floating bridge' engineer. The history of Torpoint is inexorably linked with the ferry service and the start of the building of the naval dockyard at Devonport – subsequently designated a Royal Naval Dockyard. This drew people across the river for employment and as the dockyard grew so people migrated to settle on the banks of the river near the ferry crossing. In fact, Torpoint does not appear on a map before 1700. Torpoint's links with the Royal Navy were strengthened with the commissioning of the naval shore establishment of HMS *Raleigh* in 1939. This is now the only new entrant training centre for recruits to the Royal Navy and Women's Royal Naval Service.

The town itself cannot boast many imposing buildings and, in fact, lost one large property when Thanckes House was moved stone by stone from Torpoint and rebuilt further along the coast on the headland above Portwrinkle beach as the Whitsand Bay Hotel. Torpoint's link with the past is however, reflected in its street names, many of which have connections with the Carew-Pole family of Antony House. Torpoint was once a part of the parish of Antony and indeed the land on which the town is built, originally, almost exclusively belonged to the Carew-Pole family. More recent street names, however, commemorate local heroes and well respected members of the community. In particular, Dr John Langdon Down who was the first to recognise Mongolism as a medical condition and gave his name to 'Down's syndrome'.

Torpoint is mentioned in the Guinness Book of Records – in 1852 a local doctor recorded a birth of 21 lbs which is still claimed to be the heaviest baby born in the United Kingdom. The town can also lay claim to one of the smallest parks in the country. A local reporter at the opening ceremony was heard to comment that it was barely big enough for a sparrow and today it still enjoys the title of 'Sparrow Park'. Most local anecdotes revolve around the ferry. One of its most unusual passengers was Julia the circus elephant, who leapt off midstream and swam the rest of the journey much to the consternation of her keeper who was left urging her on from the prow.

Today Torpoint remains very much a naval town. A large part of the community comprises a fluctuating population of naval families but it is a recommendation for the friendliness and peacefulness of this often forgotten gateway to Cornwall that so many people from all parts of Britain later choose to return here to settle.

❧ TOWNSHEND

Townshend must be one of the prettiest little villages in West Cornwall. A very neat and tidy village, the new houses have blended in extremely well with the older traditional cottages. Sadly now it does not even have a shop or a post office but in its heyday this busy little community had two pubs, a cobbler, butcher, blacksmith, two grocer's shops, a post office and a doctor's surgery.

Its name is taken from a descendant of the Duke of Leeds, at the end of the 19th century, who owned nearby Godolphin estate and most of the land surrounding the village, which was leased out to the local farmers. Much of Townshend faces south and was therefore an extremely good flower-growing area. Every cottage garden grew flowers to supplement their income. The local mines served as alternative employment and the Count House where the miners received their pay is still lived in today. Many villagers worked at the Troon mine, walking to work early Monday mornings and returning at the weekend, having taken enough pasties for each working day! Gilbert Stamps and C.B. Stevens' corn mill worked by a waterwheel on the river Hayle provided additional work.

Many know Townshend as Bucks Head, so called after the former pub was named, so the story goes, when two local lads went hunting deer and came back with a young buck. They then presented the head to the landlady. The inn has been a doctor's residence for many years.

Like most Cornish villages, Townshend had a wealth of musical talent. Jessie Ivey at 15 had a great musical ability and in the 1880s a harmonium was purchased for her from Truro, transported to Gwinear Road station, then to Townshend by pony and trap. This musical ability has continued in the Ivey family down through the years and Jessie's grandson, Lambert Ivey, entertained hundreds of appreciative audiences.

John Winn, another very gifted musician, was also the local blacksmith. He had an exceptional voice which never broke, and trained the choir which helped to raise funds to purchase and build the chapel organ. Much of the musical life was centred around the chapel and earlier in this century a strict Methodist upbringing often created difficulties in families. One dutiful middle aged son on acquiring the first car in the village in 1935 was under strict instructions from his mother that it must never be driven on a Sunday, until the fateful day when the preacher had to be fetched! But his long suffering wife stated, 'If I can't ride in the car on a Sunday, the preacher can't either!'

The chapel is now closed and there are plans to convert it into a dwelling. The Sunday school, a Grade II listed building, is now a very popular village hall, and a great amenity for the village.

Townshend cricket team was renowned throughout West Cornwall and won many cups, aided and abetted by a demon lefthanded underarm bowler named Will Eustice. So serious a topic did this become that if a match was lost a certain character would always wear black the following day! Townshend has had its share of 'characters'. One gentleman bought two identical cars, but only one licence!

The appeal of Townshend today, like the former settlement at neighbouring Kirthen Wood, is that it still retains its charm, peace and tranquillity.

🍁 TREBETHERICK

Trebetherick (the name means 'farm of Petroc') is called a village but it is not huddled together in a group as the name implies. It has properties spotted about either side of the lane with space around them, and a lot have wonderful views of the distant Camel estuary and Brea Hill, which looks like a large dome encroaching onto the beach at Daymer Bay in the distance. Some years ago, when the sands shifted, a Bronze Age barrow was found on Brea Hill, and Roman glass, beads and coins were found in the sandhill around the church.

The lane meanders through Trebetherick into the next village, Polzeath, whose steep hill suddenly offers the most glorious view of the magnificent headland called Pentire Point. The late Poet Laureate, Sir John Betjeman likened this point to a sleeping lion's form and, without much stretching of the imagination, the head, body and haunches of a lion can easily be seen. The wide sandy expanse known as Hayle Bay stretches out below with wide Atlantic breakers rushing in as if to swallow the small shops that huddle at the bottom of the hill. (On a high spring tide they sometimes do!)

If you walk along the sandy lane between the post office and the shops then follow the footpath past the picturesque caravan park, eventually you arrive at a romantic little cottage known as Shilla Mill. Shilla or Sullah, is ancient Cornish for 'the rock consecrated to the sun' and at one time it was a thriving grist mill. The mill building was eventually converted into living rooms and the beams of those rooms are said to have come from ships wrecked out on the 'Doom Bar'.

Lawrence Binyon found inspiration here. His poem *To the Fallen* was written whilst sitting on the Rumps in Polzeath just after the First World War. Every Remembrance Day this is read at the Cenotaph.

At Daymer Bay in Trebetherick, there is a small church called St Enodoc. Sir John Betjeman was buried in the churchyard there. Reputed to have been founded in the 3rd century, this beautiful little church is surrounded by a square hedge of tamarisk and, when seen from a distance whilst walking across the golf course, it can only be likened to a tiny postage stamp on a large green envelope.

Before being restored in 1863, the whole church had been almost completely buried in sand for several generations. In fact, to keep the church consecrated the clergy had to climb through a specially made skylight in the roof once a year to perform the special service. The oldest tomb dates from the 15th century and it is thought that many earlier ones were lost when the church was restored.

On the championship golf course of St Enodoc is Jesus' Well. Here, legend has it, Jesus himself tapped the dry ground with his staff during his visit to this country in the 'missing years' of his life and formed the well, which was credited with great healing powers.

From the nearby beach of Daymer Bay the land rises to form the Greenaway. It is at this point that the 'Doom Bar' exists, a vast sand bank that stretches across the mouth of the estuary and which has been the cause of many ships' demise. A chart has been made which shows 96 wrecks in this area, the earliest recorded being the *Britannia* in 1754.

The whole area, from Roman times to around 1858, was mined very profitably for silver, lead ore, copper and antimony. This was shipped in barges from Trebetherick to Padstow. One stormy day in 1819 a barge, heavily weighed down with such minerals, floundered and sank. Of the nine people on board only three were saved. The coastline has changed greatly over the years and this may be due in some way to the many mine shafts honeycombed throughout the area.

The National Trust has acquired a good deal of the headlands at Polzeath and Pentire. The people of New Polzeath raised the money to buy Pentire Farm and actually donated all of the land to the National Trust so that building development could not take place.

🍁 TREEN & PENBERTH

The farming village of Treen and the fishing cove of Penberth are frequently bracketed together in spite of being in the adjoining parishes of St Levan and St Buryan. The two communities are partly in the care of the National Trust which has ensured that, as yet, there is no undesirable development.

Treen is a small windswept granite village with an inn and a simple Methodist chapel, both of which are listed buildings. The chapel built in 1834 was paid for by Miss Bathsheba Richards and her brother William – before this time the worshippers had congregated in dwelling houses in the village. Originally this small chapel had a gallery and box pews with seating for 165 people.

Mentioning the Logan Rock, in the 18th century the Cornish antiquary, Dr William Borlase said, 'It is morally impossible that any lever, or indeed force however applied in a mechanical way, can remove it from its present situation.' This statement led to perhaps the most renowned of early tourists, Lt Goldsmith RN, nephew of the poet Oliver Goldsmith, who with a party of soldiers pushed the Logan Rock down the cliff. This incident caused such an outcry that the Admiralty compelled Goldsmith to restore the Rock to its original position at his own expense – £130 8s 6d, a considerable sum of money in 1824. A bill of the cost can be seen at the inn with such details as '60 men of St Just who did nothing but drink beer to the value of 13s 6d'! There is also a print in the bar of the Logan Rock inn showing the ropes and tackle being used in restoring the 65 ton Rock to its original position – holes on surrounding rocks are still visible. It is alleged that it has not 'logged' as easily as before.

The magnificent Treryn Dinas promontory was a fortification in the Iron Age and the triple line of defence can be clearly seen. Overlooking this site stands a white cairn used by local fishermen as a navigational aid to determine the position of the Runnel Stone reef. On the cairn is a plaque which records the linking of England with the American Continent via transatlantic cable in 1880.

The delightful small fishing cove of Penberth lies at the foot of the valley. A plaque states that it was 'Transferred in 1957 to the National Trust through the National Heritage Fund in memory of those who died in the Second World War'. The settlement is thought to have been established about the mid 17th century. During the 19th century the fishing concentrated on pilchards which were pressed into barrels before being exported mainly to Italy. To this day one can see a gulley in the floor of one of the fish cellars – as the pilchards were pressed the oil flowed down the gulley to be collected for cooking and lamps.

There is a wide granite-paved slipway from the beach up to the capstan which is now purely decorative as the boats are hauled out of the sea by an electric winch. This inshore fleet consists of a dozen boats involved in mixed fishing. There is a long established tradition for local involvement with the sea – in 1991 Penberth men were coxswains of both the local lifeboats at Penlee and Sennen Cove. Over the years there has been great need of these lifeboats as there have been many wrecks on this beautiful but cruel coastline.

❀ TREGONY

Tregony's peak time was probably from the year 1000 to about 1300. During this time it was a busy port – hence the name 'Daddiport' and Halbote'. The river Fal was navigable by ships up to 800 tons to beyond Tregony, and trade flourished. Outgoing ships were laden with wool and woollen cloth, hides and leather, tin and agricultural produce. Gradually the river silted up, due probably to tin streaming, and by the end of the 16th century Tregony's river trade had diminished, though it retained its importance as a market town, and a fair was held regularly until 1939.

Amongst the chief occupations were those of weaver, shoemaker, farmer, vintner, mason, blacksmith, tanner and miller; there was a mill down in the valley below the town. Hops were grown quite extensively – hence the area known as the Hop Garden. In 1631 there were 36 alehouses in Tregony!

In its early days Tregony ranked as a town. The population has varied, still being up to 1,000 inhabitants in the 17th and 18th centuries. In 1620 Tregony received its charter, with a mayor, recorder and eight burgesses – its Parliamentary history in those days was somewhat dubious being a Potwalloper's Borough', returning two MPs for the village up to the Reform Act of 1832.

Mention must be made of the Tregony Giant. In 1761 an old coffin was dug up and in it was discovered the skeleton of a man of gigantic size. On exposure to the air it mouldered into dust, but one tooth remained; it was two and a half inches long. The coffin was over eleven foot in length and nearly four foot deep. Unfortunately no part of the coffin or the tooth has been preserved to substantiate the story!

Another well-known name connected with Tregony was Cuthbert Mayne, the Roman Catholic rebel in a Puritan community. He was caught and executed at Launceston, but one of his quarters was hung on Tregony Bridge as a gruesome warning!

A well-known local character of the 20th century was Frankie Greet. In 1913 he was one of the leaders in the great strike at the china clay works. Later his energies were channelled into hard work for the public services and charities to benefit the village.

Tregony's original parish church, dedicated to St James, was by the river, but it had to be abandoned in 1553 due to flooding. Since then the parish church of St Cuby, at the far end of the village, has been the parish church of Tregony – though it is in fact just in to the neighbouring parish of Cuby! It is a most interesting old church and well worth a visit.

Tregony's historic Clock Tower, built of Pentewan stone in 1833, became a popular landmark in the village. In 1851 people were furious to learn that it was due to be sold and shipped to Australia, but the last Mayor of Tregony, Henry Jewell, saved the day when he sold the structure to John Dunstone, who later sold the tower back to the people for £12. Time had taken its toll on the fabric of the structure, and the clock itself was in need of a complete overhaul, so a Millennium Appeal Project was launched. A grant from the Cornwall Rural Community Council covered 75 per cent of the cost, but the remaining £3,500 was raised by local residents and in 1998 the Clock Tower was lovingly restored and will hopefully tick well into the new millennium.

The almshouses, known as the Gallery (at the top of Tregony Hill), were originally given to Tregony as a 'hospital for decayed housekeepers'! By the end of the 19th century only the walls and two end chimneys were standing and in 1897 it was extensively rebuilt. It now provides six pleasant flatlets for elderly residents of the village and is maintained by the Boscawen Trust. The old Tregony gaol is still in existence – the old cottage just below the almshouses.

Another interesting feature was a fine old clapper bridge crossing the stream on the track up to Reskivers. Sad to say, the large stone forming the bridge was badly vandalised some years ago and has had to be replaced with a wooden bridge.

Nowadays Tregony is largely a dormitory village for Truro and St Austell. There are still, however, some who work locally and on the farms around, and there has been some development of small-scale businesses. Over the years, new houses have been built and more people have moved into the village and today Tregony is a very active village with a life and flavour of its own.

Tregoodwell

Tregoodwell is a small hamlet just out of Camelford on the road to Rough Tor. Its most cherished possessions are the football field, in use for about 100 years for shows, matches and a circus and which contains an old ivy clad cricket pavilion still standing but sadly no longer required; and the beautiful old lime tree which stands proudly in the centre of the group of old cottages. Unfortunately, the electricity workers have no appreciation of this unusual feature and have hacked the branches into an ugly shape to allow wires to pass through!

The oldest house is about 300 years old and apparently, as the land comes under no authority, people staked a claim and built their cottage. There was no paperwork entailed and one could sell one's home for £50 cash! One house has an archway of stone from a chapel on Rough Tor, dedicated to St Michael according to a record of 1419. Another house, a few years ago, needed a new roof and when the old one was removed, dozens of pairs of tiny lace-up boots were found, so small it makes one shudder to think how they cramped children's feet. A nearby wall revealed holes where pigeons were kept and fattened up to be eaten. In another cottage the recesses on either side of the old stove were full of hedgehogs, who at night were given the run of the kitchen to catch the cockroaches! Most cottages were one or two up and down only, but raised large families and in one case, a pig was fattened to an enormous size, brought in with a tremendous effort to get through the door, then winched up and killed. The women rushed down to the river (which runs below the hamlet on the Rough Tor side) to wash the various parts of the poor creature. This of course, supplied food and fat for some time.

There is a spring which supplied everyone with pure water and still does, if required, as the Water Board recently passed it as absolutely pure. In the past pure water was taken to Camelford if the town needed it. Though the water may have been pure, this could not be said of the sanitation, for that did not come until 1966, previously just three pipes delivered the waste into the river. Most of the men worked at Delabole slate quarry or the clay works and on the land. Their means of transport were bicycles, carts or, in one or two cases, donkeys.

There has never been a shop or pub, but during the 1960s a chalet in a garden was used by Roman Catholics; a priest came out to say Mass for the locals and those from Camelford.

🍁 TREMATON

The Cornish village of Trematon and its surrounding countryside is steeped in history. It is said to take its name from Trematon Castle one and a half miles south-east of the village, Trematon meaning King's town/home. The Saxon King Athelstan is reputed to have had a castle there prior to the Normans' 12th century motte and bailey, the oval shell keep of which remains today silhouetted romantically against the skyline. There may well have been an earlier Celtic settlement here; certainly there are traces of a Celtic field system at nearby Trevollard.

The village is situated three and a half miles west of Saltash. It is small with no shop and no pub and the Methodist chapel which gave some heart to the community was sold some years ago.

The area has numerous rising springs and many wells, some of which are still used. Some recall an old tramp who every summer would live in a tin hut next to Thorn Well. This well and stream was a main source of water for

Trematon people, and is believed to have been the main spring for Trematon Castle.

This village of ancient agricultural origins still has tenant farmers and smallholdings. Some of the nearby outlying areas own and farm their own – the Kitts and the Greets who have farmed here for over 100 years. High Cornish hedges border the fields and much of the farmland with deep valleys borders the river Lynher. In the 19th and early 20th century, barges from Devonport and Plymouth would come up the river Lynher loaded with refuse and offload their cargoes of 'dock dung' as it was locally known, which was then transported by horse and cart and spread on nearby fields. Every time a field is ploughed there appears more evidence of a bygone age. By what is found reveals the use to which the Victorians put these fields – eg fields with glass and china were used for crops, whilst those with pottery for grazing. Now the river is silted up and the old stone quays almost disappeared.

Market gardening has long been a feature of the area. The Norman lord of Trematon in the 12th century set up a market in Saltash and prior to that it was held in the castle. Today Saltash greengrocers buy many of their vegetables and fruit from Trematon farmers although a lot of produce goes to Plymouth market. Over the years types of produce have changed – no more gooseberries from here, no more bunches of sage, mint and watercress, but strawberries remain and anemones have replaced primroses, with heavy crops of potatoes, swedes, cauliflowers and cabbage. Gone too are the cider apples which were sent to Whiteways long ago and with many farms making their own scrumpy. Locally some of the odd-shaped fields are explained by the custom of giving a piece of land, maybe a corner, in settlement of a debt or a wager.

One of the grander houses in Trematon is graceful 19th century Trematon Hall. Its second owner Squire Edwards owned much land in the area and was highly respected. One and a quarter miles from the village, situated on a peninsula of the Lynher estuary, is Ince Castle, the home of the late Lord (Lennox) Boyd and Lady Patricia Boyd (of the Guinness family). The only 16th century brick house in Cornwall (sadly damaged by fire), it has four low towers and an underground passage. It was garrisoned for the King in the Civil War. A popular story from the 17th century is of owner John Killigrew who made it into four independent parts, a bedroom in each tower with no overlooking window. A trusted servant had four separate keys. Killigrew had four ladies, one in each tower, each as wife, none knowing of the others. A letter addressed to Mistress A. Killigrew gave the service a problem, there being Alice and also Amelia. The letter went to the wrong 'wife' who wrote to her father. Killigrew was sentenced to four years on each count at Exeter Assizes.

Nearby Wivelscombe, privately owned, is a renovated 17th century house and the home of the new Viscount Boyd and his wife Alice, who was High Sheriff of Cornwall a few years ago. Erth was another old manor, mentioned in the Domesday Book, and with a privately owned renovated 17th century house situated on the banks of the Lynher one mile from Trematon.

Shillingham, two miles from Trematon and a mile from Trematon Castle, has an early 19th century farmhouse with remains of a 17th century mansion and grist mills by the river, and ruins near the house of a 14th century oratory. The Buller family who built the 17th century mansion were for three centuries the principal family in the parish and owned much land.

Burell, one mile from Trematon, was a gentleman's house built very early in the 17th century but it is sadly now in ruins. Many of the public footpaths and tracks skirt these former mansions giving one a glimpse of a bygone age.

🍁 TRENANCE AND MAWGAN PORTH

Trenance and Mawgan Porth in the parish of St Mawgan is a thriving settlement mainly of 'foreigners', deeply involved with the holiday tourist industry. There are two large hotels and several smaller ones, two pubs and a community hall. Its inhabitants are about equal in number to those of the parent village, and are well represented on the parish council, yet as recently as 1920 Mawgan Porth was surrounded only by farmland.

Trenance farmhouse and outbuildings stand at the top of the hill on the north; the coast road runs through, past Porth Farmhouse, down and across the wide valley, over the river on a bridge, and mounts again through Tevarrian on its way to Newquay.

The rapid increase in motor traffic after the First World War led to the discovery by tourists of this and other secluded bays. A wealthy merchant bought Trenance Farm and became its landlord, building a stone bungalow for his holidays and eventual retirement, but did not live long to enjoy it. It was acquired by a little group which had formed on a boat returning from the West Indies, all looking for new careers – a surveyor with building experience, an accountant, and an hotelier. With financial support from a prosperous West Indian barrister they started a company, 'Trenance Limited', and, employing local craftsmen, constructed a well and reservoir to supply piped water and built homes for their families and an hotel. Advertisement brought people to his quiet bay and the company was soon busily occupied building holiday bungalows. A grocery shop was installed next to the company's office, and later a post office was added. The absentee owner of Porth Farm also sold some land and in 1932 a cafe was built down by the bridge.

In 1934 overhead cables brought mains electricity and the telephone to the parish. Trial holes on a slope above the cafe, with a view to building, revealed a human skeleton. Experts decreed that there should be further investigation of the site and the scheme was abandoned; but visitors thronged to view the grave.

One stormy night a cargo ship went down off the coast, and barrels of wine were washed ashore. One lodged in a cave on the far side of Mawgan Porth and the residents trooped over with jugs to get a share. A local builder took his lorry to retrieve the barrel but the wheels stuck in the river-bed as it returned laden, and it had to be left in the rising tide until next day and then towed ashore by horses, the engine filled with sand.

The war profoundly affected Mawgan Porth – an RAF station had recently been laid out on the north towards St Eval; the tourist trade ceased abruptly; the hotels and all available houses were soon occupied by RAF personnel. The beach was barricaded, the sandhills mined against the expected invasion of Cornwall. Another vast airfield covered land to the south, cutting off main routes to St Columb and Newquay; it was manned chiefly by US airforcemen.

When it was over and the Americans had departed the big airfield was disused and open to the public. It was re-commissioned for the RAF, and a civil airport installed on part of the area. St Eval station was closed except for the married quarters and the school.

The Trenance Company dispersed; the remaining plots and the dilapidated hotel were sold to a company called Gensalve. A succession of managers, under-subsidised, failed to restore goodwill, custom dwindled and in 1959 the hotel closed. It was resold and refurbished; continual additions and improvements have brought it to a high level of popularity.

The Ministry of Works sent archaeologists to investigate the site containing the skeleton. They worked for four successive summers, 1952-6 and unearthed a burial ground and a group of 'courtyard' dwellings. A silver coin of Ethelred the Unready indicated Dark Age occupation; the blown sand over it all suggested that sandstorms had driven the inhabitants inland. The site was left uncovered and a pitch-and-putt golf course arranged around it, with crazy golf below, both popular with visitors.

🍁 TRESILLIAN

Suburban Tresillian was considerably smaller and a self-contained entity some 65 years ago. On Wednesdays, market days, a hotch-potch of traffic passed through, including Cornwall Motor Transport buses and herds of cattle in the care of such drovers as Benjy Little. There were flocks of sheep; ponies and traps; donkeys and chaise; a few motor cars – one owned by a local farmer displaying the number AF7777; motor cycles, bicycles and horse-drawn vehicles of all kinds.

Pendarves Cottages near the school were then malt houses and the aroma of malt wafting into school was very pleasant. The late Robert Shaw, the actor and writer, lived here later when attending Truro school. Angela Lansbury, the actress, was evacuated here during the war.

Before the First World War, railway navvies were quartered in the village. It was not unusual to see four or five fights occurring outside the Wheel on a Sunday after mid-day closing. Some members of the 'navvy gang' married local girls and their descendants still live in the area.

Tresillian's chief claim to fame is its bridge where, during the Civil War, General Fairfax received Hopton's surrender of his South-West army. Cannon balls and cannon have been found, but no battle was fought here – the only battle scars being two gunshot holes in the church Sunday school ceiling when the Home Guard accidentally discharged weapons in much later hostilities. Near the bridge, just beyond the Wesleyan chapel, is the Lower Park housing estate, named after the field on which it was built; Fairfax Road, part of the estate, is named after the victorious Parliamentary General. When 'The Signing of the Peace' was taking place Fairfax made the Wheel inn his headquarters and his entourage made use of nearby cottages which are still in being.

In the later part of the 19th century, the large pond on the river path between the villages of Tresillian and St Clements was often frozen over. Two skaters fell through the ice and were drowned. Superstition said that at midnight their ghosts would appear. In 1911, Richard John Rowe of Tresillian, returning home from a convivial night at St Clements, was nearing the pond when an apparition in white with arms outstretched appeared on the path before him, giving him the fright of his life. It was some time before he realised it was a swan moving from the pond to the river, stretching its wings as it walked.

Lime kilns were in use and boats were once built here. The barge *Shamrock* would cruise up river laden with stone for the county council depot.

Tresillian has grown considerably over the years, and although it is segmented by various parishes, it has a spirit all its own. The village has erected its village hall on land donated by Lord Falmouth and has many social organisations. Its inhabitants today are cosmopolitan, embracing many professions and trades.

❧ TREVERVA & LAMANVA

Treverva, meaning a place by the side of the road, is a small hamlet. It lies between Falmouth and Gweek, close to Penryn, Mabe, Constantine and Budock. It is steeped in history connected with the granite quarries but today only the closed and ghostly flooded sites are the monuments left reminding us of the brave people who worked there. The paths from the village to the quarries, schools and churches are reminders of how hard life was in the days before the motor vehicle, when traction engines and horse-drawn waggons were used.

Today in the village life goes on in the shape of a post office and stores where once the busy grain store operated. The upholsterer's workshop where the wheelwrights once stood was followed by a carpenter's and funeral director's, where two men operated the saw pit by hand. The village hall was originally a garage which was donated to the men of the village after the First World War. The hall stood beside the blacksmith's shop where folk came from surrounding areas to have their livestock shod, including the vicar of Mabe who paid regular visits. Large granite oval shapes were set around the walls of the old blacksmith's shop and these can be seen scattered around the village on walls and gardens.

'Teapot Alley' is a horseshoe-shaped lane which runs around the back of the village where now only a few granite quarrymen's cottages remain – local people can always tell a tale about their childhood days spent there, a place where everyone was always made welcome. In 1956 cottages in the alley were condemned and demolished by the local council and the occupants housed in surrounding villages.

The Methodist chapel has reached its centenary and the previous chapel dated 1843 is now two cottages overlooking the Argal reservoir, which was first flooded around 1939.

Treverva was built up on the side of an old ridgeway used by travellers going to the important market towns of Helston and Penryn. The road was used for transporting granite, first by horses towing waggons and later by traction engines. Some pieces weighed up to one and a half tons and came from local quarries for transportation by sea from Penryn to many parts of the world in the 18th century.

South of Treverva at a site called Trewoon there can still be seen traces of an Elizabethan mansion visible in the farm outbuildings. Napoleonic prisoners of war were once kept in these buildings. Pillared gates can be seen at the entrance and the path leads to the quarry where fine granite was quarried for monuments. Ross Kessell and his nephew Morley Wills, both masons, worked there in the 1920s.

The only inn, used by drovers, was the Oaten Sheaf at Lamanva and also used by travellers between Penryn and Gweek. Many a wage was spent here and never reached home. The property once was the home of Mary and Charlie Mann who built the famous military museum which housed a good collection of Second World War memorabilia.

At the far end of Treverva, near Helland Villas, is a tree nicknamed 'The Whistling Tree' where it is said a man fell off the wall after a drinking spree and was killed. To this day the tree whistles and can be heard when one walks nearby.

The village became famous in the last century by the forming of the Treverva Male Voice Choir under the conductorship of Mr Edgar Kessell, MBE and Cornish Bard. The choir has performed all over the country and toured abroad. At Christmas the village looks forward to a Carolaire Concert which is held in the Methodist chapel and is always a great success. The choir practises on Monday evenings and in the summer months their voices can be hard drifting out over the countryside surrounding the chapel.

🍁 TREVONE

Trevone is approached from the Padstow to Newquay coast road, via the hamlet of Windmill – the name derives from the windmill which still stands denuded of its sails.

Between the coastal road and the backcloth of the Atlantic Ocean, the village settles in its own little niche. To the casual visitor, the architecture of Trevone would appear to represent every decade of the 20th century and some of the 19th century too, but if they looked closer, cottages and houses of an earlier age are to be found.

Blessed with golden sands and rocky pools closeted between rugged cliffs and enclosed by the everchanging farmland scene, the village is a favourite with the holidaymaker who treasures the quieter environment. Tourism is the mainstay of the local economy and agriculture plays a very important role. Trevone's sandy beach offers swimming and surfing, but its other beach, Rocky Bay as it is known, provides a fascinating vista of rock pools where miniature marine life abounds and produces a wonderful variety of shells. It also houses a reminder of the vicious nature of our seas – the rusting hulk of a fishing boat, the *Smilin' Through*, which foundered on the rocks in 1924, fortunately without loss of life. Over 70 years on, one cannot but wonder at the workmanship of these little ships, to withstand over seven decades of constant onslaught of wind driven waves.

For those with an eye for history, there is an ancient burial ground, where a slate coffin with human remains was discovered, and under Porthmissen Beath (to give the sandy beach its rightful name) lie great oak tree trunks embedded in clay – part of an age old forest, which, thanks to winds and tides, have been revealed at least once within living memory.

Possibly unique in Cornwall, is the Round Hole – a centuries old subsidence in one of the coast fields and certainly a magnet to visitor and resident alike. Steep-sided, one can look down at the foaming briny from the middle of a field.

Trevone, literally translated from the Celtic language, means settlement and lamb, so it would seem that sheep farming was a predominant living in bygone days.

As with most villages, there is a church and a chapel, a village hall which started life as a cow shed in the days when cows were milked by hand, and of course a public house. It says much for the residents of Trevone that the war memorial plaque on the village hall never lacks the presence of flowers and foliage. The centre point of the village is the sub post office, a meeting place for everyone.

Those who have lived all or a large part of their lives here can hold one spellbound with their stories. One resident could recall sacks of flour which floated onto the beach during the Second World War from a war-damaged Canadian merchant vessel. Such a find kept many well supplied with home-made bread. 'Some 'andsome it was, too!' Another tale of war years, was of a large cask of wine washed up on the beach. The Customs and Excise men needed to be notified of such an item, and they were – after everyone had filled up all their bottles, replaced the bung and gone home in merry mood.

Trevone has had its share of strange happenings. A 'witches bottle' was found set in a wall of a farm cottage. It contained a cross and a set of small gardening tools. Superstition has it that it must remain in its niche and there it resides today.

Stranger still was the hissing noise that emanated from the far end of Rocky Beach each evening at nightfall in the 1960s. This phenomenon appeared to be issuing from a small hole caused by a rock fall. Such was the interest that people travelled far to hear the unusual noise but few would venture near the spot. Television and the national newspapers carried the story. Many theories were forwarded until the magic was dispelled with the discovery of a little owl adopting the hole as his home.

There are and were great characters in Trevone. Perhaps it is fitting to conclude with the story of one local man, who, when asked by visitors to point the way to wherever they wanted to go, would reply: 'Go right on and past the field where Mr Rabey had his turnips last year!'

❧ TREWENACK

In the year 1878, young Ephraim Eva and his wife, Fanny, carrying a baby in her arms, walked to Trewenack from a neighbouring village about five miles away to set up a business as a wheelwright, carpenter, decorator and undertaker. His business flourished, and on his death in 1930 his son took over and added a blacksmith's shop. This soon became the meeting place for the men of the village, while the women gathered in the grocer's shop or met at the village pump, two or three fields away, where they exchanged gossip and discussed the events of their day. At that time most of the men worked within walking distance on the local farms or in the Wendron tin mines, coming home at dusk to houses lit only by candles and oil lamps. They could, of course, find some comfort in the Star inn!

Ephraim would have known the Methodist chapel which was built in 1866, although preaching services were held for many years before that, first in the open air and later in a mission room. The chapel is still a thriving society, and the Sunday school hall is used extensively by the community.

One of the main events of the year was the Sunday school tea treat, when children and grown-ups marched through the village behind a brass band and carrying a large banner to the field where the entertainment was to take place. There would be games and races for the young ones; large saffron buns and gallons of tea were consumed, and the day concluded with a concert by the band.

One important link with the past is the very ancient holy well of St Euny at Trelil Farm on the outskirts of the village. There is a little granite building covering the well, with seats on either side of the arched doorway. It seems certain that St Wendron lived in a hermitage near the well at some time in the far distant past. There is a story that at one time the people wished to build Wendron church at Trelil, but crows came by night and removed every stone except the porch, which now forms the covering of the well.

If Ephraim could come back to his old home he would scarcely recognise the place! The population has risen from 100 to the present day figure of about 600. The pump has disappeared, replaced by a mains water supply in 1948. (There had been stand-pipes in the village before the main supply came.) The shop and the public house have been converted into dwelling houses. Electricity was introduced in 1950.

There is now no work for a blacksmith, and the neighbouring farmers employ mainly members of their own families. The present day villagers commute by car to their various occupations in the nearby towns and the Royal Naval Air Station at Culdrose, just a few miles away.

🍁 TREWIDLAND

The village has an approximate population of 300 people. It is situated in a picturesque hillside area of agricultural land, which abounds in wild flowers during spring and summer. Some four miles to the north is the market town of Liskeard and four miles to the south-west the coastal towns of East and West Looe. The main A38 trunk road runs two miles to the east.

At the centre of the village there is a small shop and post office, providing the hub of village life, Brown's – a thriving horticultural nursery, and also an ostrich and sheep farm.

The Methodist chapel, dated 1835, was built by the Bible Christian movement who began preaching in the area in 1817. There was an enthusiastic and dedicated congregation attending regular worship up until it was sadly closed, in 1998, for safety reasons. The land adjoining the chapel on the south side was given to the village by Mr Carn in 1930 for use as a cemetery. On the opposite side of the lane there is a second chapel, which was built in 1865 by the Wesleyan Reform Group: it fell into disuse in the late 1960s, when the Wesleyan and Methodist groups amalgamated, and is now owned by the local farm.

On the periphery of the village, Trewidland has a three-teacher County Primary school built over 100 years ago, which serves both Trewidland and nearby St Keyne village.

Historically Lanrest, the home of the Harris family, was situated within the parish. The house was demolished at the time of the Civil War, but was brought to life again by Daphne du Maurier in her book *The King's General*.

The decayed remains of the Looe-Liskeard Canal, used to transport copper and tin from the mines on Bodmin Moor, border the parish. This was superseded by the Looe-Liskeard railway, which is still in use today for passenger transport.

The village at one time supported a forge: the building still remains, but it is converted for private domestic use. Today the occupants of the village are either retired or are employed locally, a significant number being in farming.

🍁 TROON

Situated on the outskirts of Camborne, Troon is the largest village in Cornwall: practically treeless, scenically unimpressive in the centre, Troon's compensations are the wooded beauty of Treslothan, pretty hamlets of Bolenowe and Carwynnen, moorland of Chycarne and Plantation, and the unique mine landscape of Newton moor.

Troon's original name 'Trewoon' means 'Farm on the Downs'. Mentioned in 17th century writings, in 1768 the recorded population was 70; today it is well over 2,000.

There are at least six holy wells in the area. A megalithic burial chamber (now collapsed) was discovered in a field at Carwynnen. At the side of a stream (which rises on Chycarne Moor, flows through Troon and the Reens and feeds Pendarves Lake) is Reens Rock, called Carrek Veryasek, under which St Meriasek was supposed to have sheltered. The remains of St Ia's well-chapel (probably 10th and 12th century) were excavated in 1962. These are on the opposite side of the stream from Reens Rock, on an ancient trackway leading to Camborne and beyond.

Originally a few farms and cottages existed; Troon grew when terraced houses, radiating from the square, were built by miners in the heyday of tin. Larger houses were built by mine captains and businessmen. Now two council estates, three bungalow estates and private building have expanded the village.

Early inhabitants grew crops, raised livestock, and took their goods to market. With the commencement of tin mining, hundreds of men, women and children found employment in mines at Newton and Condurrow. A slump in tin trade later meant unemployment and hardship.

In the first half of the 20th century many were employed with Holman Engineering in Camborne; now Compair Holman, their workforce has been scaled down. Some inhabitants work at Culdrose air station, some travel to nearby towns for employment in factories, shops, offices etc. There is self-employment of farmers, builders and craftspeople.

Shopping facilities and amenities have altered greatly in the last century: 14 grocers/confectioners in the 1920s, a blacksmith, two wallpaper shops, coal merchants, corn merchants, barbers, a draper and tailor, plus a horse-drawn fruit and vegetable merchant, butcher, baker and milkman. Today there are four general stores, a post office, chip shop, hairdresser, butcher, shoe-repairer, dairy and Toc H charity shop.

Present day amenities include the Grenville Arms Hotel, a surgery, and a veterinary surgeon, Anglican and Methodist churches. The Anglican church at Treslothan was built by the Pendarves family on the edge of their estate.

Education in Troon began in a small dame school in Treslothan. A board school, built in the village in 1875, had separate departments for infants, girls and boys. With alterations and additions this is now Troon primary school.

Of myths and legends might be noted Uncle Ned's Rock on Chycarne Moor, where he is reputed to have buried his treasure. Tryphena Pendarves' ghost is said to haunt Treslothan because she was not buried in the family mausoleum due to her misdemeanours!

🍁 TYWARDREATH

Daphne du Maurier, a long time resident in the parish of Tywardreath, put the village on the map by calling one of her novels *The House on the Strand* (or sand) it being the literal translation of the name. Menabilly, or Manderley in Daphne du Maurier's famous novel *Rebecca* is the manorial seat of the Rashleighs where she lived and wrote for 21 years.

Across the valley from Menabilly near the crossroads to Fowey stands the ancient site of Castledore. Excavations which took place in 1937 and 1938 showed that originally there was a chieftain's hall, allegedly the home of King Mark and his nephew Tristan. This is confirmed by the Long Stone (now on the Fowey by Coombe Lane) erected originally near this spot which had a Latin inscription carved vertically upon it: 'Here lies Tristan son (sic) of Cunomoris' (Mark). This could have been the centre of the tragic love story of Tristan and Isolde. Later a famous battle in the Civil War was fought on this site called the battle of Lostwithiel.

At the bottom of the valley between Trenython and Menabilly is a row of almshouses, built by the Rashleigh family. In the middle of the 18th century the first four were built – later to have three more added on to the row. They were occupied by widows or retired retainers of the Rashleigh family, who gave them a guinea a year plus a Christmas hamper. At the end of the row a matron's house was built in 1855 which was also used as a hospital for seamen – it is alleged to be the fourth oldest hospital in the country. The rent for the almshouses for each tenant was one shilling and two pence a week plus rates.

Tywardreath had several outstanding local characters, as all villages have. One such was Jinny Broad, a white witch. The people of Tywardreath were certainly superstitious and strong believers in witchcraft.

Probably the most famous son of Tywardreath was Richard Lobb. Born about 1830, he was brought up in No 22 North Street and learnt his trade as a shoemaker. He then went to London where he saw the impression in the mud of Queen Victoria's foot as she stepped from a carriage. He carefully measured it, made a pair of boots and sent them to Buckingham Palace where Her Majesty was pleased to accept them. He established a business, through this, at St James Street, London. His shop was patronised by many crowned heads of Europe. The original bow window is installed inside the present premises which are famous throughout Europe.

Tywardreath is also known to have the oldest Flower Show in the county. It is alleged that several old cronies sitting in the shoemaker's shop had an argument about the size of the gooseberries they had grown. This led to a challenge and the establishment of the annual Flower Show resulted.

Tin and copper mining was the main industry in the 19th century. This meant that at one time it is recorded there were 16 pubs in the village. Of course, the mine owners were careful in paying the miners only half their wages in money, the other half being paid in tokens only to be cashed in their own pubs or shops.

Due to the flourishing mining industry the population of the village increased from 700 in 1801 to 3,280 in 1851. Naturally there was a need for education in the village on a bigger scale than the various private schools could provide. In 1842 the National Society stepped forward and offered a grant towards the building of a new school. According to a report in 1846, there were 84 boys, 106 girls. The girls were really neglected, as later in their school days only the boys were taught the Rule of Three, girls being taught needlework instead. It also points out that only at later stages were the children allowed to write on paper. The qualification for a suitable teacher was either 'a disabled miner or unsuccessful man of business – those in poor health but respectable in demeanour, mild and conciliatory'.

Dominating the village is the parish church of St Andrew, which started as a priory in 1092. In 1333 thieves slew the prior. It is recorded that the monks weren't behaving as they should, being extravagant and mismanaging affairs. The mother church in France recalled the monks, with the result of the dissolution of the priory. The original building was dismantled and the stones were to be shipped to France. This ship was wrecked near the Gribben Point. Local folk rescued many of the stones and used them to build their own dwellings. Some of the carvings can still be seen. There is a thriving Methodist chapel established in 1895.

Today the village is very popular with retired folk and several new housing estates have increased the population once more.

❦ VALLEY TRUCKLE

Valley Truckle lies between Trebarwith Strand and the northern edge of Bodmin Moor. Both have their many moods – calm, wild and even ghostly at times! The name Valley Truckle is a corruption of the Cornish 'Velyn Drukya' meaning a cleansing or fulling mill. This building is no longer in existence, but was at one time owned by the lord of the manor. The A39 runs straight through the village, which can easily be missed because of its close proximity to Camelford. Indeed it is only the signs which denote where the village of Valley Truckle ends and Camelford begins. It is an easy walk down into the town, therefore much of the life in Valley Truckle is affected by events in Camelford.

'Valley' conjures up a scene of a settlement clinging to a hillside but this is not so. Most of the buildings are on high ground with only a small number on the road leading to the river. This is the Camel – a river which has greatly affected the history of the area. In the early 19th century the area prospered and was the leading sheep rearing and cloth making centre in Cornwall. Using local wool both broad and narrow cloth were manufactured and the cleansing mills were a hive of activity. A local footpath takes the route from Valley Truckle down and along the river, round into Camelford.

Walking the many footpaths stirs the imagination. There are panoramic views in every direction. The absence of trees is noticeable, except in the valleys. Farming is as important today as in the past. Many of the farms are small and cannot have changed much in hundreds of years. The fields are marked by 'Cornish Hedges' of stone and earth, with the occasional tree leaning away from the westerlies! A memorial to Charlotte Dymond stands on the spot where she was murdered in 1844 and her ghost was last seen in the early 20th century by a fisherman.

There is a friendly atmosphere in Valley Truckle and Camelford, and in the winter it sometimes feels as if time stands still. The local people enjoy themselves and much effort and work goes into local events. The carnival is one such occasion, held on the second Wednesday in November. It is an old tradition and the main A39 leading from Valley Truckle through Camelford is closed to traffic. Held in the evening, the procession is lit by thousands of coloured lights, which have replaced the torches held by hundreds of children in earlier carnivals. The money collected goes to local charities.

Development is slow in coming to the area. An industrial estate borders the north-eastern edge of Valley Truckle and a new housing development is in progress. In the valley to the south is a golf course. Around 1330 a mighty deer herd roamed over 102 acres on the same ground, this sweeps down from Valley Truckle to Lanteglos. Here can be found the church where Samuel Wallis was baptised – a great explorer of the Pacific Ocean. Lanteglos is the mother church for Camelford and means 'the church outside'.

🍁 VERYAN

Veryan is a very attractive village situated on the south coast of Cornwall in Gerrans Bay, on the Roseland peninsula. The name Veryan was taken from the patron saint, Symphorian, which was corrupted to Phorian and then Veryan. The village church, dedicated to the saint, contain several Norman features. The bells have recently been restored at great expense in Loughborough.

In a coastal village death by drowning is an ever present danger, and there is a long grave in the churchyard containing 19 bodies from the German barque *Hera* which ran aground off Gull Rock in 1914. There is a tradition that a great plague once raged in Veryan and Tregony, and that 'on the graves of the many victims buried in the churchyard nothing would grow except plaguewort – *Tussilagio Petasites*'.

Jeremiah Trist, vicar of Veryan from 1782-1829, was the man who has left the most lasting impression on the village. He gave money to establish the parish school and later paid for a second school designed specifically for girls. The present infants and junior school was opened in 1872. He was also responsible for the building of the lovely Georgian house known as Parc Behan, just below the green, set on the finest site in the village. As he owned such a lot of the village at the time he was able to landscape it, and part of Veryan's appeal today is from the wonderful trees left by him for our enjoyment.

Trist was also responsible for the construction of Veryan's most famous landmark, its five Round Houses. Two were built at the green, another pair at the top of the hill leading to Gwendra, and one behind the school. All the houses are built of cob on stone foundations, four have thatched roofs and one slate. Many legends have developed regarding them; that Trist built them for his five daughters (he had three); that they were round to prevent the devil from hiding in corners; or to keep him out of the village altogether.

The village has one pub, the New Inn, whereas in 1855 it boasted four. It also has a post office and general store, greengrocer's, gift shop, butcher's shop and a small hotel.

There is a very attractive water garden in the centre, given by a former resident in memory of his late wife and known as the 'McLeod Water Garden'.

One of the more recent additions to the village is the sports centre, opened in 1984.

Homeyard Homes is a charming group of six dwellings with a separate house at the side for the matron. Opened in 1952 for the widows of Cornish seamen, the money to build and maintain them was bequested by Mrs Homeyard-Kempe, a very wealthy woman and a descendant of the Kempe family. Much of the lady's wealth was derived from the production of *Liquafruta*, a patent cough medicine.

Veryan has chiefly revolved around the farming industry in the past, but is now becoming more and more a retirement and holiday village, which makes difficulties for young people wishing to remain.

In the 1650s there was a famous smuggler at Veryan called Robert or Robin Long. He confined his operations to the channel, using St Mawes as his base. In addition to smuggling he was a pirate, and used to tow the vessels which he captured up the Fal to Percuil. He was eventually captured in 1660, and local tradition says he was hanged in chains at the junction of Ruan and St Mawes roads, a few yards from Bessy Beneath, and that he was buried beneath the gallows; the spot is still known as 'Robin Long'.

The burial registers record several deaths connected with smuggling enterprises. On one occasion two young men lost their lives while attempting to rescue brandy kegs 'on a Sunday'. On another occasion five kegs were smashed on the rocks, two were landed and their contents drunk, one man consuming so much brandy that he collapsed and died!

🍁 WARBSTOW

Warbstow was first mentioned in the Domesday Book in 1086 as Werburghastow, meaning 'land dedicated to the honour of St Werburgha'.

The parish church was built by the Normans and dedicated to St Werburgha. The church was originally cruciform but when partly rebuilt in the 15th century, a north aisle and tower were added. A Norman south transept existed until drastic restoration in 1861 when it was removed.

An animal pound, on the village green at Downinney, is a round earth bank topped by trees and a small gate.

Many events were held on the village green including Band of Hope fetes and meetings. John Wesley is reputed to have preached here on several occasions. At one end of the green is where the original manor of Downinney once stood, which was held after the Norman Conquest, for the Count of Mortain, who was half brother to William the Conqueror, by Richard Fitz-Turold, lord of Cardinham. The right hand side of the house frontage has been built around the Norman door, porch and upstairs window, which are the only remains of the manor house.

Just above the village is a pre-historic earthworks known as Warbstow Bury or Barrow. This ancient fortress or camp consists of double ramparts, the outer walls of which are almost covered with yellow gorse and bracken, with deep ditches at the bottom of each rampart and two entrances opposite each other on both levels. It is 820 ft above sea level and in the centre is an oblong tumulus. The tale is told that the giant on Launceston Castle threw a stone and killed the one at Warbstow and this is his grave. Should you start digging, it will come to thunder and lightning and you will hear chains rattle. The Bury, now taken over by English Heritage, is still the source of water supply to the residents of Warbstow: the workings are all under the Bury, the water being pumped up into an underground reservoir and piped to farms and cottages.

Mining for manganese and wolfram have been recorded around the village. One relic found was a bronze bowl which experts dated to the 1st century AD. This is now in Truro Museum.

Before the village had mains water around 1955, the only drinking water for the school and houses was collected in buckets from 'The Adit', where water gushes from a passage about three foot in diameter. No-one knows how far the passage goes, though many have attempted to explore it and it could be connected with the mining.

The population of the parish is about 400. Two new estates have been built with many retired people living here with farms on the outskirts.

🍁 WARLEGGAN

Warleggan is a small parish on the edge of Bodmin Moor, less than 3,000 acres with a population of 158. It stretches from the A30 in the north to the A38 in the south, bounded mainly by small rivers. Once known as the most remote village in Cornwall, it could only be reached from the southern half, the road ending at Callaway Water. In 1953, with voluntary help a road was made by the parishioners and linked up to a road from St Neots, so making it possible to get through to the A38. This road now skirts the new Colliford reservoir, a beautiful lake in the summer but very bleak in the winter. Going back to Callaway Water, you are at the foot of Carburrow Tor.

As you travel south you come to the hamlet of Warleggan, about ten houses, a church, a chapel and the old rectory now converted into flats. The last vicar to live in the rectory was boycotted by the parishioners and lived the life of a hermit, preaching to an empty church until one day he was found dead in his barricaded home. His story was written by Daphne du Maurier and later made into a film for television. The oldest part of St Bartholomew's was built in the

1100s and added to in the 14th century. The tower plus the steeple was struck by lightning in 1818 and three of the bells were sold to pay for the rebuilding, this resulted in a squat tower and only one bell. The organ was built in 1920 to honour the men who fought in the First World War. The chapel was built in 1821 using some of the stones from the ruined belfry and the Sunday school was added in 1969.

At one time Warleggan was busy. Should one stand on the Tor, men could be seen coming from every direction to work Treveddoe mine, Glynn Valley clay works and Gazeland quarry – sadly they have all closed. Treveddoe mine is thought to have been one of the largest mines in Cornwall but closed in 1945. On leaving the village the road winds down the hill passing a well in the wall, where butter was cooled and stored. One comes to Wooda Bridge which crosses the Beldalder river – a beautiful spot, the water tumbling over rocks as it comes down from the moor, rushing to join the river Dewey. Wooda Bridge was restored in 1904, the previous one having been washed away in a storm.

The road now climbs out of the valley towards the village of Mount, passing Treslea Downs. Mount is built on the crossroads of the original main road from Bodmin to Liskeard. Though once quite small, there was a public house, butcher's shop, grocer's, post office, school and chapel. The village hall was built in 1935 and a number of new homes have been built in recent years but the school, public house and butcher's have gone.

Going east from the crossroads, one passes Bofindle Farm, thought to have been a small village as there are ruins of cottages in the fields. The road continues to Panters Bridge, which spans over the river Dewey now joined by the Beldalder river. The bridge built in 1969 stands side by side with the original, very quaint but not made to take modern traffic. The road on the right leads to Trengoffe, an old manor house, sadly burnt to the ground in 1969. Records show that there was a building there in 1382, a king travelling from Norwich to Newlyn was said to have stopped here. The manor house that stood here was quite big; the span over the kitchen fireplace was 13 ft wide and still stands in the grounds, and there are also the remains of an avenue of trees, 39 still standing.

Going south from the village crossroads leads down to Glynn valley and the river Fowey, passing Trevorder and Sina farms – another beautiful view as the Fowey rushes past on its way to the sea.

🍁 WEEK ST MARY

Week St Mary is home to some 500 people. It is 600 ft above sea level and lies three miles inland from the Atlantic coast where there are great cliffs and wide surfing beaches.

It is hilly country hereabouts with many small farms – dairy, beef or sheep; few cereals. The fields are small and irregular, enclosed in old hedges; the lanes sunk between high banks which are covered in wild flowers in spring and summer.

The village is not picturesque, but contains many ancient houses. It has a fine church and a resident rector; the tower contains a peal of six bells and has a devoted band of ringers. It has a much loved Methodist chapel, with a Sunday school boasting 20 children, a post office and general stores, a bakery, pub, and charming small hotel. It has a splendid parish hall which is used for activities ranging from a doctor's surgery to yoga, youth club to skittles, as well as the occasional parish lunch and dance.

It also has history. Mentioned in the Domesday Book, it once had a great castle owned by a cousin of William the Conqueror, the foundations of which can still be traced. In the 16th century Thomasina, the daughter of a local family, made three brilliant marriages, one to a Lord Mayor of London and used some of her wealth to found a school here. Though it was suppressed under the Chantries Act in the reign of Edward VI, part of the buildings survive to this day and are now owned by the Landmark Trust. During the Civil War Royalist troops spent a night here before the battle of Stratton, and later Charles Wesley made it a frequent overnight stay and also preached in the church.

The cattle market has gone because of transport problems, the school has gone because of nationwide reorganisations, the railway, which approached within two miles, has gone because of Beeching. Some things have not gone but have changed; the annual carnival has gone but elements of this, of the patronal feast and the harvest festival, are incorporated in the September Revel, when a young girl is crowned queen for a year. Our benefactress, Thomasina, left a piece of land the rent from which was to be distributed to the poor; known as Poor Men's Piece, the charity still continues and the rent goes towards the Retirement Club's Christmas party. There has been some new house building and some people from other parts of the country have come to live here, and all have been received with great courtesy.

✹ WHITEMOOR

Whitemoor is not named after the white of the china clay as some suppose, but after the white puffs of marsh cotton, which once grew on the moors long before any mineral workings.

Originally a village of smallholdings – 'Goudge's', 'Farmer Bray's', 'Butcher's', 'Cap'n Dicks', 'Stormer' and 'America' – where every family kept chickens, a pig and maybe a cow. Many of these stone-built houses disappeared as the clay works, 'Dorothy', 'Dubbers' and 'Little Johns' expanded. No more conical tips but long barrows of waste sand, partially grassed over.

Whitemoor has a neat layout, with primary school, village hall, recreation ground and methodist chapel at the centre of three roads radiating to St Dennis, Roche and Nanpean. Unfortunately the village post office/store has closed but various tradespeople call and milk and papers are delivered.

Damerell's motorcycles is well known throughout the region, employing salesmen, packers for the spares trade and office staff. Allen's Garage, another family business, has expanded, doing car repairs and selling tyres, parts and accessories. These businesses along with Susan's Hairdressers are important as employers and supporters of village activities and of the school.

The fine musical tradition continues with the Whitemoor Gospel Singers, all ladies, and Halwyn A Gan, a mixed choir. The chapel, built in 1875, with its 'rings' at the back is still flourishing as a centre of worship and service to the community.

✹ WILCOVE

Where is Wilcove? The summer traveller into Cornwall via the Torpoint ferry, intent on his holiday destination, can be forgiven for missing the signs to Wilcove, situated on the right as he leaves Torpoint, well hidden from the road and tucked away in the Lynher valley looking towards Devonport dockyard.

The manor of Antony was listed in the Domesday survey, but Wilcove, then a part of Antony, is first mentioned by Richard Carew in his survey of Cornwall published in 1602. The Carews were the principal family in the area.

Within a generation, Devonport dockyard was planned and accounted for an influx of tradesmen. In the 1821 census, these families together with those of naval personnel who had settled in the area following the Napoleonic Wars, made up the population with workers in trade and agriculture. The Pole-Carews lived at Antony House, very close to Wilcove and owned much of the village.

During the late 19th century, changes had been made in the Wilcove area, including the building of a church and school at Maryfield between Antony House and Wilcove. The priest-in-charge lived at Maryfield House, thus Maryfield became important to the people of Wilcove. A custom observed up to the present day is for the villagers to go up to Antony House on Good Friday to gather primroses for the church.

Wilcove lost some cottages in the late 19th century. Their roofs were 'walked', causing them to be uninhabitable, rather than installing drainage. Older inhabitants remember playing in the ruins of these cottages, which have now disappeared together with the Methodist Ebenezer chapel built in 1806.

In inter-war years, Wilcove's population mainly concentrated on about ten families, including the Turners, the Carters, the Squances, the Lees and the Viguses. Their descendants still live in the area. The children enjoyed freedom to play and to join in the many village activities. They were also expected to fetch water (there was no running water or electricity in the village until the beginning of the Second World War), milk and to gather wood chips for the fire at home when a tree was felled.

The church was popular with a thriving, hundred-strong Sunday school. Men and boys were in the choir and acted as churchwardens and Sir John was vicar's warden. The Wilcove social club was the focal point where activities included concerts, Wilcove Girl Guide company, whist drives, dances and the highlight of the year, the children's Christmas party.

The onset of war brought further changes. American soldiers camped in the grounds of Antony House and built the concrete drive to Jupiter Point. The *Impregnable*, *Vulcan* and *Andromeda* were anchored off Wilcove and used as training ships The 'first bomb of the war' (we are unable to confirm!) fell near Maryfield House. Later another bomb fell on nearby Thanckes oil tanks which blazed for three days. Bandmaster F. Harwood RM was awarded the DSM for his work as a stretcher bearer while serving on HMS *London* during the infamous Yangtse River incident just after the war.

The only trace of scandal is the story of a Mr Prescott who, some years ago, arrived from Plymouth to collect a debt owed to him by someone at Antony House. He disappeared! Legend has it that he was murdered and his body dumped in 'Dead Man's Pool', a bottomless pit at Borough, now filled in.

The public house, the Wilcove inn, overlooks the river. The village hall is situated in a small industrial estate, once HMS *Defiance*, the shore offices of the Reserve fleet.

Cornish cross

❧ INDEX